GOD
Who Walked On Earth
The Life and Times of
SHIRDI SAI BABA

The book presents an absorbing story of a man who came to Shirdi as a fakir, was teased by children and frowned upon by sceptical villagers and remained to reign as a spiritual leader, the greatest saint of all times. He became a god who walked on earth. It is a book which every Sai devotee will like to possess as a Bible of Baba's teachings and a remembrance of the great Master whose idol or portrait adorns the *pooja* rooms of millions of homes throughout the country.

Rangaswami Parthasarathy, a journalist, retired as a Senior Assistant Editor of the Hindu, *after serving the newspaper for 32 years. He wrote the history of the* Hindu *titled* Hundred Years of the Hindu *which was released during the centenary celebrations of the paper in 1978. He subsequently wrote* Memoirs of a News Editor *describing his experiences as a News Editor of the Hindu for over 12 years. He has also written three more books on journalism,* Basic Journalism, Journalism in India *and* Here is the News: Reporting for the Media. Apostle of Love, Saint Saipadananda, *which he wrote in 1981, is a biography of Sri Radhakrishna Swamiji, his guru, and a great devotee of Sai Baba of Shirdi and disciple of Sri Narasimha Swamiji. Parthasarathy has been the recipient of the N. Raghunatha Aiyer Memorial Award for Excellence in Journalism.*

Published by
Sterling Publishers Private Limited

GOD
Who Walked On Earth

The Life and Times of
SHIRDI SAI BABA

*To Dear DEEPAK & SONIA
WITH LOVE FROM
SURINDER UNCLE*

*READ A PAGE OR TWO EVERY DAY &
SEE HOW IT CHANGES YOUR LIFE
TO MAKE A BETTER &
COMPASSIONATE HUMAN BEING.*

Rangaswami Parthasarathy

A Sterling Paperback

Dedicated to
Srichand Rajpal
a Steadfast Friend and Great Sai Devotee

STERLING PAPERBACKS
An imprint of
Sterling Publishers (P) Ltd.
L-10, Green Park Extension, New Delhi-110016

God Who Walked On Earth: Life and Times of Shirdi Sai Baba
© 1996, Rangaswami Parthasarathy
ISBN 81 207 1809 7
First Edition 1996
Reprint 1996, 1997

Published by Sterling Publishers Pvt. Ltd., New Delhi-110016.
Lasertypeset by L.C. Publishing Service, New Delhi.
Printed at Print India, New Delhi.
Cover design by Pratibha Advertising

FOREWORD

There are certain men and women who walk on this earth like us, but do not really belong here. It looks as though they have sojourned here for the sake of the suffering human beings, to bring them solace and peace and to show them the way, the way to light and blessedness. They are the salt of this earth— the great sages, saints and seers. The Saint of Shirdi, Sri Sai Baba as he is lovingly called by thousands of his devotees, was a jewel among such holy men.

True men of God talk very little about themselves but only of God and the ways that lead to Him. Their external life appears to be rather ordinary, providing very little material to history or the biographers. But, their internal life is so intense, holy and great that they can create history. In fact, the lives of such great people alone is history in the real sense. It is a very living and dynamic history that shapes the destinies of generations of people of a society or a country.

Though very little of the early life of Sri Sai Baba is known to us, fortunately for the devotees and the spiritual aspirants, a lot of material has been meticulously gathered by his disciples and admirers. This biography—*God Who Walked On Earth*—by Sri Rangaswami Parthasarathy, is one such, which perhaps supersedes all the previous ones. Written in a simple but captivating style, it takes the reader on a spiritual pilgrimage in the company of the Baba.

Sri Sai Baba lived like a beggar, like a true Sannyasin, till the last day of his life. Though pomp and pageantry followed him, it could never catch up with him!

His real greatness does not lie in the superhuman miracles that he wrought but in the succour that he brought to the suffering humanity and the strength he infused in them to face the problems of life and turn towards God. His Muslim adjuncts did help in bringing about a working harmony between the Hindus and the Muslims, enlightening them both on the true aspects of religion, as life and God-experience.

His teachings do not reflect anything new. But the way he delivered them, depending upon the context and the persons, have acquired power.

Today Sri Sai Baba of Shirdi is fairly well known. But, not many know the relevant details of his life, doings and teachings. This book fulfils that need, thereby helping the mortals to take one more step towards immortality.

Swami Harshananda
President
Ramakrishna Math, Bangalore

PREFACE

I came to know about Sai Baba of Shirdi through my guru, Radhakrishna Swamiji, who in turn became his ardent devotee through his guru, Narasimha Swamiji, the person responsible for discovering Sai Baba for his countrymen outside Maharashtra. It is an amazing fact that this man of God, who was worshipped as God by hundreds and thousands of people, was little known outside Maharashtra where he lived in a small unheard of village called Shirdi. Intellectuals, officials and the elite in society flocked to him, fell at his feet and proclaimed him God, an avatar. But he remained secluded in Shirdi and virtually unknown outside the Bombay Presidency (as Maharashtra was then known.) In Maharashtra itself the vast multitude came to know this "Muslim" fakir through ballad singers and discourses by itinerant entertainers. The available material about Baba was scanty. It was in Marathi, and much of it a mixture of fact and fiction. The exception was *Sai Satcharita* by Hemadpant which is an authentic source material for the life and times of Baba. The real biographer of Baba is Narasimha Swamiji, who in his search for a guru, after renouncing a princely life, stumbled on Baba more than 12 years after his samadhi and surrendered to him. It became his life mission to propagate the ideals and teachings of Baba and he succeeded in this to such an extent that today there are thousands of Sai Mandirs in all parts of the country and Baba's idol is worshipped in millions of homes. Narasimha Swamiji gathered around him a band of dedicated disciples to help him in Sai *prachar* and foremost among them was Radhakrishna Swamiji.

In attempting to write this book I have largely relied on the writings of Narasimha Swamiji and on *Sai Satcharita*. Besides Narasimha Swamiji's prolific outpourings on Baba there are not many authentic and objective literature on Baba. My effort has been to supply a crying need in this respect and if I succeed in this task even to a small extent it will be my crowning achievement. This book could not have been written but for the inspiration and encouragement given by my brother devotee, Sri Srichand Rajpal, and I express my deep sense of gratitude to him. I wish also to thank Mr Kesava Rao, President of the All India Sai Samaj, for going through the manuscript and offering valuable suggestions. My wife, who introduced me to Radhakrishna Swamiji and was very much attached to him and Baba, has given me the strength and confidence to venture on this formidable task and I thank her. My thanks are also due to Sai Venkatakrishna, who got the manuscript typed and helped in various other ways, and to Rama Ram Mohan, Lakshmi, Suchitra Madhavan, Radha Thirumalai and Usha who assisted me in getting the manuscript prepared.

Rangaswami Parthasarathy

CONTENTS

CONTENTS

1

IN SEARCH OF SAI BABA

MAN is born in fear, fear of the unknown, fear of the morrow, fear of the future and fear of the dark forces around him. He seeks protection, safety and security in a world which seems to him to be hostile and full of suffering and sorrow. He is tossed in the ocean of *samsara* and struggles aimlessly, helplessly against the tide of adversity, of disease and death. He desperately tries to appease the forces of nature by deifying the elements and throwing up his arms in suppliance to a superior power and he sends out a prayer for deliverance from the shakles of disease, poverty and ignorance. He seeks from God, the all merciful, compassionate, omnipotent and omnipresent solace for the tragedies and misfortune which engulf him. His prayers are sometimes answered, sometimes he has to wait for a long time but he clings to faith and hope and it is this undying faith in an unknown, invisible and unfathomable superior power which is just and impartial and which comes to his rescue in times of danger and calamity that makes life bearable with all its misery and torture. To overcome fear man lives in faith. To help him discover faith prophets, messengers of God, have appeared at various periods in time, and through religion and rituals opened his eyes to the spiritual path which will make it easier for him to go through the obstacle race which is life on this earth.

In the line of those great prophets came one towards the end of the 19th century, who founded no religion, who had no credentials to be recognised as a prophet, whose appearance and dress and nomadic ways of living provoked people to call him a mad fakir. He appeared a fakir all right but he was not surely mad. He was a highly self-realised soul, whose parentage, antecedents, caste or religion nobody knew, nor would he reveal. He had no name either and he carried all his life the name given to him by his devotees. He had extraordinary powers, which he was reluctant to exhibit but was compelled to exercise them by a mean act of some petty traders who played a prank on him by denying him oil to light the mud lamps in the dilapidated mosque where he lived. This was a turning point in his life and from a mad fakir he became a living God to the simple folk of Shirdi, an obscure village of Maharashtra near Nashik. They worshipped him as they did their own personal deities (*ishta devatha*) and he became a living God to them. They did not have to wait for answer to their prayers as they had to in their puja rooms or in temples but this man-God granted them on the spot. He was their protector and guarantor of their safety, security and well-being. His message to them was : "Don't be afraid. I shall take care of you." The only thing he wanted from them was *nishta* and *saburi* (faith and patience). And this he got from them in abundance and those who surrendered to him including intellectuals, scholars and government officials of status and high position, never regretted and found fulfilment of their desires and aspirations. One of these intellectuals said: "He symbolised my conception of God."

They affectionately called him Sai Baba (Great Saint) and today this name is respected and revered in most parts of the world. But he was not known outside Maharashtra for a long time even after his death in 1918 and it was left to a Tamil ascetic to discover him and recount his life and teachings to most parts of India and especially to the South. Nobody knows exactly when Sai Baba came to Shirdi but it must have been in the latter half of the 19th century. Nor does anyone know how old he was then. It is an established fact that once he settled in Shirdi, which was bereft of decent civic amenities and was no more than a cluster of mud houses, he never left it even once. Except for stray visits to a neighbouring village, he continued to stay there till the end of his life.

Although books were written about him, they are in Marathi and no attempt was made to carry his name and fame outside Maharashtra. Ballad singers and itinerant storytellers sang his glory and divinity and were responsible for the rush of devotees in hundreds and thousands daily to Shirdi. The Marathi books and the ballad singers have provided unimpeachable evidence of Sai Baba's divinity and his unique position as a representative of God on earth, nay, as God himself. The experiences of devotees and the accounts of those who were close to him and were his beneficiaries are a treasure-house which reveal to the world the story of a great but simple man of God, who lived in poverty but who was never in want of money who lived in a mosque in ruins and rejected offers of a palatial residence and who personified in himself all the attributes of God.

It is this material which Narasimha Swamiji tapped and which he used to write the first regular, comprehensive, authentic and complete biography of Sai Baba almost 12 years after his passing away. The story of Narasimha Swamiji itself is one of renunciation and sacrifice and search for truth. It is during this adventurist part of his life when he was in search of a guru who could bring peace and solace to his embittered and rebellious soul that he came to Shirdi and found at Baba's *samadhi* what he had been searching for months and years. Here his quest ended. He felt Baba's presence all over his body and he was transformed into a new personality. He felt at peace within himself and a great surge of compassion and devotion flooded his mind and heart. At that moment was born an ardent devotee of Sai Baba and his chief posthumous disciple too.

B. V. Narasimha Aiyer, as he was known before he renounced the world, was a flourishing lawyer and politician in Salem in Tamil Nadu which under British rule was called Madras Presidency, embracing a much wider area than the present state of the Indian Union. He was a staunch nationalist and an active member of the Indian National Congress. He was a member of the Madras Legislative Council which enjoyed no powers except the freedom to discuss and debate subjects brought forward before it. The Governor, an Englishman, presided over its deliberations and Narasimha Aiyer frequently crossed swords with him fighting for the right of members. Once the Governor stopped him when he began speaking in Tamil as members were allowed to speak only in English. Narasimha Aiyer asserted he had every right to speak in his mother tongue and continued to speak in Tamil until the presiding officer asked him to go out of the chamber. Narasimha Aiyer gathered his papers and walked out. His action was considered daring and reckless in those days when Mahatma Gandhi had not yet arrived on the scene and nationalists were docile and lacked the fighting spirit.

Narasimha Aiyer was born in an orthodox Brahmin family in Bhavani in Coimbatore district on August 21,1874. His father,

Venkatagiri Aiyer was also a lawyer and he moved to Salem to set up practice there, when Narasimha Aiyer was still an infant. Narasimha Aiyer graduated from the Madras Christian College and later took a B.L. degree from the Madras Law College. He began his profession as a lawyer in 1895 and soon became leader of the bar and retained that position till 1925 when he gave up practice in response to an inner call for spiritual quest.   In politics he was an admirer of the Maharashtra leader, B.G. Tilak, who was considered an extremist. He was elected to the Madras Legislative Council in 1914 and continued to be a member till 1920.   He joined the Home Rule Movement of Annie Besant.

Tragedy struck Narasimha Aiyer's home in 1920 when he lost two of his children in a drowning accident. That came as a terrible shock to him and he decided to give up his practice and withdraw from politics. His mind was troubled and restless and he hungered for spiritual solace. He returned his *vakil sanad* to the High Court in 1925, resigned from the Legislative Council, gave away his property and concentrated on rebuilding the Lakshminarayan temple in Salem. He left home sometime later in search of spiritual guidance and it took him to Ramana Maharshi in Thiruvannamalai. He stayed in his ashram for three years (1928-30). He led a life of seclusion, studying Hindu scriptures. He wrote a book on the life of Ramana. At the end of three years he discovered he had lost the bhakti in which he had made good progress before he left Salem. Between 1930 and 1931 he resumed his efforts to regain his *bhakti* and began visiting temples and holy shrines which took him to Pandharpur and Nashik. At Nashik he met Mehr Baba, a disciple of Upasani Baba, and on his advice went to see Upasani Baba at Sakori, a short distance from Shirdi. Upasani Baba made him stick to the bhakti path and develop knowledge through *japa, bhajan,* discourse, etc., and to lead a life of poverty and asceticism. When practising his *sadhana* in accordance with his advice Narasimha Swamiji found to his surprise that there were elements in Upasani Baba's teachings and methods which were against his own idea of a correct religious life. He left Upasani Baba in 1933 intending never to return to his ashram. But Upasani Baba told his disciples that Narasimha Swamiji would return, "Where will the Madras Swami go?" he asked. "I shall draw him back here again." And so it happened.

Narasimha Swamiji went on pilgrimage, visiting sacred places, including Dwaraka. In the course of his pilgrimage he came to Hubli in Karnataka and met a *sadhaka* at the Siddharudha mutt who was eager to go to some place where he could settle down to a religious life. Narasimha Swamiji promised to help him and it appeared that Sakori was the only place for the sadakha and that was where Narasimha Swamiji took him. Although he wanted to avoid meeting Upasani Baba he was compelled by circumstances to bow before him. He stayed in Sakori for some time studying the teachings of Sai Baba and Upasani Baba. Shirdi was only three miles away from Sakori, an easy walk from there. Narasimha Swamiji carried on his research on Sai Baba and realised that it was Sai Baba who was drawing him through Upasani Baba. The completion of the research and development of one pointed bhakti towards Sai Baba resulted in full surrender to him. Narasimha Swamiji says, till that time he did not know what it was to surrender and what was meant by banishing ego. He had been visiting hundreds of places and contacting hundreds of saints and *sadhus* and none of them could put down his ego and make him surrender. He came to believe that Baba was really Rama or Krishna in a new *avatar*, that his power for good was as potent even after his death as it had been when he was alive and that he was worthy of worship as God incarnate. He found in Baba the personification of the Trinity and took upon himself the mission of propagating the Sai faith.

Narasimha Swamiji says that a calamity in 1953 as great, if not greater than, the one in 1921 proved to be the turning point in his spiritual life. It made him realise the truth of Baba's saying that he gives everything to him who surrenders everything to him. "Baba looks to the devotee who solely looks to him with perfect and complete confidence and reliance," says Narasimha Swamiji. Swamiji says the second calamity was essential to develop his personality and make him write the biography of Sai Baba about which he had taken a vow long ago but could not fulfil owing to some reason or other. Narasimha Swamiji says that it was in 1931 that he heard about Sai Baba, saw his picture and resolved to visit Shirdi and Sakori. He was in search of some spiritual or religious institution where the facilities and atmosphere for his sadhana were suitable to his condition and stage of development. The quest took him to a number of places noted for their sanctity such as temples, sacred rivers, ashrams of sadhus and saints. He visited Pandharpur, Nashik, Brindavan, Kashi, Gaya, Prayag, Sakori and Hubli. In none of these places could he find what he was seeking. "In all these places satisfaction eluded me because the conditions and atmosphere suited to my requirements were absent." In the course of his travels, Narasimha Swamiji met N. P. Avasthi, a judge in Pune who introduced him to his father, Purushotham Avasthi, who was a great devotee of Sai Baba. Purushotham Avasthi introduced Narasimha Swamiji to about 60 devotees of Sai Baba who had personal experience of moving with Baba. Most of these devotees could speak only in Marathi with which Narasimha Swamiji was unfamiliar. Avasthi helped him by translating their statements into English.

Narasimha Swamiji says : "From the very beginning I was determined to collect, test, sift such materials, to arrange them on their strength, that is, on their inherent reliability and credibility and compile a biography of Baba that would benefit earnest souls all over India if not also beyond." Narasimha Swamiji says a miracle occurred at this time. He had typed out the statements made by devotees and left the bunch of papers with his friend, G B Datar. Later when he returned to Pune to collect them he was told by Datar that the bunch of papers had been lost. As Narasimha Swamiji had no copies of the statements with him their loss would have been disastrous. However, having faith in Baba and praying to him he went to Datar's house and searched his table where he had placed the papers. Very soon he was able to find the missing papers mixed up with legal documents of Datar.

Narasimha Swamiji says : "More than one devotee warned me against accepting statements of bogus devotees and faked experience and asked me how I, a stranger to the men, manners and language of Maharashtra, hoped to ensure the purity and reliability of the information I received. I have one and only one device. Sri Sai Baba was my guide and he would not allow humbugs to pass into my sacred collection. At least in two cases I received strange and unexpected warnings and revelations indicating what I should reject. Some statements were thus wholly rejected and some in part. It was quite obvious to me as also to my Bombay friends that Baba was favouring the publication by me of his biography and was removing the obstacles thereto step by step."

Narasimha Swamiji discovered a mass of information about what Sai Baba had said and during his lifetime and about the experiences of people who had met and talked to him. There was even greater mass of evidence of experiences of devotees after the samadhi of Sai Baba in 1918 who treated him as their true God or Ishta Devatha. Unfortunately, very few who met Baba or benefited by him till 1918 made use of their contact with him to collect and record facts about him. Baba's thinking and nature were totally unknown to anyone. No one was with him all through his life, noting as Boswell did about Johnson, everything Baba did or said. But says Narasimha Swamiji, there is a fair record of his sayings and doings up to 1918 when he passed away. There were equally a large if not larger mass of material of his *lilas* and utterances after 1918. Till Narasimha Swamiji came on the scene there had been no good biography of Sai Baba containing a fair, full and faithful description of his life.

A number of intimate devotees of Baba who may be called his apostles have written about Baba and their experiences. Among them are Dabolkar, also known as Hemadpant, who wrote a book *Sai Satcharita*, G H Khaparde, whose diaries provide invaluable information about Baba, Das Ganu Maharaj whose poems and songs on Baba spread his name and glory far and wide, and Marthand, son of Mahlsapathy, who wrote about his father's intimate association with Baba.

When Dabolkar told Baba of his desire to write his biography Baba gave him permission to do so and also gave him advice on how to go about it. He told him a biographer should not write with self-conceit and in the spirit of controversy. He said: "Let there be no taking of sides and no aggressive debate." He said the biographer must drown himself in the contemplation of Sai Baba and must write after full surrender of self and egotism. The biography would then have really been written by Baba himself, he said. Baba added : "I fully agree with you regarding the writing of *Sai Satcharita*. You do your duty, don't be afraid in the least. Steady your mind and have faith in my words. If my lilas are written the *avidya* will vanish and if they are attentively and devoutly listened to, the consciousness of the worldly existence will abate and strong waves of devotion and love will rise and if one dives deep into my lilas he would get precious jewels of knowledge".

Baba, then in a mood of ecatasy, said : "If a man utters my name with love I shall fulfil all his wishes, increase his devotion. And if he sings earnestly my life and deeds I will be in front of him and back and on all sides. Those devotees who are attached to me heart and soul will naturally feel happiness when they hear these stories. Believe me, if anybody sings my lilas I will give infinite joy and everlasting contentment. It is my special characteristic to free any person who surrenders to me completely and who worships me faithfully and who remembers me and meditates on me constantly. How can they be conscious of worldly objects and sensations who utter my name, who worship me, who think of my lilas and my life and who thus always remember me? I shall draw out my devotees from the jaws of death. If my lilas are listened to all diseases will be got rid of. So hear my lilas with respect and think and meditate on them, assimilate them. This is the way of happiness and contentment. The pride and egoism of my devotees will vanish, the mind of the hearers will be set at rest and if it has whole-hearted and complete faith it will be at one with supreme consciousness. The simple remembrance of my name as Sai will do away with the sins of speech."

Narasimha Swamiji believed that devotees were the best observers of the powers and doings of their gurus from the viewpoint of the chronicler. He said : "Their love of exaggeration, credibility, over-sensitiveness in trying to avoid anything like strict examination of seeming miracles and mysteries and usual want of the scientific attitude account for the unreliability of their testimony." Therefore, Narasimha Swamiji, carefully and vigorously scrutinised the statements obtained from devotees and to shift the grain from the chaff and arrange all the mass of evidence collected. He presented what after inquiry and investigation could be accepted as true and beyond reasonable doubt. The amount of trouble he must have taken in collecting and processing the information and finally producing a narrative in accordance with the norms of scientific and objective inquiry was truly amazing. The biographer of Narasimha Swamiji says : "Only one blessed with divine grace could have summoned to his aid the enormous patience, perseverance and faith without which the task undertaken would not have become an accomplished fact." The biographer, Saipadananda Radhakrishna Swamiji, says it was Narasimha Swamiji's "immense and meticulous effort since 1936 that discovered for us Sai Baba as a world saviour whose presence in our hearts helps us to ward off danger and cast off fear".

It is true, says Radhakrishna Swamiji, that the rapid spread of the Sai faith was due to the emphasis which was laid on the mundane benefits derived from devotion to Baba. "But it is mainly through conferring material benefits that God always attracts and draws devotees to himself, secures their love and devotion and places them on the path that leads them to their moral and spiritual advancement. Were he not our refuge and strength, our helper amid the flood of moral ills prevailing in the world nobody would care for God."

Narasimha Swamiji has said in his biography of Baba that at the time of his samadhi in 1918 he was little understood and there was hardly anything worth calling a real account of his life. Even in 1936, the number of people seeking solace at the feet of Baba was small and it was only in the late thirties and forties that the Sai movement gathered tremendous momentum spreading all over the country and reaching even beyond the frontiers of India. The rise and spread of the Sai movement is entirely due to the initiative and devoted and single minded efforts of Narasimha Swamiji.

Narasimha Swamiji first wrote about devotees' experiences in articles published by the *Sunday Times* in Madras and they appeared in 40 issues of that English weekly. It then occurred to him that he should try to write a reliable but orthodox biography of Baba in Tamil, his mother tongue. He says : "So far as I know a clearly intelligible picture of Baba's nature, his powers and the course of his life were presented in my book *Introduction to Sai Baba.*" The first edition of the book came out in 1938 and within 11 months a third edition was published. It was later translated into Tamil, Malayalam, Telugu and Kannada. Thousands and thousands of people in the South in the space of a few months became devotees of Baba. People from all parts of the country wrote to him their experiences and these were later published in another book, *Devotees' Experiences.*

Narasimha Swamiji then started writing in English a comprehensive biography of Sai Baba which came out in four volumes, the last two posthumously. Writing about this he says he had been thinking of writing an English biography for over 12 years but something or other prevented the work from being undertaken and carried through. He had a serious accident in 1953 which confined him with a bone fracture to hospital for 60 days which was followed by a severe attack of dysentery. This continued up to the middle of 1954 and then, in his own words, "it was a wonder to the author that his life had been spared and that sufficient remnants of energy, mental and physical, had been left to him. It was clear that the remaining energy and life were intended to be devoted to Baba just as the previous decades of the author's life were. So the matter of this big book was all in his memory and fairly easy to recall, at least with some little effort. He started recalling and strange to say though he had no strength to sit and write Baba provided him with a stenographer."

Narasimha Swamiji says his health since October 1954 being extremely unreliable the work would have been impossible but for the provision of medical help. "Baba designated a doctor in very good position and with excellent knowledge and made him to attend on him repeatedly without receiving any recompense at all and that doctor was still attending on him as he was writing the book."

Before he was hospitalised in 1953 Narasimha Swamiji had been engaged in propagating the Sai faith through extensive tours in the north and by founding the All India Sai Samaj in Madras and publishing a journal *Sai Sudha*. Earlier, before his discovery of Baba, he had gone to Sri Narayan Maharaj in Nashik and said to him: "I am a diamond merchant. I want a flawless diamond. Where can I get it?" Narayan Maharaj said: "You will get it soon. Go West." At Shirdi, which he reached after meeting Upasani Babu, he felt like a man possessed at the samadhi of Baba and he had a vision. It was then that he took the decision that he would do *Sai prachar* (propagation) throughout the length and breadth of the country. But he had no resources. Where would he go for the money? And miracle of miracles, a South Indian merchant came to him and left Rs.11,500 with him to be utilised for *Sai prachar*. By this gesture of Baba Narasimha Swamiji was more than ever convinced that Baba wanted him to carry on *Sai prachar*.

The year was 1934-35. He offered the money to Sai Sansthan to utilise it for *Sai prachar* but to his great surprise it was said on its behalf that Baba never favoured propaganda and his offer was rejected. And for sometime there was a campaign against him and motives were attributed to him. But subsequently amends were made, the charges were withdrawn and today his portrait adorns the picture gallery of Baba's apostles in Sai Samadhi Mandir.

Narasimha Swamiji undertook the prachar work single-handedly and delivered 600 to 700 lectures on Baba in various parts of the country; he brought out pamphlets and books on the life and teachings of Baba. He recalled that at Shirdi before Baba's samadhi he had prayed to him for an indication of his approval of his mission by making a bird sit on his head. A bird did come and perch on his head to his great delight. He began writing in the *Sunday Times* in 1935, started the *Sai Sudha* in 1940 and the All India Sai Samaj in 1941 which was however registered only in 1956 shortly before his death. Narasimha Swamiji passed away on October 19, 1956, at the age of 82 after achieving what he set out to do—the launching of the Sai movement which today has spread throughout the country and is drawing thousands to the worship of Sai Baba in temples and shrines built for him in hundreds of cities, towns and villages.

Writing about Narasimha Swamiji K. R. R. Sastri, a veteran educationist, said: "He resembled in features and appearance an old rishi of the vedic age. He never wasted a minute either during the day or the night except for a very short time when he slept. He spent his time either in writing something about Baba or giving a talk on him to any devotee who came to him. Even during journeys on train he continued to write. The extraordinary labour and trouble he undertook to collect data about the life and teachings of Sai Baba in Maharashtra have rarely been excelled in modern history."

Narasimha Swamiji's chief disciple Radhakrishna Swamiji to whom he gave the title of Saipadananda, wrote : "The inspired zeal and matchless dedication of Narasimha Swamiji discovered and presented to a troubled world Sai Baba the saviour par excellence. It is my firm belief that a great majority of sadakas and aspirants to spiritual progress can profit more by a study of the lives and doings of saints and seers than by the mastery of the dry doctrine of any system of philosophy. For in such a study they cannot find practical guidance for overcoming difficulties and complex situations that often confront them in their lives and in their spiritual quest."

Radhakrishna Swamiji asked the question : How was it that a person like Narasimha Swamiji who had the benefit of personal contacts with a living sage like Ramana Maharshi had been drawn towards Sai Baba, a saint who was no more and whose method of teaching differed considerably from that of Ramana Maharshi? He got the answer when Narasimha Swamiji visited Udhagamandalam in the course of his *Sai prachar*. Radhakrishna Swamiji put the question to him. Narasimha Swamiji explained to him the circumstances and reasons which guided his footsteps in his search for a final resting place where his heart could abide in complete faith with a mind which "is in repose because it is no longer assailed by doubts."

Radhakrishna Swamiji, who was called Radhakrishna by his parents, came from a village near Karur in Tamil Nadu and was marked for the spiritual path from very early in life. He had no love for the formal type of education but he developed extraordinary love for the Hindu scriptures, the *Vedas* and the *Upanishads* and the *Bhagavad Gita*. It was amazing how he learnt Sanskrit and English and began writing commentaries on the *Upanishads* even in his teens which, however, he did for his own satisfaction and not for others to see. His biographer happened to see scraps of paper in his brother's house where they were preserved in which he had explained the message of the *Upanishads* and the *Gita* in beautiful and flawless English. It was this precocious young man brimming with knowledge and ability, whom Narasimha Swamiji met in Udhagamandalam. He was struck by his devotion to Baba and his enthusiasm for *Sai prachar*. He invited him to Madras and an intimate and close association between the master and disciple began at the All India Sai Samaj. Narasimha Swamiji sent him to Bangalore to take up *Sai prachar* in Karnataka. Radhakrishna Swamiji settled down in Bangalore and established the Sai Spiritual Centre which has been doing yeoman service to propagate Sai faith.

Radhakrishna Swamiji says it was through Narasimha Swamiji that Baba's "loving kindness" was showered on him. "Baba has paved the way for me for a worthy living to realise truth. Baba is all in all to me, mother, father, relative, friend, knowledge, wealth (spiritual) and all. He gave me plenty of opportunities to realise *samatva*, enough power to bear *sukha* and *dukkha* (pleasure and pain) equally without hurting myself. Equally he has showered patience on this humble self on the path of spirituality."

Narasimha Swamiji told Radhakrishna Swamiji : "Remember Baba's words 'Sit quiet'. Have patience and at the end you will have the reward. Concentrate on Baba's feet first and then go on upward, concentrating on every part of his body till you reach the whole. Go up and down in your concentration from foot to head and head to foot and with your mind at his feet for eternal refuge. You will get the grace in full with all ananda (bliss absolute). There is no difference between Brahma, Vishnu and Maheswara and Baba. The three combined in one you will find in Baba, the pure, unadulterated, omnipotent soul. Remember, he is the one who dances his joyful eternal with all its freedom everywhere. The mystics and saints enjoy his dance. You too can enjoy it in full. He lavishes his grace freely upon all devotees who take shelter at his feet. He is your mother. He knows your hunger and will feed you at all times. Like a compassionate mother he can hear his child's cry of hunger. He will fill your heart's hunger too. But remember that you should understand that the salient benefits of higher attainments cannot be acquired without the practical realisation of purity, of all kinds."

Radhakrishna Swamiji came to know all about Baba through Narasimha Swamiji who became his guru in 1942. "Baba's loving kindness was showered on me through the revered Narasimha Swamiji, the great apostle of Sai Baba," he wrote in his biography of Narasimha Swamiji. "After my introduction to Baba there were many experiences which have helped me in my evolution in the spiritual path." He wrote, his guru was the personification of dedication, devotion, emancipation and enlightenment. His life was an example of absolute surrender to his guru God. He said it was Narasimha Swamiji's inspiration, zeal and matchless dedication that discovered and presented to a troubled world Baba the saviour par excellence. Radhakrishna Swamiji's biography of Narasimha Swamiji was published in 1973. He was deputed by Narasimha Swamiji to go to Shirdi for liaison with the Shirdi Sansthan on his behalf and to ensure proper facilities for pilgrims from the South. He later served on the Shirdi Sansthan Committee as a member for some years. He came to Bangalore in 1952 as desired by Narasimha Swamiji for

Sai Prachar. Radhakrishna Swamiji said:"I was leading a comfortable life in Ooty. Then my contact with Narasimha Swamiji brought me to Madras. Swamiji gave me a plank of wood to sleep on and I used my arms as a pillow."

Radhakrishna Swamiji has said the last words of his guru to him in Bangalore in 1956 were : "Trust in Lord Sai. Worship and adore him. Let your faith be not shattered. Great changes are going to take place. Hold on to the feet of Baba, you will be blessed, nay, you are blessed." Three years earlier Narasimha Swamiji had written to him saying: "Hereafter you will be known as Saipadananda," and when his guru attained samadhi in Madras in 1956 Radhakrishna Swamiji in Bangalore saw a vision of his guru entering Sri Rama's portrait in the Sai Mandir. Radhakrishna Swamiji set up the Sai Spiritual Centre in Bangalore on April 4 , 1954. The present premises of the centre was opened on June 17 , 1965. Until then Radhakrishna Swamiji had lived in a small room spreading the message of Sai Baba. He soon was able to draw hundreds of devotees who helped him to build the Sai Spiritual Centre. Radhakrishna Swamiji became a powerful spiritual force in Karnataka and a number of Sai mandirs sprang up in various parts of the state Baba's name became a household word. In addition to being President of the Sai Spiritual Centre in Bangalore Radhakrishna Swamiji also took charge as President of the All India Sai Samaj in Madras and he kept this post until his samadhi in 1980. Through his efforts and the work of dedicated devotees the All India Sai Samaj became a national centre for Sai worship and *Sai prachar* with many branches and associate members in all parts of the country, Today, the Baba shrine at the Samaj premises draws thousands of devotees and has become a haven of solace and spiritual guidance for the sadhakas and common people who come to seek Baba's blessings and his favours.

We may conclude this chapter with R. R. Diwakar's stirring words on Baba : "The Universality of Sri Sai Baba's soul and the child-like purity of his consciousness made him the darling of thousands and he was the resting place of the afflicted."

2

THE FAKIR FROM NOWHERE

I N THE closing years of the 19th century the rustic folk of
Shirdi, a small village in Maharashtra not far from the
Godavari, observed a young fakir sitting under a neem tree on
the outskirts of the village, not talking to anyone, and deeply
absorbed in meditation. He wore a kufni (robe) which had seen
better days and a cloth tied round his head like a handkerchief.
He appeared to be a mysterious person who roamed about in
the nearby forests for hours and slept under the neem tree in a
pit he had dug for himself. Nobody knew what he did for his
food and how he sustained himself, for he never entered the
village and moved with people.

A very old woman, mother of Chopdar, said in 1900 that
when she was very young she had seen the fakir at Shirdi and
he was then an attractive lad of 16 or 20 without a moustache,
about whom nothing was known. He was seen frequently sitting
under the neem tree, called "Gode Neem". He would wander
in the fields and show no interest in worldly matters. She said
sometime later he moved from place to place and led a nomadic
life till he returned to Shirdi once again and settled there
permanently. He was generally considered a mad fakir and he
was harassed by children who thought him crazy and threw
stones at him. But the fakir did not retaliate and tried to play
with them There were, however, some residents who realised
he was no ordinary fakir, that he was a highly evolved soul and
was of a divine nature. Among them were Mahlsapathy, a
goldsmith and priest of the Khandoba temple in the village, and
his friends. There was also a woman, Bayyaji Bai, who
captivated by his purity and innocence, pursued him to the
jungles and fields to feed him. So much was her devotion to him
that she would not eat until she had fed the fakir.

Suddenly the fakir disappeared and there was no trace of him for the next year or two. The people of Shirdi saw him again in 1872 when he returned with a wedding party from neighbouring Dhupkeda village which was in the Nizam's Dominions. Thereafter he made Shirdi his home for the rest of his life.

There is a story connected with Chand Bai Patel of Dhupkeda who led the marriage party to Shirdi taking the fakir with him. Patel had met the fakir some weeks earlier in unusual circumstances. He was looking for his horse which had been missing and in the course of his search he came to the neem tree under which the fakir was sitting. He entered into conversation with the fakir and told him he was in search of his missing horse. The fakir told him : "Don't worry, you will find the horse near the stream." Patel went to the spot indicated by the fakir and the horse was sure enough there. Unable to contain his surprise and gratitude Patel rushed back to the fakir and thanked him. The fakir asked him to stay on and share a smoke with him He then took out his pipe and hit the earth with the short stick he had with him and water gushed forth as if from a spring. With this he cooled the pipe and then he again hit the ground with the stick and there was a flame jetting out and he lighted the pipe. He offered it to Patel to smoke and then had a puff himself. Patel could not believe his eyes at what he saw and recognised that this was no ordinary fakir. He invited him to accompany him to his village and take part in a wedding of one of his relatives. The fakir agreed, went with him, stayed in the village for the marriage and returned with the marriage party to Shirdi.

Mahlsapathi recognised him as the lost fakir and greated him "Aao Sai" (welcome saint). And from then onwards, the fakir came to be known as Sai Baba and to the end of his days nobody knew what was the name his parents gave him. A devotee who saw him then described him as having long hair flowing down his back. He wore a green *kupni,* (a skull cap) and over it a *bagawi topi* (ochre-coloured cap). He carried a small *danda* (stick) in his hand with a *chillum* (pipe) and a matchbox. He got his food by begging, the devotee said. Mahlsapathy and his friends told the villagers that Baba was no ordinary fakir and he was a pure and holy man who deserved

their respect and veneration. They began to take care of Baba
and supply his requirements.

Baba slowly came out of his shell and began treating the
sick and the ailing in the village. He mixed with the sadhus and
the spiritually-minded people. His real worth and high spiritual
quality were known only to these sadhus and to the very few,
like Mahlsapathy who attended on him. One sadhu told the
villagers that Baba was "a diamond lying neglected in a
dunghill". Another said the world would one day come to
know Baba's real worth as an eminent devotee of Rama.
However, the villagers continued to treat him as a Muslim fakir
of no importance. In his treatment of the sick Baba usually
gave them herbal medicine but he sometimes adopted
unconventional methods to cure a patient. It is said in one case
that when a patient came to him with a diseased eye he pulled
out the eyeballs, cleaned them and reinserted them. Truly a
surgical feat unheard of anywhere in the world. If a patient had
no one to look after him he acted as his nurse and took care of
him. Later Baba gave up the practice of giving medicines and
distributed *udhi* (sacred ash) instead. This was after he took his
residence in an abandoned mosque. Referring to this Baba said
: "I used to give medicine before but thereafter gave up
everything and went on chanting the name of Hari and by a
ceaseless muttering of the holy name I became Hari."

Shirdi was then a small village of 400 houses with a Hindu
majority and a small percentage of Muslims also. It is near
Kopargaon and midway between and equidistant from Rahata
on one side (south) and Nimagoan on the other side (north).
Baba never went beyond these places throughout his life. He
never saw a railway train nor did he travel by one. Shirdi is in
Ahmednagar district in what was then called Bombay Presidency.
It was not well known even in the district. It consisted mostly
of mud houses with narrow lanes and surrounded by an
abundance of babul and prickly pear trees and other wild growth.
There was hardly a single building fit for occupation by anyone
visiting it for the first time. There were no shops except some
tiny ones which sold foodgrains and oil. There was no temple
except the Maruthi shrine next to the mosque which itself was
dilapidated and its rafters were falling one after another. The
villagers led a quiet life engrossed in their agricultural operations.
The only event which caused excitement and brought cheer to

their lives was the fair or the bazar held every week. A tonga (horse carriage) was a rarity and if one was sighted children and elders would crowd around it in admiration.

In an article published in *Sai Leela* in 1932 Balakrishna Viswanath wrote that the name Shirdi was a corruption of the name, Shiladhi or Shailadhi. When he visited Shirdi in 1910 there were about 400 houses, big and small. There were two public wells, a Marathi school (up to Seventh standard) and Marathi Mission School. There were two orchards, a flower garden, nine temples, two mosques, a dharamsala, a sugar mill and a flour mill. There was a population of about 2,600 consisting of both Hindus and Muslims. But at the time Baba arrived in Shirdi there were hardly 80 or 100 houses and there were no facilities or amenities for the villagers. The more important village, Rahata, was three miles away and it was also not a place of importance and not known to many.

Shirdi was wretchedly poor and the only consolation for the people was the occasional visit of a fakir or sadhu who talked to them on religion and God. The Muslims who were not many were very poor and were mostly artisans or labourers. They did not own any property. At the head of the village society was the Hindu village headman, called Patil. There were no roads or street lights. For drinking water the people had to depend on a public well. There were one or two *chavadis* (choultries) which were used as schools and also to accommodate visitors. The Khandoba temple was on the outskirts of the village.

It was amidst these unprepossessing surroundings and abject poverty that the "mad fakir", as the innocent illiterate villagers called him, decided to pitch his camp and serve the people. As Narasimha Swamiji said : "Practically nothing is known about the parentage and early life of Baba. There is a cloud of mystery hanging over every period of Baba's life and Baba allowed it to remain so evidently because there was no necessity to remove that mist." Many years later after Baba settled down in the mosque in Shirdi and thousands came to worship him daily, an accused in a theft case stated in court that Sai Baba had given him the stolen property. The magistrate issued summons to Baba to appear in court and give evidence. Baba threw the summons paper in the *dhuni* (sacred fire) at the mosque. His devotees, afraid of the consequences, approached the magistrate

and told him that Baba was being worshipped as God by a
large number of people and the issue of summons and warrant
was improper and undesirable. They said that if his evidence
was necessary a commissioner might be sent to Shirdi to take it
from Baba. This was agreed to and the commissioner came and
questioned Baba. The following conversation took place :

Commissioner	:	What is your name?
Baba	:	They call me Sai Baba.
Commissioner	:	Your father's name?
Baba	:	Also Sai Baba.
Commissioner	:	Your guru's name?
Baba	:	Venkusa.
Commissioner	:	Creed or religion?
Baba	:	Kabir.
Commissioner	:	Caste or race?
Baba	:	*Parvardigar* (God).
Commissioner	:	Age?
Baba	:	Lakhs of years
Commissioner	:	Will you solemnly affirm that what you are going to say is the truth?
Baba	:	Truth.
Commissioner	:	Do you know the accused?
Baba	:	Yes, I know him. I know everyone.
Commissioner	:	The man says he is your devotee and that he lived with you. Is that so?
Baba	:	Yes. I live with everyone. All are mine.
Commissioner	:	Did you give him the jewels as alleged by him?
Baba	:	Yes. I gave him. Who gives what to whom?
Commissioner	:	If you gave him the jewels how did you get them and came in possession of them?
Baba	:	Everything is mine.
Commissioner	:	Baba, here is a serious charge of theft. That man says that you delivered the jewels to him.
Baba	:	What is all this? What do I have to do with all that?

The dialogue ended there and the Commissioner was
perplexed and did not know what to do. However, he was

saved from embarrassment as it was later established that the accused was not in Shirdi at the time he was alleged to have received the jewels from Baba and Baba had never left Shirdi. The commissioner placed these facts before Baba who said they were true. Baba was not asked to sign any document or put his mark on any paper. In fact, Baba did not put his signature or mark on any paper at any time.

So who was Baba? Mahlsapathy, his intimate devotee, has recorded that Baba once told him : "I am a Brahmin of Pathri and when young my parents gave me to a fakir for being trained under him." Pathri is a village in the former Nizam's dominions. Baba is reported to have told another devotee: "I was only eight years old when I left my parents and came to the Ganges (Baba always referred to the Godavari as Ganga). Then I came to Shirdi." This devotee adds that the neem tree under which Baba sat was on the outskirts of Shirdi near the debris of the old village wall where people used to throw their rubbish, where a stream of filthy stinking water ran and the thorny cactus abounded—Baba stayed here uncared for and unnoticed by the villagers for a year or two. No one knew how he fed himself. But from the admonition he administered to one of his devotees once it appears he lived on margosa leaves for more than 12 years. He had said to the devotee : "What ! You can't put up with a day or two days of starvation? I myself lived on margosa leaves for as many as 12 years."

It is established that Baba was born to Brahmin parents. It is also established that his parents handed him over at a very early age to a Muslim fakir and his wife (whose names have not been revealed) and for what reason we do not know. It is also known that after some years the fakir died and before his death he asked his wife to hand over the child to a petty chieftain of Selu in the Nizam's dominions who was called Gopal Rao Deshmukh. It is believed that Baba must have been eight years old then. Deshmukh, a Brahmin who was also called Venkatesa (Venhusa as Baba called him) worshipped Venkatachalapathi of Thirumala and had developed siddhis. He became Baba's guru and Baba served him with bhakti and devotion. We will hear more about Baba and his guru in another chapter. A picture of Baba's stay with his guru at Selu is given by Das Ganu Maharaj in one of his books. Das Ganu says he wrote the account based on Baba's own statements and on what residents of Selu told him. The villagers told him that an old saint who lived there trained a fakir boy. Some of his disciples did not like this and tried to kill him. One day when Baba and his guru were in a garden some of the disgruntled disciples threw stones at the master in an attempt to kill him. One of the stones was about to hit him but the master, through his yogic power, made it stop in mid-air and then, since it had to be disposed of, allowed it to hit him on the head, causing a bleeding injury. The man who hurled the stone was struck with fear and died. The disciples who had caused the incident fell at the master's feet and prayed to him to revive the offender who had died. The master said he had given all his powers to his young disciple and asked Baba to bring back to life the dead man. And Baba, quite unaware of his powers, prayed for the man's life, chanting the guru's name. The dead man got up and fell at the feet of the guru. This was one instance of Baba reviving a dead body and as far as we know there was another case which will be mentioned in a later chapter.

Meanwhile the guru bandaged the injured part of his head with a piece of cloth which he tore from his dress and then he told Baba:"I see the time has come for me to part with you. Tomorrow at 4 p.m. I shall leave the body not as a result of this injury but by my yogic power. I shall therefore now vest my full spiritual personality in you." For this purpose the guru asked him to fetch milk from a nearby black cow. Baba was, however, told by the owner of the cow that it had not calved and was barren but the animal was brought before the master anyhow. The guru passed his hand over the cow from the horns to its tail and then asked that it be milked. To the great surprise of everyone present the cow yielded copious milk which was given to Baba by the guru who then blessed him. The guru passed away the next day as foretold by him and Baba left Selu in the direction of Shirdi as he had been instructed by his guru. The young man who must have been about 16 years old at this time was greatly attached to his master and the master was deeply interested in his ward. Baba was with his master at all times, either in the field or at puja, whether he was in the garden or in office. Baba did not receive any formal education. As mentioned earlier the master was a pious and religious man very much attached to the deity, Venkatachalapati at Tirumala, whose idol he worshipped daily in his castle. He patronised learning and sadhus and his young disciple had plenty of opportunity to pick up real education. Baba always referred to his guru as Venkusa which is a contraction for Venkatesa, the *ishta devatha* of his master.

After leaving Selu Baba wandered through jungles, hills and villages and came to Shirdi in obedience to his master's directive that he should go due west from Selu. Shirdi is due west of Selu on the banks of the Godavari. Baba's stay with his parents was far too short for any noticeable development. He lived with his foster, parents the fakir and his wife, for four or five years and this appeared to be the most impressionable period of his life. However, very little is known of what happened during this period but the fact that in later years, whenever Baba referred to his guru or God he used the term fakir, showed his regard and reverence for his foster-father whom he treated as a guru. He left Shirdi after some time and again wandered till he returned to Shirdi at the age of about 20 to stay there permanently. Nothing is known of what he did during this period or where he lived. There are, however, many reports current which speak of his having done penance in caves and learning at the feet of Muslim saints but none of these is authentic and cannot be confirmed.

After he returned to Shirdi for the second time Baba was in search of a suitable habitation for himself. He visited the Khandoba temple and was impressed with it and its surroundings. He thought it was an ideal place for him to stay but it did not occur to him that since he was recognised as a Muslim by the villagers and Mahlsapathy, the temple priest who had high regard for him, he would not be permitted to stay in the temple. And that was what happened. Mahlsapathy told Baba he could not allow him inside the temple as he was a Muslim. He suggested he could go to the nearby mosque which was in a dilapidated condition and was not being used. Radhakrishna Swamiji, giving an account of the incident, quotes Baba as telling Mahlsapathy:

"The creator God is one and the same for both communities, Hindus and Muslims. This is a mere verbal difference. Sadhakas should not attach importance to it. But let each one attend to his own group, its ways and customs. Do not neglect them. But see one God, Sat Chit Ananda in everything. He that is called Allah Ilahi by Muslims is the same as Seshasayee for the Hindus.

Your Khandoba is also the same. Ask your Khandoba how being a bania by caste he came to marry the shepherdess of the name of Banoo. From this the conclusion has to be drawn that the wise ones do not attach importance to differences of caste, etc. There are temples and mosques. Good men do not neglect either of these. Respecting your decision I shall have *darshan* from outside, from a distance. In your *Puranas* you have the story of Chokia Mahar who became hundred times dearer than his pujari to Pandarinath. He who is pure in heart is pure and holy wherever he is."

Not many months later it was the same Mahlsapathy who invited Baba to the temple and said the whole place had been purified because of his presence.

After his conversation with Mahlsapathy Baba returned to the old neem tree and made it his resting place. He made no arrangement for food but this was taken care of by Bayyaji Bai whom we have already mentioned. She was the wife of the village headman, Ganapati Rao Patil Kothe, and the couple undertook to feed him. H.S.Dixit described Baba under the neem tree in these words:"With rags to wear he would sit wherever he chose and though he appeared to be a mad man he was one who had realised the entire universe within him. At times he sat on one side of the stream, sometimes in the fields of someone and at other times underneath the neem tree. At times he appeared to be in great anger, a line of conduct which to the worldly-minded rustic folks appeared to be that of a mad man."

Baba soon moved on to the dilapidated and crumbling mosque and made himself comfortable there. The place which was later called Dwaraka Mayi was to be his home till his death. He dug a pit and started a fire which was called the dhuni and it was kept burning day and night and it continues to burn even today at Shirdi. Baba sat by its side and received his devotees. He ploughed the village common land and raised a flower garden which was later called Lendi. He watered the plants and carried pots of water on his shoulders for the purpose. He distributed the flowers to temples and Muslim places of worship.

In his earlier days Baba loved art and music and at nights often went to the Muslim rest house, intended for travellers, and he sang and danced with anklets on his legs. The songs were mostly those sung by Kabir and sometimes they were also in Arabic and Persian which the local people did not understand.

An incident occurred in the mosque after Baba took his residence which completely transformed the attitude of the local people from one of derision and suspicion to total surrender and worship. It was the practice of Baba to put up earthen lamps in the mosque in the evening and he got the oil to keep them burning from the local vendors who supplied it free. One day these vendors who continued to think Baba was a mad fakir decided to play a trick on him and watch the fun. When Baba came in the evening and asked for oil they told him they had run out of stock and could not oblige him. Unruffled and without showing any sign of distress Baba walked back to the mosque with the empty tinpot. He poured some water into the tinpot and stirring a little bit of oil sticking to it drank it. He then poured water into the earthen lamps and lighted the wicks and wonder of wonders, they burnt brightly and throughout the night.

The oilmongers and the shopkeepers who had followed Baba to see how he would manage the situation were stunned to see the miracle and they fell at his feet and sought forgiveness for their mischievous prank. Baba readily forgave them and advised them never to tell a lie. "Falsehood displeases God," he told them. He said their conduct was unsocial and wicked. The lamps in the mosque, he said, were intended to help visitors to the mosque and they would be inconvenienced if the mosque was dark. He asked them never again to take pleasure in others' distress.

The miracle of the lamp opened the eyes of the people of Shirdi and they realised that the man whom they took for a mad fakir was in fact a man of divinity, one to be worshipped, not derided. It was the signal for the villagers to flock to the mosque for Baba's darshan and it was an unending mass of people who clamoured to see him. They offered him flowers and fruits. Some waved lamps with burning camphor before him and some poured coloured rice on his head and applied sandal paste. It began to take the form of regular worship however much Baba tried to prevent them from worshipping him as God. It was thus that the fakir from nowhere became the God or Godman of Shirdi.

Since this kind of worship is not observed in a mosque the local Muslims objected to it and they asked Baba why he permitted it. Baba told them he had to bend to circumstances.

If Hindus wished to please themselves by worshipping him why not allow them to do so, he asked. He said if Hindus worshipped a Muslim in a mosque it was no loss to Islam but only a loss to Hinduism. It is to be noted that almost everyone thought Baba was a Muslim and Baba made no attempt to identify himself either as a Hindu or a Muslim. In fact, at one stage the local people referred to Baba as the "Muslim Vishnu." A young man who attended a study class of scriptures one day came to Baba and complained that his teacher had defamed Baba saying he was no God. Baba merely said: " What is the harm in that? I am only a fakir, I am not God. Who can compare with God?"

The change that came over the people of Shirdi is described thus by one devotee: "While eating, drinking and working in their backyards and in the fields and while doing various household chores the people of Shirdi always remembered Sai and sang his glory. They knew no other God except Sai. The poor women in their pure love of Sai composed poems and songs in praise of Baba in simple rural language."

Baba was often confronted by Muslims who wanted him to go their way. They complained against his actions and gestures which were against the tenets of Islam. Once some of them wanted Baba to come outside the village for saying the kutha prayers. Baba at first said: "Yes, let us go," but when they came to fetch him Baba declined to go with them. On another occasion they came and offered prayers in the mosque but Baba did not join them. During Moharram some Muslims came to Baba and said they wanted to bring into the mosque a *tajia*. Baba allowed it to remain in the mosque for a couple of days and then dragged it out and placed it on the dhuni saying : "I do not want a corpse in the mosque." An orthodox Muslim brought a *sera* (an ornamental arrangement of flowers) to decorate the niche in the mosque and asked for Baba's permission. Baba said: "Take it and put it on Hanuman." The Muslim replied, he being a Muslim could not decorate a Hindu idol. Baba became furious and the sera was taken away.

On one occasion when Mahlsapathy wanted to apply sandal paste to Baba as a mark of worship there was a howl of protest from Muslims who, waving their sticks, threatened to assault him. Mahlsapathy ran outside the mosque in fear but Baba called him back and said : "Let me see who stops you. You proceed to anoint me with sandal." The Muslims retreated.

Baba attracted larger and larger devotees from neighbouring villages and from distant places too. A devotee who frequently came to the mosque for Baba's darshan was Madhavarao Balwant Deshpande who later came to be known as Shama. He was a teacher in a school adjacent to the mosque and he had a grandstand view of what was happening in the mosque. He said he used to hear many languages, including English, spoken in conversation at dead of night in the mosque between Baba and unknown voices. He very soon became an intimate assistant to Baba, preparing his pipe and looking after his other needs. In course of time he was so much attached to Baba that he left his job and took to serving Baba full time. He controlled the flow of devotees and was a reliable guide for all those who wanted to secure the blessings of Baba. One devotee remarked that although the entire village had come to put implicit faith in Baba still very few happened to be very intimate with him. Owing to his serene yet austere outlook no one dared to take undue liberty with him.

Meanwhile the worship of Baba gathered in strength. At first the worship was individual in character, each devotee going to Baba, placing flowers at his feet and prostrating in reverence. Baba tried to dissuade them from worshipping him and asked them to worship the idols in temples and in their homes but they would not listen. They told him : "You are our talking and walking God." Baba ultimately promoted this worship for he foresaw individual benefit to millions and also national benefit to the cause of religion and humanity. The individual worship developed into congregational worship and it took complicated forms as seen in Pandharpur and Tirupathi. There were rituals, music, processions with palanquin, horse and other paraphernalia with a *pujari* to conduct the rituals. This began round about 1908. According to one devotee the Hindu worship of Baba began in 1908 with a child's homage to him. The woman devotee who revealed this said : "My brother, Babu Rao, who was then a child of four, used to go every morning to the mosque and put a flower on Sai Baba's head and worship him. That was the beginning of the regular worship of Baba as he had not permitted others to do it before that." The child was honouring Baba as he had seen idols being worshipped in temples, she said. From that time grew the practice of full ritual worship of Baba as was done to an idol. The devotee said Baba had a tulsi brindavan constructed in the centre of the yard outside the mosque about three feet high with a tulsi plant in it. K.G. Bhishma drew up the rituals for Baba worship on practically the same lines as at Pandharpur and he introduced a set of *aratis* (ritualistic verses) for use at Shirdi. Baba got them approved by Nanasaheb Chandorkar. Congregational worship implied there would be someone to officiate as *pujari* or head priest. The story is told that the man chosen to be the first *pujari,* Megha, declined to accept the job as he could not serve Baba whom he though to be a Muslim.

But Megha was persuaded to go to Shirdi and the moment Baba saw him he shouted: "Why should this idiot be sent to me?" Megha returned to his place only to fall ill and he thought it might be due to his refusal to serve Baba. He rushed back to Shirdi, fell at Baba's feet and became his ardent devotee.

To make congregational worship more colourful and attractive Radhakrishna Ayi, a young widow, who devoted her life to serving Baba (we shall hear more of her in a later chapter) came forward to take up the task. She organised the devotees and drew up a plan to transform Baba and his place of residence as befitting a Maharaja and in God's real image. All the pomp and ceremonies observed in temples and Maharaja's durbar were there. She brought silver whisks, silver maces, silver umbrellas, a silver chariot, a palanquin with silver appurtenances, a horse and other regal paraphernalia. What was required in a durbar was valuable presents in cash and kind to those attending the durbar like scholars, poets and pandits and entertainers such as acrobats,wrestlers and nautch girls and Baba arranged for funds to pay them all.

Shirdi presented the appearance of a very prosperous durbar from 1909 to 1918. Baba disliked all the pomp and display of affluence. He refused to sit in the chariot or use the palanquin and they became part of the show. Baba preferred to walk to the chavadi barefoot when he went there on alternate nights, for rest in a procession. He would not put on his head the regal crown which his devotees had got for him or be adorned in a regal dress, disappointing his devotees who wanted to see him as a Maharaja. When some of the small silver horses decorating the palanquin were stolen Baba asked his devotees: "Why was not the whole palanquin stolen?" All the paraphernalia were kept with Ramakrishni Ayi and on her death were taken care of by an association.

The worship of Baba in the mosque by unsophisticated villagers stiffened the backs of the orthodox Hindus who abhorred the worship of a Muslim (as they thought Baba to be) by Hindus in a mosque. This explained the fact that the railway employees at Kopargaon station, nearest to Shirdi, tried to prevent people from going to Baba saying he was a "dangerous and immoral man". This false propaganda was helped by the lack of authentic information about Baba, his life and work which could have dissipated the fears and doubts fostered by the orthodox community.

Two annual festivals were celebrated at Shirdi and these were the Sri Rama Navami festival and the Muslim Urs procession. Very often they were celebrated on the same day and there was perfect communal amity and harmony. First the Hindus would come to the mosque to worship Baba to be followed by the Muslims. Ordinarily 5,000 devotees gathered at the mosque for the Sri Rama Navami celebrations and sometimes the crowd swelled to 7,500. On one of these occasions Baba was called upon to perform a miracle to provide drinking water to the people. There were two wells in Shirdi, one was completely dry and the water in the other was brackish. The villagers came to Baba and told him of their problem. Baba turned the brackish water in the well into sweet water by throwing flowers into it.

The first man to offer *arati puja* to Baba was a sub-judge from Pandharpur named Laxman Krishnaji alias Tatyasaheb Noolkar. He came to know of Baba through Chandorkar, went to Shirdi and offered oranges to Baba. Baba did not receive him and showed his temper but the judge was unwavering in his faith that Baba was God and spent most of his time in Shirdi. One day he lighted two lamps with ghee and waved them before Baba and thus began the *arati puja* of Baba. After he retired from service he stayed permanently in Shirdi serving Baba, and died there. When he passed away Baba said: "Now Tatya has gone ahead and he won't be born again." As mentioned before there were no fixed rituals for *puja* and no songs for arati until Krishnarao Bhishma, a devotee of Pandharpur deity and a *kirtankar* of great renown, came on the scene and wrote songs for being sung at arati. Later some songs of Das Ganu Maharaj and Upasani Baba were sung. Babusaheb Jog, who was an official of the Bombay government, took over the *arati puja* to Baba after Megha's death. Retiring from service he settled in Shirdi with his wife in 1909.

There is an interesting anecdote about Baba in connection with the Shirdi Bazaar which used to be held every Sunday and which was attended by people from neighbouring villages in large numbers. Stalls and booths were set up in open spaces where wares and commodities were displayed and sold. On that day the mosque would be crowded with devotees and there would be hardly space to stand. On one such occasion Dabolkar (also known as Hemadpant) sat before Baba massaging his legs and chanting God's name. Shama, Dixit and some others were also present. Shama told Hemadpant: "Some grams seem to have stuck on the sleeves of your coat." He touched the coat and some gram fell. Hemadpant straightened his arm to see what the matter was and to the surprise of everyone some particles of gram rolled over to the ground and were picked up by those sitting nearby. When everyone was wondering how the grams got into Hemadpant's coat Baba said: "The fellow has got the bad habit of eating alone. Today is Bazaar Day and he came here chewing gram. I know his habit and these particles are proof of it. What wonder is there in the matter?" Hemadpant said he had not been to the Bazaar and then how could he buy and eat gram? Baba's miracles had a touch of humour too.

In the early days most people,as we have already seen ,took Baba to be an ordinary mortal, a begging fakir who was living in the mosque. But there were some *sanyasins* like Devdas who recognised that Baba was a saint of rare merit. Another was Ganga Gir Bua of Punthanba who treated Baba as a precious gem. Many were attracted to Baba when they found he possessed powers like clairvoyance, clairaudience, ominivision and knowledge of the past and future and wished to benefit thereby.

In the first decade of the century Baba's name and fame spread especially through the works of Chandorkar and Das Ganu Maharaj who spread his message through discourse and ballads and through pamphlets. N.G. Chandorkar, Deputy Collector, and his orderly, Das Ganu Maharaj, paid their respects to Baba in 1892 and were struck by his wonderful powers and simple life, and his love and compassion. As a result of their efforts there was a regular and increasing stream of people flocking to Shirdi, especially the better class of people like intellectuals, officials and businessmen. They included B.G.Tilak, whose meeting with Baba we shall describe in another chapter.

G. S. Khaparde, a biographer of Baba wrote: "The wonder of wonders is that of a person so universally admired and worshipped, not even a single human being knew his real name. He dropped into Shirdi, so to say, from the blue, helped a person to find his lost horse and took up his residence there for a whole lifetime helping everybody that came along without any distinction, securing the love and reverence of all without exception. He appeared to know the innermost thoughts of everybody, relieved their wants and carried comfort to all. He fulfilled my idea of God on earth."

3

PIED PIPER OF SHIRDI

L IKE the Pied Piper of Hamlin, Sai Baba drew devotees to
Shirdi, many of them at first unwillingly. He said: "I bring
my men from long distances under many pleas. I seek them and
bring them to me. They do not come of their own accord, I bring
them to me. However distant even thousands of miles my people
might be, I draw them to myself just as we pull birds to us with
a string tied to their foot."

When a devotee objected to devotees going to Baba for
temporal benefits like employment, money, children and cure of
diseases Baba said: "Do not say that. My men first come to me
on account of that only. They get their desire fulfilled and
comfortably placed in life. They then follow me and progress
further." Baba made use of the devotees' needs to turn them
into highly grateful devotees who were prepared to march
forward under his guidance. Having assumed responsibility for
the disciples he regarded them as his trust and himself as their
trustee. He said: "I will not allow my devotees to be lost. I will
account to God for all those who have been given to me"

Baba said of himself: "This is a Brahmin, a white Brahmin,
a pure Brahmin who will lead lakhs of people to the *subra marga*
and take them to their goal right up to the end." One devotee
remarked: "By first conferring temporal benefits Baba drew unto
himself countless souls caught up in samsara and then later
opened their eyes to the true meaning of life and brought about
their spiritual awakening. He made people realise the transitory
nature of human life and the worthlessness of earthly objects."

Baba told a devotee who thanked him for saving him from a
serious accident: "What am I to do? I spread four hands at a time
to save my devotees. I will not allow any harm to befall them."
He was asked: "You said just now you were only a father, how

can you have four hands?" Baba merely smiled. Four hands are
typical of Godhead. The questioner was more than ever convinced
that Baba was God. Those who came into contact with Baba
knew enough about him to declare that Baba knew everything,
everywhere at any time, that he had power to do anything
everywhere, that he had power to control the movements and
hearts of all creatures and even the elements of nature like rain,
fire, etc., that he had a mastery of knowledge of the past, present
and future even centuries away from the present and that he
had the highest moral principles of selflessness and service and
love for all including the lowliest of beings. In Narasimha
Swamiji's words: " Baba is undoubtedly a beneficent universal
power responding to prayer and appeals of every sort by those
who are sincere, true, loyal and faithful."

His many-sided nature helped Baba to deal suitably with an
infinite variety of people of all castes, creeds and age approaching
him for various purposes. He responded to their needs in the
way they wanted and satisfied them. A visitor once asked him:
"Do you look upon all equally?" Baba replied: "Yes. I look upon
all equally." He said he was impartial and did not prefer one to
another. However he responded more vigorously and constantly
to those who had been attached to him and loving him in
previous births as in the cases of Chandorkar, Tatya Patil, and
M.B. Rege. He said Chandorkar had been his disciple for four
births and that was why he sent for him (the story of how
Chandorkar was drawn to Baba is related in another chapter).
Similarly, in the case of Tatya Patil his parents were greatly
attached to Baba from the very beginning of his visit to Shirdi,
when he was unknown and did not exhibit his powers. Baba
said Tatya's mother had been his sister in a previous birth and
had served him with great devotion. Tatya was called nephew
by Baba and Tatya called him 'mama'. Tatya used to sleep by
the side of Baba in the mosque for many years. Baba would
massage his feet and stroke his head and ensure that he did not
come to any harm. This was because Tatya was a rustic youth
who had no education and left to himself would have gone
astray, but Baba's company kept him from spiritual and moral
shipwreck and developed his culture and morality. There were
factions and bickerings in the village in which Tatya was involved
and Baba helped him to come out unscathed. In one instance
Tatya and his friends were sentenced to imprisonment in a

criminal case and Tatya wanted to appeal but his lawyer said he had no strong case. Tatya appealed to Baba who asked the lawyer to file the appeal. When the appeal was taken up by the Divisional Magistrate he set aside the conviction and sentence even before the proceedings started.

Baba said he was an agent of God and he told a devotee: "I can do nothing except what God orders." He declined to give *a sanyasi* robe to a devotee saying: " The fakir (God) has not permitted me to give you the robe." As an agent he said he had vast powers, that is, divine powers, and these were utilised for the benefit of mankind and for promoting the welfare of individuals. That was obvious, seen and well understood. But there were also general benefits that were not so obvious or seen and well understood.

Baba was so much attached to Tatya that he would not get up from his bed till Tatya came and lifted him and prepared his pipe and lit it for him to smoke. Tatya was his pet and he gave him money with which he later built a house for himself and purchased land. Baba said Tatya would die in 1918 but he saved him and it was said that Baba himself (who passed away in that year) gave his life to save him.

Baba was not always happy about people who came to him for material benefits. He once said: "I have been considering long and thinking day and night. All are thieves. But we have to deal with them. I prayed to God night and day for their improvement or removal but God delays and does not approve of my attitude or grant the prayer. I will wait for a month or two and then see. But living or dead I will have what I have been praying for. People are not good and devoted. They are unsettled in mind and have become bad and give trouble. They are pestering me for money. Moreover they become shameless. Now I am disgusted." Once Baba told a zamindar about the disgusting way in which some devotees behaved in Shirdi and said he wanted to leave Shirdi. Baba wanted to regulate the lives of those who fully surrendered to him. However, the work of moral regeneration was not and could never be complete. He advised devotees to "behave with integrity and probity". He moulded his ankita (children)—as he called his devotees—internally and he used not merely words but also his gaze, touch or even his aura or will-power to remove undesirable tendencies and influences and replace them by useful and holy

ones. Any worldly help rendered by Baba was accompanied by
sowing a spiritual seed and the beneficiary remembered Baba
with faith, love and admiration, for his powerful guidance and
kindness. Baba's message to them was that God is one who is
nothing but love, who is common to all whatever their religion.

Baba's objective was that a devotee should not merely get
relief but also a full belief in him (Baba), that he was the Guru
God for the devotee so that the devotee might attach himself to
Baba and develop his life thereafter with his help. It was with
this in mind that Baba utilised his siddhis. Temporal reliefs
were given by means of *chamatkar* (miracles) and there was
always a string attached to the temporal help. The man who got
a temporal benefit was at the same time pushed in the spiritual
direction.

Baba's concern and love for the lowliest was exemplified in
an incident when an old woman wanted his darshan but could
not enter the mosque, because of the crowd of devotees. Shama
went out and brought her to Baba who exclaimed: "Mother !
How long I waited for you. Have you brought anything for me
to eat?" The old woman said she had brought a piece of stale
bread and onion. She added that on the way she felt hungry and
ate part of the bread and the onion. She offered the remaining
piece of bread to Baba who ate it with gusto and said: "How
sweet oh, Mother is your bread!" Does this incident not remind
us of how Krishna welcomed Kuchela and ate the parched rice
he offered him?

When Chandorkar was transferred to Pandharpur and
intended to visit Baba to take leave of him, Baba knew of this
and asked devotees present: "Let us do *bhajan*. The door of
Pandari is wide open. Let us joyously do bhajan." As they were
singing Chandorkar entered the mosque.

One day when Shama was wiping Baba's wet hands with a
towel Baba playfully pinched his cheeks. Shama pretended to be
angry and said: "Sir, is it proper for you to pinch me like this?
We don't want a mischievous God who pinches us like this."
Baba said: "Shama, during the 72 births you were with me I
never pinched you till now and you resent my touching you."
Shama said: "We want a God that will ever give us kisses and
sweets to eat. We do not want any wealth or heaven from you.
Let our faith in you be ever awake and alive." Baba said: "Yes.

I have indeed come for that. I have been feeding and nursing you all these lives and I have love and affection for you."

A woman devotee wrote, "Whenever I went into Baba's presence I forgot everything. I had no anxiety, no care, no fear. Everything was blotted out and I passed through a blissful time in his company."

A ninety-five-year-old devotee, Goulibuva, who worshipped the deity at Pandarpur, came to Shirdi every year for, darshan of Baba. He gazed at Baba and said: "This is Pandarinath Vithal incarnate, the merciful lord of the poor and helpless."

Baba talked and laughed with his devotees and always chanted the words "Allah Malik" (which was a tribute to his foster fakir father). He did not like discussions or disputations. He was always calm and controlled although at times he was irritable and burst into anger. Prince and pauper were treated alike by him. He preached *vedanta*, and the devotees said that though he had a human body his deeds testified to his Godhood.

Devotees who acted according to Baba's instructions given at the time of their taking leave of him fared well while those who disregarded them suffered many a mishap and accident. Implicit obedience to Baba's orders was always found to be the safest course. When Baba was in a cheerful mood he sang merrily. He had a mellifluous voice. One song was about udhi which went like this: "Oh; playful Rama, come, come and bring with you sacks of udhi." Baba discouraged empty bellies. He said that God's quest should not be made on an empty belly.

Baba adapted himself to the capacity of people who went to him for help and protection. Most of them were superficial people seeking mostly some material gain or advantage and to them he did not reveal his inner nature. But when anyone capable of going beyond material benefits came to him he revealed more of himself and his powers. One of his disciples said: "Baba was not the man to stifle legitimate enquiry. Everything he said or did was full of significance but I could not understand him always."

Baba told several people about their past lives and what happened to them. He told Prof. Narke (about whom we will learn more in a later chapter) of his past four lives. He revealed this in the presence of others who however could not know or understand that it referred to Prof. Narke. Baba had the peculiar way of giving information to particular individuals in the midst of a group that those concerned alone could understand and not the others present.

When once a devotee asked Baba for udhi he told him he would get it later. As predicted the devotee got it later on a train from a fellow passenger who gave him udhi which had been given to him by Baba.

A devotee named Damodar Saveram Rasane said: "My mind is always dwelling on Baba. Sometimes Baba abused me and beat me, but I know that blows and abuse have an auspicious ending. So I never resented or grumbled and remained greatly attached to him."

One day Baba, who was sitting in his usual place in the mosque, suddenly shouted "Oh!" for no apparent reason. The next moment his headdress and kufni were found drenched and water dripping from them for more than half an hour. Soon there was a pool of water and the devotees were perplexed. They silently swept the place and dried up Baba's dress. Baba did not tell them anything about it nor did they have the courage to ask him. On the third day Baba received a telegram from a devotee, Jehangirji Frami Daruwala, thanking him for saving him. The full story connected with this incident was revealed later. The devotee was a naval captain during the Russo-Japanese war and he found all his ships except three sunk by the enemy and he feared the other three including his own would also be sunk. He took out a photograph of Baba and with tears in his eyes prayed to him to save him and the ships. Later the ships were all safely towed to port.

One of Baba's favourite devotees was Lakshmi Bai who brought food for him at the mosque. One day as she sat before Baba he suddenly turned to her and said: "Mother Lakshmi, I am very hungry. Please go home and fetch me some food." Lakshmi thought that Baba must indeed be hungry for it was not his usual time for food and she rushed home and prepared a meal for him and hurried back to the mosque with it. Baba carried the food brought for him to the courtyard and beckoned a dog which was standing there and gave the food to it. The dog ate it with satisfaction and ran away. To Lakshmi who was pained and surprised that what she had specially prepared for Baba should have been given to a dog, Baba said: "Mother, listen to me. Do not get angry with me. By feeding this dog in this manner you have appeased my hunger too. You have done a meritorious act. I appreciate your alacrity in obeying me. The same *atman* dwells in me and in the dog also. Learn this truth from me today. Be happy with this knowledge."

Baba did not enter any of his devotees' homes while on his begging rounds but he made an exception in the case of Lakshmi Bai. One day he entered her house and said: "Mother, I want to drink *payasam (a sweet dish)* today, can you prepare it and serve me?" Lakshmi prepared the *payasam* with pleasure and gave it to him. Baba gave his last *dakshina* (offering) of nine silver coins to Lakshmi Bai before he passed away. He called her a few minutes before his death. She was taken to him and on seeing her he took out the coins and gave them to her and blessed her.

A woman devotee, Mrs Manager, wrote about a leper devotee of Baba. "We used to sit near Baba in the mosque. At the usual time anyone can go, bow to him and sit there. On one occasion as I was seated a short distance from Baba a leper came for his darshan. His disease was far advanced. He was stinking and he had little strength left in him, so much so, that it was with much difficulty and very slowly that he clambered up the three steps of the mosque, moved on to the dhuni and then to Baba and placed his head at his feet. It took much time for him to complete the darshan and I, feeling the stench from him intensely, hoped he would clear out. At last when he got down slowly carrying a small parcel wrapped in a dirty cloth, I felt relief and said to myself: 'Thank God, he is off.' Baba darted a piercing glance at me and I at once knew that he had read my thoughts. Before the leper left the place Baba called out to him and sent someone to fetch him back. He came back making the slow climb up the steps, emitting foul stench all the time. As the man bowed before him Baba took the parcel from him saying: "What is this?" and opened it. It contained some *pedas* (sweets) and Baba took a piece and gave it to me   alone of all those present and asked me to eat it. What horror! To eat a thing like that brought by a stinking leper! But it was Baba's order and there was no option but to obey. So I ate it. Baba himself took another piece and swallowed it and sent the man away with the remainder. Why the leper was recalled and I alone was chosen to be the recipient of his *peda* none there could find out. But I knew full well that Baba had read my thoughts and was teaching me a valuable lesson, namely, humility, fraternity, sympathy, endurance and trust in his supreme wisdom rather than in my own notions of hygiene and sanitation for saving me from disease". Mrs Manager wrote the above account in her book of reminiscences of Sai Baba.

Once a blind woman appealed to Baba: "I want to see you with these eyes." By a miracle she regained her sight and was able to have a darshan of Baba. But no sooner did she go out of his presence than she became blind again. Who can fathom Baba's lilas?

One day a princess of a princely state came in a palanquin to see Baba. One of her attendants carried a vessel which was placed before Baba. Baba asked Mahlsapathy, who was present what was in the vessel. Mahlsapathy looked into the vessel and said it contained gold. Baba pointing to himself said to Mahlsapathy: "Is this (Baba) the real gold or is that?" Mahlsapathy said: " You are the treasure." Baba said: " Then send it back." The vessel was promptly returned to the palanquin.

In 1910 Baba was angry one day. He said loudly: "Rascal, coming to see me, what have I got? I am a naked fakir with human organs." People around him wondered to whom he was referring. In a short while a party of officials was seen coming towards the mosque. It included the Revenue Commissioner of Bombay, Sir G. Seymour Curtis and his wife. As the party arrived at the mosque an official told a devotee: "Ask Baba to finish his morning routine quickly as the sahebs wish to see him." The devotee said: "Such a communication to Baba is unthinkable. If you have any business with him you must await his pleasure."

After half an hour Baba passed that side and Mrs Curtis bowed to him and said: "We wish to have a little talk with you, Maharaj." Baba said: "Wait for half an hour. I have to go and beg," and he moved away. But he returned within ten minutes. Mrs Curtis again bowed to him and repeated her request. Baba said: Wait one hour," and he passed on. The white officials were in a hurry and left the mosque. It had been Mrs Curtis' desire to seek Baba's blessing for a child which she longed for and it remained unfulfilled as her husband could not wait. The incident was a lesson in humility and typical of Baba's bizarre humour.

The story is told of a devotee of Baba, Megha, an orthodox Brahmin and an ardent devotee of Baba who was the cause of a Baba miracle. Megha had a bath in the Godavari (which in that region was called the Ganga) daily and fetched a pot of water from it to be poured on a Shiva idol he worshipped. One day he decided to pour the water on Baba's head as he considered Baba to be Shiva. Baba told him the head was the chief thing and asked him to sprinkle a few drops on his head and that would suffice. But Megha insisted on pouring the water over his head. But strangely enough not a drop of water fell on Baba's body. All the water fell on Baba's head and disappeared mysteriously without wetting his body.

Sometimes Baba said to his devotees: "Stay with me and keep quiet. I will do the rest." Thereby he assured them security and inward peace. Prof. Narke, an ardent disciple of Baba, wrote that the duty of the devotee or aspirant was firstly to keep himself chaste, pure, simple and upright so as to be fit to receive the guru's grace and secondly to have full faith in the beloved master to raise him to various higher and higher experiences till at last he was taken to the distant goal whatever that might be. "One step enough for me." was the right attitude for the devotee. He need not trouble himself to decide complicated metaphysical and philosophical problems about ultimate destiny. He was as yet ill-prepared to solve them. The guru would lift him up, endow him with higher powers, vast knowledge and increasing realisation of truth. Prof. Narke said: "All this was not uttered by Baba in one breath either to me or within my hearing out the various hints I got from his dealings with people and his occasional words on the subject add up to this and common sense points the same way."

Baba made no distinction between one devotee and another and if anybody thought he was being treated less favourably Baba would try to set the balance right. He always said in his "durbar" that there was no differentiation between one devotee and another.

Baba used to say : "My lila is inscrutable." He had infinite love for his devotees and his mode of instruction was born of compassion. Because of his omniscience he could understand and follow the sorrows and sufferings of his devotees and could ward them off. He never gave a beginner in the quest for spiritual enlightenment the higher lesson. To each he imparted knowledge according to the capacity of the recipient to absorb it. Sometimes he would give him a *mantra* (incantation) that seemed just right for the devotee or approve a mantra with

which the devotee was already familiar. At his first meeting
with M. W. Pradhan Baba uttered the mantra, "Sri Ram, Jai
Ram, Jai Jai Ram", thus confirming his recognition of the mantra
given to Pradhan by the family guru.

Baba told one devotee : "Do not read books, but keep me
in your heart. If you harmonise head and heart that is enough."
Baba was opposed to his devotees borrowing money to come to
Shirdi. He insisted that in any social function no near relative
should be excluded and he rebuked a devotee who failed to
invite his father-in-law to a function which Baba was to attend.
Baba often made his devotees feel, see and realise him in his
portrait or picture and many saw or felt his presence in their
homes. They regarded him as their God and felt his presence
in themselves, their fellows and in the animals and reptiles they
came across. All of them experienced renewed faith in their own
religion. To his Hindu devotees he was a living God inspiring,
aiding and guiding them at every turn in their day-to-day life
and also at critical moments of their existence. Baba told them
: "It is popularly supposed that I am different from you and you
from me. This view is wrong. You are in me and I am in you.
My devotee feels me in him and in all creatures. This wall of
separation keeps you from me. If you pull it down then we will
see each other clearly face to face. Saints do not recognise this
differentiation. If you wish to serve me give up discrimination
and differentiation."

Baba gave sound advice to his devotees about how they
should conduct themselves in their daily life. He told a disciple:
"If anybody comes and abuses you or punishes you do not
quarrel with him. If you cannot endure it speak a simple word
or two and leave the place. But do not battle with him and give
tit for tat." "I feel sick and disgusted when you quarrel with
others." Baba told a woman devotee : "If anyone talks ten words
let us answer with one word if we reply at all. If anyone is
angry with another he wounds me to the quick. If anyone
abuses another I feel pain. If anyone bravely endures the abuse
I feel highly pleased." In this connection, it is appropriate to
mention an incident which showed Baba's exemplary patience
in the face of an insult. On one occasion a crazy sadhu, Nana
Wali, came to Baba and said : "I want to sit in your seat. Get
up !" Baba quietly vacated the seat and the impertinent sadhu
occupied it. After a few minutes the sadhu realised his mistake,

got down from the seat and fell at Baba's feet and requested him to reoccupy the seat.

Did Baba ever really offer his head to save his devotees? "Yes, a number of times," says Narasimha Swamiji. On one occasion the local Muslims joined together and decided to stop by force what they considered the desecration of the mosque by Hindu worship of Baba with sandal paste. Mahlsapathy alarmed at the prospect of being clubbed to death decided to come out of the mosque and do his worship of Baba from outside the compound wall. But Baba invited him inside and directed him to go on with his normal worship. Baba challenged the Muslims to use force if they wanted. Baba ran a great risk by throwing out this challenge for the Muslims were armed with sticks and looked dangerous. But the very daring of Baba cowed them and they retreated and there was no violence. Twenty years later (1914-15) in a similar situation when Baba was sleeping at the chavadi with his intimate devotees, a Muslim fanatic at dead of night shouted that he would cut the throats of the Hindus sleeping in the chavadi as they were "spoiling" Baba and he appealed to Baba to permit him to do so. Baba told the Muslim that the Hindus were not to blame for worshipping him, that it was his own "madness" that spoiled them and resulted in their worship of him. He offered his own throat for being cut. The fanatic beat a retreat.

A year or two later another Muslim fanatic named Rohilla who called Baba God because of his wonderful powers, was at the same time outraged at Baba's tolerance of Hindu image worship with music, mantras and rituals. He came to kill Baba with a club. But just a glance from Baba was enough to subdue him and he sank to the ground.

Among the material benefits which devotees sought from Baba were children for childless couples, marriage for daughters, employment and promotion in jobs and cures for ailments and diseases. In dealing with devotees who wanted children Baba adopted a peculiar procedure in conferring this blessing. Every woman who sought his blessing for a child brought a coconut and presented it to him. Baba gave it back to her and she would receive it in one end of her sari and it was an indication that she would bear a child within a year's time. If Baba disposed of the coconut otherwise it meant the request had not been granted. In one instance, Baba returned the coconut signalling that the devotee's request had been granted but as he did so Baba looked agitated and there were tears in his eyes. The woman in course of time gave birth to a son but the mother died 18 months thereafter. That was perhaps why Baba shed tears when he presented the coconut to her.

A woman devotee, Mrs. Aurangabadkar did not have a child even after 27 years of married life. The doctors told her she was barren and would not conceive. She came to Shirdi and prayed to Baba to grant her a child. Baba blessed her and said she would deliver a son in 12 months and so it happened and the woman was happy with a son.

Baba changed his method in the case of another devotee, D. S. Rasane, who prayed for a son. Baba gave him four mangoes and said : "Take these mangoes, eat them and die." Rasane was taken aback by Baba's words but it was explained to him by others present that to beget a son was equivalent to dying and being replaced by another. To plunge into the life of the world is death, to remain calm and aloof is life, Baba said. He added : "Don't eat them yourself, give them to your wife (Baba meant the second wife of the devotee).

In one instance Baba helped a woman devotee to deliver. Sitting in the mosque one day Baba complained of severe pain in the abdomen and asked his devotees to tie a cloth around his waist and pull it tight. "Tighter, tighter," he cried. "I can't bear it. The pain is frightful." Then suddenly he felt relaxed. "All right," he said with relief, "the pain has gone now." And it later transpired that a woman devotee had been having a painful delivery and had prayed to Baba for help.

Baba was equally at the service of his devotees in getting their daughters married. His help in this direction endeared him to them and they called him their Aye (mother) or as their match-making *Ayi* or mamma. A devotee, Ganesh Keshav Rege desperately searched for a bridegroom for his fourth daughter. One day as he was sitting in his house burdened with care he heard a voice which said: "Go to Jirapur". The words were loud and clear but he could not see anyone uttering them. This was one of the ways adopted by Baba in his service to his devotees (a voice without a body) and create a strong conviction that the voice was that of Baba. Rege concluded it was Baba who had asked him to go to Jirapur. While he was wondering what he should do in Jirapur where he knew no one and had not visited it before he got an order from his employer posting him to Jirapur. He went to Jirapur and soon was able to find a suitable match for his daughter in a village nearby.

Baba's cures for ailments and the sick were miraculous but his methods were strange, crude and unconventional and were such as would outrage the sensibilities of a doctor and even a common man and woman. Here are some instances of his unique way of treating patients. He cured Shama's inflammation of, the eye by applying pepper to the eye! Mrs Manager gives an account of her experience. "Wondrous was his curing deep-seated organic diseases abruptly and suddenly without any visible application of remedy or treatment. Scientists and medical men may disbelieve this but having actually seen it in my own case and noticed it in those of others who came to Sai Baba I cannot disbelieve such cases and what is most peculiar, this drawing of diseases on to himself through sheer will—power. My eyes have been giving me trouble constantly. On one occasion while I was at Shirdi they were greatly paining me and water was freely flowing from them. In such a condition I went and sat before Baba. He looked at me. My eyes ceased to pain and water. But his eyes were shedding tears."

A devotee suffering from diarrhoea came to Baba carrying a pot of water for use if needed. On seeing him Baba got into a rage and the devotees around him fled. The devotee with the pot felt the need to go out and carried the pot of water with him. Baba stopped him and gave him some groundnuts which someone had left there. "Come on, let us eat groundnuts," said Baba and both Baba and the patient ate groundnuts. Baba asked the sick man to drink water after this. This is not the treatment usually given to diarrhoea patients but Baba said: "Your annal sphineter is now tightly closed." And the devotee was indeed cured at that instant.

Baba was once taken to treat a leprosy patient in a devotee's house. He gave him a mixture of poison taken from a cobra which he had asked the patient to catch, as cobras were believed not to bite lepers. The patient improved but since he disobeyed Baba's injunction not to have relations with his wife Baba stopped treating him.

A devotee's son suffering from an incurable disease, tubercular bone abscess, known in medical parlance as chronic osteontetis, was brought to Baba. Baba said : "Those who come to the mosque won't suffer in this life nor in their future lives. Give up your cares and worries now. Apply udhi on the abscess and the boy will recover within a week. Believe in me and in God. This is not a mosque but Dwaraka Mayi and he who steps into her shade gets eternal peace and happiness." The boy sat before Baba who glanced at him and passed his hands over his diseased limbs. Within seven days the boy was cured.

Baba's intimate and millionaire devotee, Bapusaheb Buti on one occasion suffered from dysentery and the medicine and drugs he took did not help and he was not able to visit the mosque for a darshan of Baba. Baba sent for him and made him sit before him and said loudly: "Now take care. You should not purge any more": and waving his index finger added: "The vomiting must also stop." Buti was rid of the disease.

A six-year-old girl suffering from chronic asthma got cured in a very unusual and unimaginable way through the grace of Baba. Baba simply asked the child to take a puff at his clay pipe and the asthma was gone. Devotees said epileptics were cured merely by looking at Baba.

Epidemics were very common in Shirdi and towns and villages of Maharashtra and the main cause was plague. People came in large numbers to Baba to seek relief from it. On one occasion when Shirdi was in the grip of the epidemic Baba advised the people to clear the roads, sweep the tombs and cremation and burial places and to feed the poor. Baba was himself seen cleaning the mosque. In 1911, when there was an outbreak of plague in Shirdi devotees noticed seven or eight buboes on Baba's body and he began to develop a high temperature. Expressing concern they asked Baba what the remedy was. Baba said burnt cotton wool dipped in ghee should be applied to the buboes. He followed the remedy himself and assured the devotees he was safe and added that nobody in Shirdi would come to grief either. He said he had taken upon himself the calamity that had descended on Shirdi. And it turned out that no one in Shirdi died of plague. More remarkable was the fact that in spite of so many buboes on his body there was no change in Baba's routine.

Plague broke out in the house of a devotee in Nashik and he frantically asked Baba for instructions. Baba asked him to stay on in the house. And he did so in the face of advice from doctors and friends and in spite of dead rats continuing to fall in the house. And nothing happened to him and his family. Baba's simple advice was : "Why should we give up our residence?."

Once a devotee, Appa Kulkarni, had darshan of Baba. Baba casually told him : "Thieves have entered our village. The way of these thieves is peculiar. They do not upset the whole house. They are after principal things only. Taking these they walk away without being discovered. Such arch villains they are. You will be the first object of their attack now. So take precautionary measures." Kulkarni did not understand the purport of Baba's warning and thought it referred to the security of his property and so he strengthened the security staff at his residence. But what happened was an outbreak of cholera in the village and Kulkarni became its first victim. The villagers rushed to Baba and sought relief. Baba told them: "In the village of Shirdi seven men will die and thereafter cholera will disappear." And so it happened.

Baba's manner of speech was highly symbolic on many occasions. He often spoke in parables, not clarifying them, leaving his devotees to assimilate the meaning. Even stray comments or answers to questions were also cryptic. Some understood what he was saying while others found great difficulty in following him as the devotee from Shirdi who fell a victim to cholera found to his cost.

A devotee has said : "People were immensely benefited by the darshan of Baba. Some became hale and hearty, wicked people were turned into good ones. *Kushta* (leprosy) was cured in some cases, many got their desires fulfilled, blind men got back their sight without any drops or medicine being put in their eyes and some lame ones got back their legs."

One day Baba asked a devotee what he had eaten that day. He said it was *ekadesi* day and he had taken nothing except *kandamula* (sweet potatoes). Baba picked up some onions and asked him to eat them. The devotee, not wanting to displease Baba, said he would eat them but Baba must eat them first. Baba agreed and ate some and the devotee followed his example. Baba then made fun of the devotee saying he ate onions on ekadasi day (onions are forbidden on religious days). The devotee said : "Baba ate it and I ate it." Baba said he had not eaten the onions and to prove it he vomited and what came out

were not onions but sweet potatoes! Baba said : "see, it is not
onions I had eaten but sweet potatoes." Baba showed he was
human and could enjoy some fun at the expense of his devotees.

Baba always set an example in hospitality. He would never
taste even the food he had begged without letting others have
a share of it. Dogs and crows always had their share as also
beggars and fakirs.

A Muslim devotee, Abdullah Jan, said his darshan of Baba
brought about a transformation in his mentality. He said :
"When I came to Shirdi I regarded Hindus as enemies. After
staying with Baba for three years this feeling of animosity passed
away and I began viewing Hindus as my brethren."

As stated before Baba lived in a dilapidated mosque which
was crumbling all the time. Some devotees took upon themselves
to renovate it and make it more habitable. But Baba would not
have it. They said they would build another residence for him
and he rejected the idea altogether. They went on pressing him
to agree to repairs of the mosque but he did not yield to this
request. Then one of the devotees began dumping cartloads of
bricks in front of the mosque and said he was going to begin the
work of renovation. Baba asked him to take away the bricks
and utilise them to carry out repairs to the local temple. This
was not done and Baba was ultimately forced to agree to the
work being carried out. But he frequently interfered with the
work and destroyed what had been done much to the dismay
of the devotees. The devotees then decided to carry on the
work at night when Baba went to the chavadi to spend the night
there. The work then was at long last finished.

Two brahmins came to see Baba one day and Baba narrated
an incident which he said happened to him. He spoke of his
wandering on the seashore and his arrival at a rich brahmin's
house where he was fed and shown a clean and nice place near
the cupboard to sleep. When he was sound asleep a man pulled
out a stone slab from the wall and took from Baba's pocket a
bundle of currency notes. When Baba noticed the theft he was
upset and began weeping. He thought the brahmin had stolen
the money. He lost all interest in food and drink and stayed on
the verandah of the house for 15 days. On the 15th day a
passing fakir saw him crying and made kind enquiries. Baba
told him everything that had happened. The fakir told him of
another fakir and asked him to seek relief from him. He would

restore the property to him, the fakir told Baba. Baba followed his advice, met the fakir and got back his money. Again he went to the seashore and there was a ship by which he had to travel. He got on board the help of a peon and thereafter he got into a train and came to DwarakaMayi.

As Baba was telling about his experience the two brahmins were wondering what he wanted to convey because they knew that Baba never left Shirdi and had not seen the sea or seashore. Their puzzle was cleared when they realised that what Baba had narrated was what they themselves had experienced and it was their story that Baba had described in such vivid detail and it was absolutely true in every respect.

Then there is the story of the two goats. Baba once bought two goats for Rs. 32 and his devotees thought he had been duped, for the animals were worth only Rs.8. Baba spent some money in purchasing lentils for the goats, fed them and then sent them away to their original owner. He told his devotees who were mystified : "You think I have been duped. No. Listen to the story of these goats. In their former births they were human beings and my neighbours. They loved each other and they loved me. Later they became enemies, fought with each other and killed themselves. They have now been born as goats. As they passed they looked at me and I at once remembered their past history. My love for them was renewed and I spent all this money to have them near me once again and to feed them sumptuously. As you do not like my bargain I sent them back to the shepherd."

4

GURU IS GOD

To Sai Baba Guru is God. For anyone who surrenders to his guru body and soul nothing else is required. He need not be learned, he need not read scriptures nor be proficient in religious disputations, nor need he worry about material wants and desires. The guru will take care of him, protect him and lead him on to spiritual salvation. It should be total surrender to the guru with emphasis on the word "total" and any doubt or mental reservation on the part of the disciple will be unproductive. This is reflected in the many incidents involving spiritual aspirants who were made to realise by Baba that guru worship meant worship of God and it should be uninhibited and complete. Baba told his devotees of his own total surrender to his guru and how his guru was everything to him, the very personification of God.

Baba told the story of how he met his guru in an allegorical way which was meaningful and symbolic. He said: "Once I and three others were studying the scriptures and we discussed how we were to get realisation. One of us said we should depend on ourselves and not on a guru. Two others spoke of qualifications or requisites for Brahma *jnana*. I said that surrender and love to guru were the only solution. Let us do our prescribed duty and surrender our body, speech and life to a guru who is all pervading. Faith in him is what is needed."

Baba said: "As we rambled through the forest we met a *vanajari* (one who works in the forest) who said: "Where are you going in this heat in the forest?" He kindly warned us against getting into the trackless woods and that too needlessly. He asked us to share his food. We disdained his advice and marched on. Soon in the vast and dense forest we lost our way. The *vanajari* met us again and said by relying on our cleverness we had got into the wrong way and that a guiding finger was needed to show us the way. He said: "Do not despise offers of food. Such offers are auspicious signs of success in one's endeavour." He again invited us to take food with him. Again we declined and moved on. I soon felt hungry and I went to him, accepted a bit of bread, ate it and drank water. The guru then asked : "What was your dispute?" I told him about our discussion. The others left him but I reverently bowed to him. Then he took me to a well, tied my legs with a rope and suspended me head downwards from a tree by the side of the well. My head was about three feet above water which I could not reach. The guru left me there and went away, God knows where. He returned after four or five hours and asked me how I fared. I answered : "In great bliss was my time passed." The guru was mightily pleased with me, drew me near him, passed his palm over my head and body and spoke to me tender words, dripping with love and he put me in his school where I entirely forgot my father and mother and all attachments and desires. I loved to gaze at him. If he were not there for me to see I would not like to have eyes at all. I did not wish to go back. I forgot all other things but the guru. My life was concentrated in my sight and my sight in him. He was the object of my meditation. In silence I loved. Realisation flashed upon me of itself without effort or study purely by his grace. Guru's grace is our only *sadhana*. *Jnana* comes as experience in its wake."

Arthur Osborne in his book, *The Incredible Sai Baba*, has interpreted Baba's story of the journey in the forest thus. He says the story was symbolical and adds that the forest mentioned by him is the jungle of the mind in which the quest for truth takes place, and the four friends are the four modes of approach. The forester is the guru and the food he offers is his grace. After the youth accepts the food he discovers that the giver of it is the divine guru. Therefore he bows reverently, that is, accepts his authority. Tying him head downwards over a well is overturning the ego, binding it, and holding it within sight of the cool waters of peace. It is because of this that the ordeal is blissful. It is suffering beatified by the end for which it is endured. Baba said divine knowledge is to be realised, not taught. Prostration, enquiry and service are the methods to be followed to obtain the grace of the guru. Love of God and Guru was the only thing

Baba cared for. The *siddhis* which incidentally accrued to him and which would turn the head and ruin the hearts of many did not interest him. He kept them, it seemed, ill—developed and unmanifested for a long time. *Hari nama smaranam* (chanting) was everything to him and the *siddhis* were distractions.

In the early days after he came to Shirdi and sat under the neem tree some villagers asked him why he sat there alone. Baba said the tree was sacred to him as his guru's tomb lay underneath it. He asked them to take care of the tree and keep the surroundings clean. The villagers agreed to do so. Later Baba asked a devotee to dig under the tree and a tomb was unearthed. Baba declared it to be that of his guru, not in this life but in a previous incarnation.

Baba never touched a book in his life and did not know the alphabet of any language and yet was supreme intellectually and could interpret any part of the scriptures. How did he get this knowledge? It could have been only through guru's grace. When Baba was handed over to Gopal Rao Deshmukh, a zamindar of Selu, he met a devotee of God Venkatachalapati or Venkatesa of Tirupathi. He adopted him as his guru and stayed with him for 10 or 12 years This was the most important period of his life. Gopal Rao treated him as the reincarnation of Kabir and he knew he himself was in a previous birth Ramananda of Kashi who was Kabir's guru. The love of Ramananda for Kabir, pure and unalloyed without any worldly taint must have continued in the present birth between Baba and Venkusa as Baba called his guru. Baba said: "For 12 years I waited on my guru who is peerless and loving. How can I describe his love for me? When he was in *dyanastha* (love-trance) I sat and gazed at him. We both were filled with bliss. I could not turn my eye on anything else. Night and day I pored upon his face with an ardour of love that banished hunger and thirst. The guru's absence even for a second made me restless. I meditated on nothing but the guru and had no goal or object other than the guru. Wonderful indeed was the art of my guru. I wanted nothing but the guru and he wanted nothing but this intense love from me. Apparently inactive he never neglected me but always protected me by his glance. That guru never blew any *mantra* into my ears. By his grace I attained my present state. Making the guru the sole object of one's thoughts and aims one attains *paramartha*, the supreme goal. This is the only truth the guru taught me. The four *sadhanas* and six *sastras* are not necessary. Trusting the guru fully is enough." The process of love which Baba described as subsisting between himself and Venkusa his guru was the one course calculated to produce transformation of the pupil into the perfect likeness of the master. The long sojourn of 10 or 12 years at Selu, it could be presumed, sufficed to complete the course or training which Baba had to undergo for reaching perfection of sainthood or guru status. This prepared him for his lifelong work of transforming all those who came into contact with him or who would come into contact with him decade after decade and even for centuries after his death. Baba made this reference to Selu on one occasion: "My fakir's wife left me with Venkusa and I stayed with him for 12 years and left Selu."

Das Ganu Maharaj once asked Baba for his age. Baba did not take notice of the question but he however told him that his guru was called Venkusa and that he had attained his yogic state as a result of Venkusa's grace.

Swami Sivananda wrote: "Those who approached Sai Baba in dead earnest to achieve the highest that life holds for them were and are anxious to view him as a guru in which capacity he would be of the greatest use to them for achieving the goal of life. It is as guru to all persons of all faiths and places that one can meet at his feet." Baba's method of teaching his devotees has not been exhaustively studied but one of them is known as the Dakshinamurthi method. In this at the foot of a banyan tree disciples are seated at the feet of the guru. The guru observes silence and does not utter a word. The doubts of the disciples are however cleared and dispelled. One may ask, how is that possible? It has been explained that it is a way of conveying thoughts and impulse to action without utterance of a single word. it is called "radiating thought." A person before such a guru feels that his whole being is permeated, controlled, communed with and moulded by the guru without the use of words and without any direction that any book should be studied or any practice should be followed. One disciple of Baba said: "Baba graciously conveyed to me without any words the feeling that all differences (between various souls) were unreal, that the one real thing was that which underlines all."

Baba's training, teachings and achievements varied widely and were adjusted to the nature and condition of those who approached him. Baba has repeatedly undertaken to guide his devotees, life after life promising to be reborn for that purpose. Baba's guru showed him that he was not the mere body, that his interests were not to be confounded with the thousand and one things of the organism or one's artificial or sentimental personality closely associated with the organism. According to Narasimha Swamiji if a person once realises that he is not this organism and the body but is something which is very much wider it may be due to Baba having trained him to pitch himself into all others' hearts and identify himself with those souls. Then the present "necessities, desires and aversions formerly found in oneself all drop off. The scales fall from one's eyes. The world looms as something totally different from what it did. One sets about it and acts in a different way. Baba gives the needed push and sees to the proper progress of everyone according to his nature and circumstances. It does not matter whether one's progress is achieved completely now or later. If progress is not complete in one life the *jnani* reaches God after many births."

Baba throughout followed the rule of secrecy and except under sheer necessity did not reveal his spiritual eminence. He did not reveal his name, his antecedents and other particulars and only almost at the end of his presence on earth did he disclose his Brahmin parentage and his being brought up by a fakir. Even his guru's name was rarely mentioned. On these occasions he spoke about his previous births without indicating the places and dates.

M. B. Rege said Baba did not prescribe one uniform spiritual exercise or practice for all. He suited himself to the state, circumstances and conditions of each. Baba used to tell his devotees : "If you are a Rama *bhakta* keep to it. If you want only Allah keep to it." He taught both by example and precept that real happiness and success in life here and hereafter came only to the man who did not grasp but renounced, who surrendered all to his God and Guru. Baba helped the true devotee to make this surrender by attending to every want of his once he made his surrender or even started making it.

On one occasion talking to a devotee after the noon *arati* Baba said : "Be wherever you like, do whatever you choose, remember this well, that all you do is known to me. I am the inner ruler of all and seated in their hearts. I envelope all creatures, the movables and the immovables in the world. I am the controller, the wire puller of the show of this universe. I am the mother - origin of all beings, the harmony of the three *gunas*, the propeller of all senses, the creator, preserver and destroyer. Nothing will harm him who turns his attention towards me but *maya* will lash or whip him who forgets me. All the insects, ants, the visible, movable and immovable world is my body or form." Making these pronouncements, which remind one of Krishna's message in the *Gita*, Baba must have acted as God in ecstasy.

According to Baba the disciple or devotee who comes to the feet of the guru in complete surrender has no doubt to be pure, chaste, and upright but he does not need to continue any active practice of japa or meditation. On the contrary, any such practice or intellectual process which involves the postulate : "I am doing this", is a handicap. All sense of *ahamkar* or ego in the disciple has to be wiped out, swept out of memory and mind as it is an obstruction to the guru's task. The guru does not teach. He radiates influence. This influence is poured in and absorbed with full benefit by the soul which has completely surrendered itself, blotting out the self, but it is obstructed by mental activity, by reliance on one's own exertion and by every kind of self-consciousness and self-assertion.

Baba's devotees have said, Baba was well versed in all yogic practices including the six processes among which were *dhanthi* (stomach cleaning by a moistened piece of linen three inches in width and 22.5 inches in length) and *khanda yoga*, that is separating his limbs and joining them and samadhi.

To many people some of his actions and sayings were confusing and perplexing. For instance, he said : "I am not at Shirdi but everywhere. He who thinks that Baba is in Shirdi alone has totally failed to see Baba." On one occasion he said : "I am Allah (God)." Such statements appeared to some like eccentric outbursts of a mad man. His queer unconventional ways, his habit of accommodating himself to all sorts of people including Hindus, Muslims and others and "unorthodox originality" failed to impress many of his visitors, says a writer.

Baba told one of his disciples : "You want to escape from samsara. I cannot escape from it myself. As long as there is the body samsara is there. One cannot be released from samsara by running away to a jungle or by other similar processes."

Baba set a good example in service when he was forcibly taken away by a Muslim sadhu, Javar Ali, who taught him Islamic scriptures. Though Javar Ali was not morally superior to Baba he was very well equipped and learned in the Quran and the shariat. Baba who followed a policy of non-resistance to evil was forced to be his disciple. He served him by carrying faggots, lighting fires, cooking, sweeping the floor and doing all kinds of menial jobs. Baba's devotees were alarmed by his prolonged absence and they went and requested Javar Ali to release him and allow him to return to Shirdi. Javar Ali agreed but said he would also stay with Baba at Shirdi. He however did not stay long in the mosque for in an argument with a Hindu sadhu he was worsted and he left Shirdi for good.

Not only did Baba reject dead tradition and accept traditions which were good but he also interpreted them afresh as we shall see in his interpretation of the word *athithi* (guest) in a subsequent chapter. He had great faith in the *Ramayana* as is evident in the following conversation Shama had with him on it :

Shama	:	Is it true that one crore of *vanara* (monkey) army assembled at the time of Rama's war against the demon king Ravana?
Baba	:	Yes.
Shama	:	How could so many assemble in one place ?
Baba	:	Even as ants do one above the other and so on.
Shama	:	Were you there then to see it?
Baba	:	Yes.
Shama	:	I see you here in the mosque now. How could you witness what happened so long ago? If you were there then how were you?
Baba	:	Innumerable births went by for you and for me. You don't know them but I do. I was as I am now.

Baba's personal attendant, Abdul, has written that Baba often uttered words about avatars of God. Those utterances showed that he believed in the avatars of Rama and Krishna, Abdul wrote in his diary. Baba also told him: "I have helped you to cross the ocean of birth and death." In certain unusual ecstatic moments Baba used to exclaim, I am God. I am Allah." But his usual role was that of a devotee entrusted with vast powers to carry out the wishes of the Fakir (God). Baba held Brahmins in high esteem. He said: "Brahmins earn much pica (*punya*) by their ways." Baba spoke of his service to his master and said he followed his wishes strictly to the letter. He said: "I would tremble to come in the presence of my guru." There was no one in Shirdi to serve Baba in that way. Baba asked once : "Who dares to call himself my disciple? Who can serve me adequately and satisfactorily?"

Baba the saint set an example of living in society and moving and working like common people. He even turned a stone grinder to make wheat flour. He was not for desertion of society as ascetics were wont to do. He wanted people to continue their *grihasta* lives and did not want them to renounce society and take to *sanyas*. He was always in a state of detachment in the midst of numerous distractions. His life was marked by *vairagya* (detachment from the world) and *nishkamya karma* which would lead one to God.

Baba did not always respect orthodoxy. Das Ganu Maharaj said his (*ganu's*) orthodoxy kept him away from onions but Baba liked onions and seldom had a meal without onions. Baba asked Das Ganu to prepare a dish of onions, give it to him and himself eat part of it. When Das Ganu prepared the dish and gave it to Baba the latter asked him if he had eaten some of it. Das Ganu said "Yes", but what he really did was to touch the dish with his finger and make a pretence of eating it. This he did thinking that Baba would not know it. However, Baba knew what he did and he showed to others who were present how he did it. Baba said: "He pretends he eats but only touches it with his finger and applies the finger to his chin." Baba told Das Ganu he should really eat onions. He said if one digested onions and overcame its lust-producing tendencies it did no harm. Das Ganu says he began taking onions thereafter and as long as Baba lived except on ekadasi days.

When Baba talked about religion it was pure advaitha, the doctrine of non-duality which is the very essence of spiritual teaching. Arthur Osborne wrote : " Even apart from his miracles there was something bizarre about Sai Baba. A strange figure, teaching Hindus and Muslims alike, keeping a sacred fire burning in a mosque, raging at his devotees, even beating them with sticks, answering unspoken thoughts, flinging stones and abuse at an unbelieving visitor to drive him away or performing a miracle to attract him, openly asking for money to give away to others, he was a spiritual gargantuan — one before whom Gargantuan himself is dwarfed to a schoolboy. He would fly into a towering rage for no reason that could be seen, pouring out abuses but the storm would pass and he would suddenly speak graciously to someone who had just arrived or was taking leave. In all things Baba was picturesque. He taught in symbols, not in words."

Prof. Narke says as far as he knew Baba never spoke of maya. Baba took the common sense view that this world and the world beyond were real and we had to make use of them here and hereafter. "We must sow good seeds (results) in this life and the next," Baba said. This was the truth that underlay many of the stories he told. He believed in rewards and punishments for acts done in this life. These are Hindu doctrines and beliefs. Although he never declared he belonged to any religion, caste or creed he mentioned and did several things, says Prof. Narke, which showed his relation to Hinduism. He says he had heard Baba say : "My guru is a Brahmin". He had great regard for the *Bhagavad Gita, Ramayana,* the *Puranas* and *Yoga Vashista.* In his talks Baba often made references to these scriptures.

Das Ganu who called Baba an advaitin personified said nothing distracted him. Thirty-two dancing girls would come and dance before him daily but he would not even care to look at them. He was detached and in his *ananda* state.

A devotee once asked Baba what was Brahman like. Baba did not reply but sent someone to Bagechand, a Marwadi, to fetch Rs.100 from him. The Marwadi did not give the money but sent his *namaskara* to Baba. Baba sent another person to the money-lender with the same result. Then Baba asked Nana Chandorkar to get the money for him. Chandorkar sent a chit to the Marwadi who at once sent the money. Baba merely commented: "All is like this in the world." Das Ganu later told the devotee who had asked the question that the demand made to the money-lender and his response was the answer to his question. When others asked for that money it was not forthcoming but when Chandorkar wanted it, it was furnished at once. Similarly the man who wanted to know Brahman did not get it. It was he who was qualified to know it that got it. The lesson was: deserve before you desire Brahman.

Radhakrishna Swamiji gave this interpretation to the demand by Baba for Rs.100. The world (*prabancham*) is like Rs.100. Hundred is written as one followed by two zeros. Similarly prabancham or the world consists of one Sat, the real to which is added prabancham in the shape of names or forms which are but appearances (and not substantial). Sat (reality) is one and the two zeros are names and forms that are added. If the zeros in 100 are taken away the remaining one (1) still has value and does not perish whereas by taking away one (1) from 100 what remains is useless. Names and appearances are merely external and so they are Soonya or zero or worthless.

What did Baba think of pain and pleasure which every living being experiences? He said : "When waves of pain heave and disturb your mind they are all delusions and cause confusion. Do not give room to these. There is no wave without water and no light without a lamp. Similarly, for these waves of pain and pleasure there must be some basis. These waves are produced by the six internal enemies, *kama, kroda, lobha, moha, madha* and *matsarya*. These waves cover or delude the *swarup* or real nature of the soul and make the unreal appear as real. The rich wear golden bangles. Seeing it the poor man is pricked as a result of which the wave of jealousy arises. By reason of greed this wave heaves up with the thought : Let me have that (golden bangle). In this way all these occur. How can I describe to you the extent of the mischief caused by these ? Therefore at their onset you must curb and crush these shadripus (internal enemies). When the force of these six enemies is subdued and quelled they cease to raise the waves that agitate the mind. But if the force of these shadripus is not totally quelled (if even a little of these is allowed to work) then it will succeed in enslaving all the rest in its course. Hence you must get knowledge to control these six slaves and with knowledge keep discretion for supervision."

A Baba devotee points out that Baba had to keep his ego to carry out his obligations to the thousands who were connected with him by pre-natal obligations spoken of by him as rinanubhanda. The very idea of rinanubhanda implied that Baba considered himself as a person dealing with a number of limited *jivas* receiving from them and returning to them various obligations. Baba entered the worldly life for that very purpose and came to Shirdi at the age of 16 to draw to himself the thousands that were to benefit by his contact in this birth again after their contacts in previous births.

Baba's path of self-realisation was through guru worship. His life and lilas throw a flood of light on the significance and value of *guru marga*. It is through guru worship that saints achieved perfection and what they learnt they endeavoured to impart to others. Baba had the ability to conceal his real nature and the working of his mind and body in line with the dictum in the scriptures that eminence must be concealed. His action as a *sadguru* and *samartha sadguru* was unknown to the thousands of people who met him in life or heard of him. it was only through the revelations of devotees experiences that people realised that he was a *samartha sadguru*. The path Baba followed has puzzled many as it did not fall into any of the accepted paths followed by saints and sadhus. The path he adopted could be called bhakti marga, that special form of it that is described as Guru Marga in the *Guru Gita*.

Guru, a Sanskrit word, is one who imparts knowledge or trains a disciple. *Gu* means darkness and *Ru* denotes the action of destruction. Guru therefore means a dispeller of darkness or ignorance. Baba used the Persian equivalent of the word guru, murshad. He said once : "My murshad has taken me away from this body which is but my house." This meant the guru had destroyed the identification of self with the body and made Baba realise that the *atma* was not the body just as the fire which burns the fuel is different from the fuel and the seer is not the seen.

According to the *Guru Gita* gurus are classified under seven heads: *Suchaka, Vachaka, Bodhaka, Nishiddha, Vihita, Karana* and *Parama. Suchaka* is the ordinary schoolmaster who teaches the three Rs. *Vachaka* is one who imparts ethical teachings. Bodhaka is one who teaches mantras for various purposes. *Nishiddha* is one who teaches mantras and other methods for achieving ignoble purposes such as killing, seducing, preventing movement, etc. *Vihita* is one who teaches detachment and prepares one for achieving spiritual welfare. *Karana* is one who teaches the message of the *Upanishads*. *Parama*, the last and greatest of all, teaches the disciple to absorb the truth of the scriptures, for achieving self-realisation and escape samsara and rebirth. He is also called the Moksha guru. There are gurus who are seen and others unseen. There are gurus who merely impart knowledge and do not care for results. They are those who do not undertake any responsibility for their disciples. There are others who give definite undertakings and carry them out at all costs and if necessary, life after life seek the disciple in subsequent births for the purpose. Baba was the best example of such a guru.

A guru, as we have seen, is one who teaches something, secular or religious. One who teaches about God or Sat is called Sat Guru. He who uses all his siddhis and superior powers to carry the disciple right up to the goal is called Samartha Sat Guru. Baba belongs to this type of guru. Parama Guru is a Samartha Sat Guru who looks after the entire welfare (secular and spiritual) of his disciple. The scriptures clearly say that without a guru *Brahmajnana* and *moksha* cannot be attained. It is not always true that *sishyas*(disciples) go out to find the guru. The reverse is often true. Baba himself drew hundreds of thousands to himself inwardly and unnoticed by them. He said: "No one comes to me except by my drawing them. I draw people to me under various pretexts such as the worldly objects they want. When a boy ties a bird with one end of a string can the bird refuse to come?" This drawing of people to himself Baba ascribed to rinanubhanda (personal ties and obligations). One disciple called it the "irrestible pull of destiny".

Guru marga may be defined as that form of *bhakti marga* in which faith in and devotion to the guru is the only sadhana for achieving every end, including salvation (*mukti*), conquest of samsara, all yoga siddhis and temporal welfare. Baba realised that a guide was needed and mere talk with bookish knowledge was no use at all to help one to realise God. It was not an intellectual task. The problem was how a particular soul was to be helped towards self-realisation and that was essentially a matter of moulding the mind and character of the sishya(disciple). What was wanted was humility, receptivity and a powerful desire to reach the goal with the aid of the guru and therefore a readiness to surrender everything to him. Baba surrendered everything, body, mind, possession to the guru as a result of the intense love he bore him. In ancient days the guru's return of love was equally strong. The guru had vast powers including the power to ward off death and to revive the dead and it was the guru's duty to use his powers to save his pupil from death. In Baba's case his guru averted his death from a brick hurled at him by making the brick stand still in midair. Baba himself averted death in the case of a number of his devotees. It was the guru's responsibility also to help his disciples achieve success in other fields.

Baba has proved in a number of cases (several of which have been recorded) that he could provide everything and that he undertook to provide everything to his devotee. He told one devotee: "Why have you any anxiety? All care is mine." On every occasion and in every matter Baba looked after him, the devotee has stated.

It is not so much the personality of the guru that matters as the extent of the disciple's faith in him. Baba told a woman devotee that she would find great benefit by putting faith even in a potsherd and that the most important thing was the faith of the sishya and not the merit of the guru.

The wrong choice of a guru may lead to unhappy results as a village official who later became a devotee of Baba found. This official was told by his guru that he must install a brand new image of a goddess in place of the old one that he worshipped in his family temple. The motive was to make profit out of the installation and the ceremonies connected with it. The official who had grave doubts about the advice of his guru approached Baba who advised him against replacing the old image. The official, however, did not follow Baba's advice and decided to install a new image as directed by his guru. Baba had cautioned him against disregarding his advice and mentioned that in a similar case disregard of his advice against the purchase of a cow had resulted in an epidemic breaking out in the village. As foreseen by Baba an epidemic did break out in the official's village and the first victim was the official's wife. The official appealed to his guru to help him but the guru demanded that he should gift to him half of his landed property. It was then that the official realised that his guru was an avaricious person and a hypocrite and he rushed to Baba and said he would follow his advice not to install a new image in the temple.

However, normally, when a guru was not a person who was sinful or wicked Baba's advice was not to shift loyalties. He said people should stick to their own guru however little merit there might be in him and not change over to another guru who might have greater merit.

Among Parama gurus there are two kinds, the *mouni* and the *vagmi*. The mouni enjoyed the bliss of perfection but did not impart it or help others to achieve it. The vagmi expressed his thoughts as far as possible and helped the disciple to share them and achieve self-realisation. The vagmi is to be preferred by the disciple at the initial stage though finally the mouni might suit his purpose better.

What are the qualifications of a sishya? It is said in the scriptures that *upadesa* or instruction should not be given to (1) the covetous, (2) the miserly, (3) the fickle-minded, (4) a person without devotion of faith and (5) one who does not care to render service to the guru. There are incidents in Baba's life to show how he adopted disciples. On one occasion a rich man with Rs 250 in his pocket had heard that Baba could impart Brahmajnana to anyone he chose and would not demand payment for the upadesa. He engaged a carriage from the railway station to Shirdi and back. On arrival at Shirdi he told the carriage driver he would be back in a few hours and went into the mosque and saw Baba. He told Baba he had come for Brahmajnana and wanted it immediately as though it was a parcel to be handed over across a counter in a shop. Baba told him he understood his need and asked a boy who was near him to get a loan of Rs 5 from a moneylender on his behalf. The boy returned after a few minutes saying that the moneylender was not to be found. The boy was again sent with a similar demand to some other moneylenders and he came back with the same reply—not to be found. In this way half an hour had elapsed and the rich visitor was getting impatient and afraid that the carriage driver would now demand more because of the delay. He thought of lending the money Baba wanted but was not sure if it could be recovered and so he gave up that idea. He then asked Baba why he was delaying giving him upadesa. Baba asked him: "Have you understood nothing? I have been all the while trying to impress you with Brahmajnana. You see, I want five things surrendered to me. The five are *manas* (mind), *buddhi* (reason), *ahamkar* (ego), *chitta* (thought) and will. Unless a man thoroughly surrenders himself and is free from the love of money and love of worldly things he cannot attain Brahmajnana. When the dawn comes there will be light and not earlier." The visitor then realised that Baba had read his mind and that he was too avaricious ever to get Brahmajnana.

For Baba, two things necessary for a good sishya were "Nishta" (faith) and "saburi" (patience). Baba said his guru asked him for a dakshina of two paise and when he gave the coin to him he was satisfied. Explaining nishta Baba said no progress could be made by any sishya who had no faith in his guru or in the scriptures, vedic mantras, etc. No guru would accept a sishya who lacked the proper attitude and spirit and betrayed lack of faith. Unless a man had the necessary humility he could not approach the guru. A guru had to test a newcomer to make sure that he had or would soon have sufficient humility and receptivitity. If one did not have sufficient faith in his guru he would not accept what the guru said. It has been said that mantras do not bear fruit unless the one who chants them has faith in them.

Once a railway station master, who had no faith in Baba and thought that he was being honoured too much, was taken to visit Baba who was then cleaning pots and placing them on the ground face down. Asked why he did so Baba said: "Persons who come here are like that. Just as a vessel with its mouth upside down cannot receive anything some persons come to me in an unreceptive mood." That was the case with the station master and Baba knew it. Persons with wavering faith have first to develop stronger faith before they could get any benefit from Baba.

It has been said that if a guru is treated merely as a man the disciple's sadhana will be a perpetual failure. The guru who has realised his soul as identical with *Parabrahmam* works at the soul of his disciple and after seeing that it is duly prepared at the right moment utters a word or makes a gesture and the effect is instantaneous. The sishya is drawn into the same state of *sachitananda*. This is done in one minute or half a second, says Narasimha Swamiji. As the *Guru Gita* says : "In a moment or half a moment the guru and the sishya are in that realised state as a result of the guru's action and the disciple's faith.".

Narasimha Swamiji says the technique by which the guru prepares the disciple through working inwardly on the soul of the disciple and the actual means by which the grand denouement is effected is extremely subtle and peculiar to each guru. Baba concealed this technique but revealed it partly. Gurus not infrequently employed devices when a person approached them to be accepted as a disciple. From 1908 onwards Baba started asking for *dakshina* (offering) from those who aspired to be his disciples. The idea was that a man too much attached to wealth would be frightened at this demand for dakshina and might stay away. On the other hand a person ready to pay dakshina showed his readiness to part with worldly things and might also be ready to part with his worldly avocations and attachments and thus be prepared for intense love towards the guru and surrender to him. (Baba's habit of demanding dakshina is treated in greater detail in the next chapter.)

Narasimha Swamiji says that despite the great sacrifices that Baba made there was no one who was fit to become a complete sishya and his successor in point of spiritual eminence or at any rate possessing a sufficient portion of his qualifications to continue his mission of service. The loyalty of a sishya to his guru must be more powerful than the loyalty of a chaste wife to her husband, says Narasimha Swamiji. A flagrant breach of ties with the guru may have serious consequences on one's spiritual progress. Baba therefore dissuaded devotees from leaving their own gurus and seeking contact with him. To doubters and critics Baba's reply was, what was needed was not external gestures or reasoning but working on the mind internally without words, and unseen. It took away and wiped out clean all traces of the critical spirit and substituted it with a humility which said in effect : "I am a worm. Thou art all power and mercy."

What brought Baba and his disciples together? What was the cementing force? Baba said to G. S. Khaparde: "You, Kaka, Shama, Bapusaheb, Jog, Dada Keldar and I were living together with our guru in a blind alley in our former birth and I have therefore drawn all of you together in this birth."

5

TAX COLLECTOR

S AI BABA was in the habit of collecting dakshina (offering) from devotees who could afford to pay and he used this device with a twin-objective, one to keep away those who were solely interested in getting worldly benefits and the second to convey a spiritual message to those who needed it. Baba began to ask for dakshina from 1908. He asked his visitors for payment of sums ranging from Rs. 2 to Rs. 500. Almost everyone who was asked paid. Many sent money of their own accord, one devotee sending Rs. 6,000. The total amount collected in a day was quite big, sometimes running into thousands. The total collection amounted to a Governor's salary on which the Government wanted to levy income tax. But Baba retained nothing for himself and he disposed of the money collected on the same day. He fed 200 beggars every day. Those to whom he gave money became wealthy and bought landed property and they paid income tax. Baba himself had only Rs.16 in his pocket at the time of his death which he had kept for his funeral expenses.

Baba had an utter disregard for money. His necessities of life were sufficiently provided by his *biksha dharma,* that is, by being a true fakir. He went out daily to beg for food. He stood before four or five houses in the village and shouted : "Pora *Puri* (boys and girls) *roti dhal lavo* (bring bread and dhal)." Housewives invariably provided him with pieces of flat cakes which he carried in his cloth and poured lentils and vegetables in a tin pot. These formed his meal till the last moment of his life. Occasionally when he was too ill to go to beg he asked some of his devotees to do the biksha for him.

He at first slept on the bare floor and later he lay on a rough and cheap mattress, called *gadi,* with some cloths spread on it.

He possessed no property and felt no need to possess any although his devotees offered him large sums of money which as stated above he distributed the same day they were received.

Referring to Baba's practice of asking for dakshina Shama told M. B. Rege : "You do not understand Baba at all. He does not care a rap for your rupees. What he wants is your mind, your heart, your time and your soul to be devoted to him. That is the meaning of dakshina." H. S. Dixit told Rege that when Baba asked him to go to somebody to get the dakshina Baba intended to teach him, that he should not consider being poor, or begging for money or asking for anything to be a humiliation. The lesson was : "Don't feel it to be infra dig to do anything for the master."

A poor clerk once asked Baba why he constantly asked him for Rs. 2 as dakshina when he was only a petty clerk. Baba replied : "It is not these coins that I want. I want nishta (faith) and saburi (patience). Give me these." Baba never got angry or showed displeasure if anyone did not pay dakshina. He never showed any special favour to those who gave dakshina or donations. He gave his love and attention to all. He refused to establish a mutt or ashram or be the head of any institution or estate or property or even recognise anyone as his disciple to succeed him. He left no estate for anyone to succeed to it.

Baba often made the demand for dakshina as a gesture by which he wanted to teach valuable lessons to his devotees, to help and guide them in their day to day lives and lead them on the path of self-realisation. Once when a devotee thought he had given all that he had with him as dakshina to Baba he remarked : "You have still a two-anna piece in your pocket." The devotee searched his pocket and the two-anna coin was there and he gave it to Baba. In another instance Purshotham Avasthi, a devotee, who was a judicial officer, came to Shirdi with his wife and son on his way to his son's wedding in another town. He had kept Rs. 400 with him and Rs. 300 with his wife. Baba took all the money from Avasthi and his wife in the form of dakshina in instalments leaving them with nothing. Avasthi returned to his quarters gloomy not knowing how he was going to meet his expenses. Then he met Bapusaheb Jog who asked him how much he needed. When Avasthi said he required at least Rs. 100 Bapusaheb gave the money to him and said : "As Baba got Rs.600 from you I am sure you will get by his grace a promotion and an increment in pay by Rs. 50 per month." And Avasthi got his promotion and increment as Bapusaheb had predicted.

Baba often used to say : "Whoever gives me one, I give him five, whoever gives me five I give him ten. I never take anything gratis. I never ask anyone indiscriminately. I only ask and take from him whom the fakir (my guru) points out. If anyone is indebted formerly to the fakir money is received from him. The donor sows his seed only to reap a rich harvest in future. Wealth should be the means to work out dharma. If it is used for personal enjoyment it is wasted. Unless you have given it before you do not get it now. So the best way to receive is to give. The giving of dakshina advances vairagya and thereby bhakti and *jnana*. Give one and receive tenfold."

Baba's devotees found his words true. On one occasion Balakrishna Upasani, brother of Kashinath Upasani Baba, was asked for dakshina by Baba and he said he had nothing with him to give. He left after paying his respects to Baba. On the second day when he went to take leave of Baba, Baba again asked him for dakshina. Upasani said he had only the train fare with him to return home. Baba then pointed to the silver watch he was wearing and asked for it as dakshina. Upasani gave it to him after some hesitation. Baba gave away the watch to a fakir standing nearby. Baba told Upasani : "You are not going to be worse off. Do not worry." After Upasani returned home he narrated the incident to a friend. He asked him what a new watch would cost. At that very moment his friend's brother sent his gold watch to Upasani and requested him to accept it as his present to him.

On another occasion two devotees from Goa had come to see Baba. Baba asked one of them for dakshina of Rs. 15 which was readily given and accepted. The other man voluntarily offered Rs. 35 as his dakshina but Baba refused to accept it and when asked for the reason he said: "I take nothing from anybody. This *masjidmai* calls for the debt, the debtor pays it and becomes free. Have I got any house or property to look after? I require nothing. I am ever free." He then revealed in the form of a story that the man from whom he had received the dakshina had vowed to pay the first month's salary to his God after he got a job. But after he got a job and received very good increments he forgot his vow and it was only that money that Baba had asked for as dakshina. The man who paid the dakshina confirmed Baba's story. Baba has been quoted as saying : " I take away the wealth of those I love."

Hemadpant says that for a long time Baba did not take anything from devotees. He stored burnt matches and filled his pockets with them. He never asked anything from anybody whether he was a devotee or otherwise. If anyone placed before him a paisa or two he purchased oil or tobacco with them. He was fond of tobacco for he always smoked a bidi or pipe. In course of time some devotees thought they should not visit Baba empty handed and they made offerings of copper coins to him. If a paisa was there he would pocket it but if it was a two-paisa coin he would return it immediately. And as his name and fame spread and thousands of people flocked to see him Baba began the practice of asking for dakshina from them. This he did in order to teach his devotees the lesson of charity and to remove their attachment to money and thus to purify their mind. But there was this peculiarity. He said he had to give back hundred times more of what he received. There were many instances in which this happened.

The famous Marathi actor, Ganapatrao Bodas, said in his autobiography that on Baba pressing him for dakshina he used to empty his money purse before him. He said the result was that in later life he never lacked money as it came to him in abundance. Another devotee, B. V. Deo said Baba did not ask for dakshina from all. If some gave dakshina unasked he sometimes accepted and at other times rejected it. He asked for it from some devotees only. He never asked for it from those devotees who thought that Baba should ask for it and they would pay. If anybody offered dakshina against his wish he never touched it and he asked the devotee to take it away. He asked for small or big amounts from devotees according to their wish, devotion and convenience. He asked for it even from women and children. He never asked for it from all the rich or from all the poor.

If any dakshina was sent through a friend who forgot to give it to Baba he was sure to remind him about it and collect it. But how did Baba know of the devotee's instruction to his friend? That will remain a mystery. On some occasions Baba returned part of the dakshina to the devotee and asked him to

68   *God Who Walked on Earth*

keep it in his shrine for worship. This procedure benefited the
devotee or donor immensely. If anyone offered more than he
originally intended to give Baba returned the extra amount. In
some cases Baba demanded more dakshina than the devotee
originally intended to give and if he had no money at the moment
to pay he would ask him to beg or borrow from others. From
some Baba demanded dakshina three or four times a day.

Out of the amount collected as dakshina Baba spent very
little on himself except, as we mentioned before, to buy tobacco,
oil to light the lamps and fuel for the dhuni. All the rest he
spent on charity in varying proportions to various persons.

Baba once told a rich devotee: "Unless you rid yourself
completely of your avarice or greed you will not get the real
Brahman. How can he, whose mind is engrossed in wealth,
progeny and prosperity, expect to know Brahman without
removing his attachment for the same? The illusion of attachment
or the love for money is a deep eddy (whirlpool) of pain, full
of crocodiles in the form of conceit and jealousy. He who is
desireless alone can cross the whirlpool. Greed and Brahman
are as poles asunder. They are eternally opposed to each other.
Where there is greed there is no room for thought or meditation
of Brahman. For a greedy man there is no peace, neither
contentment nor certainty (steadiness). If there is even a little
trace of greed in one's mind all the sadhanas are of no avail.
Even the knowledge of a well-read man who is not free from the
desire of the fruit or reward of his action and who has got no
disgust for the same is useless and cannot be helped in getting
self-realisation. The teachings of a guru are of no use to a man
who is full of egoism and who only thinks about the material
objects. Purification of mind is absolutely necessary. Without
it all our spiritual endeavours are nothing but a useless show of
pomp. It is, therefore, better for one to take only what he can
digest and assimilate. My treasury is full and I can give anyone
what he wants but I have to see whether he is qualified to
receive it. If you listen to me carefully you will certainly
be benefited. While sitting in this masjid I never speak any
untruth."

One day a man approached Baba for money. Baba had
money in his pocket but he told the man he had no money with
him. Later, after the man had left, Shama who was present
asked Baba : "When you are a fakir with no attachment for

money and wedded to truthfulness why did you hide the money and tell him a lie? Do you not always exhort us to be truthful?" Baba replied that the man should not be given the money as it was not good for him and he would not believe Baba's words if he told the truth; thus it was for the man's own good that he had to be thus treated.

Prof. Narke said : "Baba's language was highly cryptic, full of symbology. It would be taken literally by superficial people who would conclude that Baba was a worldly man and very avaricious at that. One day Baba asked me several times to give him Rs.15 as dakshina. I had then no money and he knew it full well. When I was alone with him I said : 'You know I have no money, so why do you ask me for Rs. 15 as dakshina?' Baba said he knew my impecunious condition well enough. But he added : 'You are reading a book now. The part you are now reading is specially important. Get me Rs. 15 dakshina from that'. I was then reading *Yoga Vashista*. Getting money out of it meant deriving valuable lessons therefrom and giving the money to Baba meant lodging the lessons in my heart."

Baba regarded money as a danger or obstacle to spiritual progress and did not allow his devotees to fall into its clutches. An example is the case of Mahlsapathy who was very poor and could hardly make both ends meet. Baba never allowed him to make any money nor gave him anything. Once a kind and generous merchant gave Mahlsapathy a large amount as gift in Baba's presence but Baba did not permit Mahlsapathy to accept it.

M. B. Rege, one of Baba's intimate devotees, recalled that in 1912 he went to Shirdi with Rs. 100 in his pocket, to meet Baba. Baba asked him for Rs. 40 as dakshina which he gave. Sometime later Baba again asked a dakshina of another Rs. 40 which was also readily given. Finally Baba asked as dakshina the remaining Rs. 20 and Rege surrendered it also. Afterwards Baba sent for him again and asked for dakshina. Rege said he had no more to give and Baba suggested he should get the money from someone. Rege agreed to do so but wanted to know whom he should approach. Baba said : "Go to Shama." Rege went to Shama and asked him for money. Shama said Rege had not understood Baba correctly. Rege reported the conversation to Baba. He smiled and said : "Go to Dixit and ask him." Dixit told Rege that Baba's direction to him should be understood in the circumstances as a lesson to him that he should not feel the absence of money or the begging for money or anything else to be a humiliation and that he should not consider himself to be above begging. Baba then asked Rege to go to Nana Chandorkar who told Rege how he tackled such situations in which Rege found himself in. He said : "Whenever I go to Shirdi I start with a certain sum and leave some money at Kopargaon. On this occasion I came with Rs. 200 of which I left Rs. 100 at Kapargaon. It is painful to say no when Baba asks for dakshina. So I go on giving dakshina out of the stock in hand and when it is exhausted I send for the reserve at Kopargaon. You must act like this." After Baba learnt from Rege what Chandorkar had said he sent for Chandorkar and asked him for dakshina of Rs. 40. He paid it and left. He was sent for again and asked to pay Rs.40 more. That was paid and Baba asked for the remaining amount with Chandorkar as dakshina. Chandorkar sent for the reserve at Kopargaon and Baba wanted that too. Chandorkar felt humiliated at having to say no to Baba since it took some time for the reserve money to arrive from Kopargaon. Rege said : "The lesson that was then taught to me and others was that it was presumptuous on the part of anyone to think that he himself was the great provider supplying the needs of Baba or that anyone could give all that Baba may ask for. Baba thus showed me how differently the demand for dakshina was interpreted by devotees. The real explanation of Baba's demand in this case was not what Shama, Dixit and Chandorkar had said it was. It was evidently a lesson to teach me, Chandorkar and others. Baba really did not care for money or for presents. What he really wanted was love that was deep, intense, passionate and wholehearted. To give him that was my aim. He knew it and read it in my heart and responded to it as only he could respond."

Another devotee from whom Baba took the last paisa in his possession as dakshina said it was a valuable lesson to him in humility. He said the demands for dakshina were often found to have allegorical and esoteric meaning on which light was thrown by the circumstances or accompanying remarks. Baba said once : "Whatever money is spent for any good purpose all that reaches me. This is true, this is true, this is true, I say this thrice."

6

A DAY WITH SAI BABA

S AI BABA was about five feet six inches tall, neither stout nor lean. His complexion was golden yellow, his eyes bluish, which shone bright mysteriously in darkness. Indeed, his eyes were the object of wonder to devotees. His nostrils were prominent. At the time when Sai Shardanandaji, who has given the above description of Baba, saw him Baba had some of his teeth missing and the rest were not pure white. He never brushed his teeth but only rinsed his mouth with a little water every morning. He did not drink coffee or tea but did not ask his devotees to abstain from them. He never told anyone how he got into the habit of smoking a pipe. He always used the same clay pipe although devotees offered him many pipes which he did not use but stocked them in a hollow of the masjid wall.

The piece of cloth tied round his head was very rarely changed and never washed. When he decided to change his kufni he sent for the tailor and said : "Get me a kufni." When it was given to him he always paid the tailor more than its worth. Left to himself Baba spoke very little. Mostly he was calm and quiet, speaking only when absolutely necessary. He never laughed loudly but smiled quietly. Most of the time he sat with his eyes closed. When a devotee approached him for darshan he glanced at him. Sometimes he did not even do that. He was always playful in the presence of children. He never sat leaning against the wall in the mosque. Even when he sat with his legs outstretched he always sat a few feet away from the wall. He did not lie down during the day. He seldom visited any temple in Shirdi.

Marthand, son of Mahlsapathy, has said that on certain occasions Baba sent for a barber, Balanari, and had his head shaved.   After the haircut Baba would put his hands in his pocket and pay the barber whatever came to his hands. But it was always much in excess of the normal payment for a shave. Baba maintained a small beard. He had a high forehead. He wore a plain kufni. The clay pipe which he used for smoking was a crude thing which had to be frequently renewed owing to its inferior quality. He used to sit around his devotees on the ground and pass the rustic pipe round to them. Khaparde notes in his diary :"Today I shampooed the legs of Sai Baba. The softness of the limbs is wonderful."

A woman devotee has recorded this impression of Baba's personality : "There was such power and penetration in his glance that none could continue to look into his eyes. One felt that Sai Baba was reading him or her mind through and through. Soon one lowered one's eyes and bowed to him. One felt that he was not only in one's heart but in every atom of one's body. A few words, a gesture would reveal that Baba knew all about the past and present and even the future and about everything else.   There was nothing else to do for one except to submit trustfully and to surrender to him.   And then he was to look after every minute detail and guide one safely through every turn and every vicissitude of life. He was the Antaryami, call him God or Satpurusha or what you like. But the overpowering personality was there and in his presence, no doubts, no fears, no questioning had any place and one resigned oneself and found that was the only course, the safest and best course."

Baba's words were always short, pithy, deep, full of meaning and well balanced. He once said: "Though I have become a fakir, have no house, or wife and though leaving off all cares I have stayed at one place, the inevitable maya teases me often. Though I forget myself I cannot forget her. She envelops me. This maya teases God Brahma and others, then what to speak of a poor fakir like me? Those who take refuge in the Lord will be freed from her clutches with His grace."

A devotee said many saints went into a trance or samadhi, forgetting their body and they would display their supernatural knowledge and power. But in the case of Baba he never had to go into a trance to achieve anything or reach any higher position. Every moment he was exercising a double consciousness, the ego called Sai Baba and the antaryami, superseding all egos and resting in the Paramathma. He was at the same time exercising and manifesting the powers and features of both states of consciousness. He was in the all knowing state always. The devotee said :"When I sit in his presence I always forget my pain, nay, the body itself with all its mundane concerns and anxieties. Hours would pass and I would be in blissful condition unconscious of the time passing. He was all in all for us and we could never think of his having limitations."

Baba slept in the mosque and the chavadi on alternate nights. In the mosque, when he got up in the morning, he would sit near the dhuni and talk to devotees about distant places he visited overnight and of his activities there. He frequently referred to his "travels" over great stretches of space and time. Many of his disciples who slept near him in the mosque were well aware that he was physically present at Shirdi the whole night. The local schoolmaster who lived near the mosque said that during the night he could often hear conversations in a multitude of languages, not only Indian but also English of which Baba was ignorant. The schoolmaster could not explain the phenomenon and Baba did not enlighten him either.

Sitting near the dhuni Baba would wave his arms and fingers, making gestures (which conveyed no meaning to the onlookers) and saying "Haq" (God). Baba washed himself once in three days. And when he did people noticed the extraordinary control he had over his physical frame. Every third day he went to a well near a banyan tree and washed his mouth and body. When he cleaned his mouth and rinsed it with water some lepers and others suffering from various diseases approached him and collected the water that he spat and sprinkled it on their heads. Devotees said one leper was cured completely by it.

One story about Baba that was current was that when he washed himself he vomited his intestines, cleaned them and swallowed them again.

After the morning breakfast Baba went for a stroll to the Lendibaugh (garden) which he himself had laid out in the early days. Devotees followed him wherever he went but they were not allowed to go with him to the garden. What Baba did there remained a mystery for a long time. The only one to be permitted to be with him was his Muslim attendant, Abdul.

On some occasions, Baba bathed twice daily. A devotee kept a stone seat for him to sit while taking his bath but he never used it. The stone has now been preserved in the mosque.

Returning to the mosque by about 10 a.m. Baba spent an hour and a half with his devotees and visitors. Sometimes during this period he would go out on his begging mission. The noon arati was performed by devotees at the end of which Baba distributed udhi to all those present and the gathering dispersed for lunch. Many devotees offered lunch packets or delicacies specially prepared for him. Baba distributed them to the devotees present and kept a little for the devotees who had offered them to him. Baba then sat for lunch in the mosque along with his close associates behind a curtain. Devotees said the lunch session was very often the occasion for Baba to manifest some of his divine powers.

One notable instance was when a portion of the mosque, which was in a dilapidated state, started to crumble with a loud noise while Baba and his devotees were taking lunch. Baba lifted his hand and said loudly :"Sahar, Sahar" (wait, wait). The noise stopped, and after the meal was finished and everyone came out, a big portion of the mosque came down with a shattering noise exactly at the place where Baba and the others had sat for their meal.

After lunch Baba spent sometime alone. Devotees did not disturb him at that moment as he was believed to be in mystic meditation. However, some devotees who managed to enter the mosque at that hour noticed that Baba was engaged in a strange mystic rite.

Writing about this Das Ganu Maharaj said :"Baba was occasionally doing something strange between 1 and 2 p.m. at the mosque with a cloth screen in front of him and when he was alone. He would take out of a pouch 10 or 15 old coins. They were of various denominations, three paise, one anna, two, four and eight annas and one rupee. He would rub his finger on them constantly, yet gently, (whether with or without mantra, I cannot say). The surfaces of the coins had all become worn out and were smooth. He would say as he rubbed his finger against the coins : 'This is Nana's, this is Kaka's, etc.' If anyone approached him he would gather the coins, put them back in the pouch and hide them."

At about 2.30 p.m. devotees and visitors again assembled at the mosque and represented their needs and offered prayers to him. Towards evening Baba walked to the front yard of the mosque and stood there for sometime, leaning against the me outer wall and talking to the passersby on the road. At about 5 p.m. he again went for a stroll to the garden and returned in time for the evening arati when devotees waved sacred lamps and burnt camphor before him. Baba spent some time with the devotees chatting and narrating parables He then distributed the daily gifts of money to beggars and some devotees, emptying the day's collections from his pockets. Then he sent the devotees, and visitors home for the evening meal after giving them udhi. Some however stayed on with him a little longer. At night they would all return to their lodgings leaving Baba to take rest.

At first Baba used a sack cloth as a seat during the day and as a bed at night. Several layers of cloth were spread over the sack cloth when it was used for sleeping. Later, a devotee gave Baba a wooden plank 4 feet long and about 3/4 of a foot wide. Baba used it as a hanging bed. He suspended the plank from the ceiling seven feet above the ground, tying it with pieces of worn out cloth which could hardly bear any weight. On the four corners of the plank he kept four mud lamps burning all through the night. And Baba slept on this plank. Devotees wondered how Baba could climb the plank at such a height, how such a small narrow plank could accommodate him and how it bore his weight without the shreds of cloth holding it not snapping. Also how he got down without upsetting the lamps and injuring himself. Devotees, including Das Ganu Maharaj, were curious to watch Baba doing this feat but they never managed to do so. When their curiosity became a nuisance Baba, in a fit of anger, broke the plank into pieces and threw them into the dhuni. Dixit offered to give a cot to Baba but he rejected the offer. He said: "I do not want it. Am I to lie on a cot leaving Mahlsapathy on the floor? Far better would it be that I should lie on the floor and he should sleep higher, higher." Dixit said : "I shall give you two planks, one for you and one for Mahlsapathy." Baba said: "He will not sleep on a plank. He will sleep on the ground. Sleeping on the plank is no joke. Who will sleep keeping his eyes open, all awake like me ? Only such a person can lie on the plank. Even when I lie on the ground I ask Mahlsapathy to sit by me and keep his palm on my chest. I lie down making mental *namasmarna* (remembrance of Lord's names) and I say to Mahlsapathy : 'Feel it, the chanting of the Lord's names by placing your hand on me here. If you catch

dozing wake me up.' Such was and is my order to him. So
you see a plank will be of no use to him."

Baba never allowed anyone else to stay with him at night in
the mosque except his closest devotees and among these were
Mahlsapathy and Tatya Patil. The three slept with their heads
towards the east, west and north with their feet touching one
another at the centre of the mosque.

Inside the mosque between 1 and 2 p.m. Baba was engaged
in what would normally appear to be inexplicable rites which he
never explained. His disciples were not allowed to be present
and he would conceal himself from view with a cloth screen.
Another of his habits was that he sat behind a pillar in which
a lamp was lit and kept burning day and night. His personal
attendant would fill mud pots with water and place them near
him. Baba would sit with two of the pots beside him and
continuously sprinkle water in various directions. It seemed to
be a kind of cleansing operation. Balakrishna Upasani had
recorded in 1910 : "Baba was standing near the dhuni and
occasionally turning round himself." What Upasani meant was
that Baba was doing *pradakshina* which is part of every Hindu
ritual. Chandrokar noted that all mantras that Baba muttered
were either in Arabic or Persian but not in Sanskrit. Baba
sometimes blew the conch which produced the sound 'Aum'.
This was seen by Khaparde.

We have already mentioned Baba's narration to his devotees
about his invisible travels during night with an invisible body
covering great distances of space and time. Prof. Narke said his
statements were literally true and were occasionally verified
and found true. Again Baba would frequently talk of post-
death experiences. Baba's ability to travel in invisible body to
distant places of the world, to traverse realms other than the
earth life and note or control what took place there and to seek
the past and future alike revealed one great fact about his nature.
He occasionally asked Prof. Narke :'where are you? where is
this world?" Pointing to his body or touching it and referring
to it he would say : "This is my house. I am not here. My guru
has taken me away." Prof. Narke said : "As even in the flesh
in this earth life he was not confined to his physical body it may
be truly said of him that in death he is truly alive. He is where
he was when alive. Even then he was where he is now." Baba
referred several times to his control of the destinies of departed

souls indicating thereby his function in the cosmic order. Prof.
Narke said Baba never spoke untruth, never uttered meaningless
jargon. But only those who were familiar with his ways could
make out the meaning of what he said or did when they were
intended for their understanding.

In the morning, as we have noted, Baba went on his daily
begging mission which he never abandoned all through his life
except in the later part of his life when his health was greatly
impaired. He never ate in anyone's place. He never kept any
food in reserve for the next meal. He remained a mendicant all
his life, although his devotees poured money and brought food
which he distributed among his devotees and to the needy. One
of the houses where he asked for alms was Tatya Patil's. Tatya,
when a child, used to assemble near the entrance to the mosque
with other children and annoy Baba by throwing stones. When
Baba scolded them they laughed at him. When Baba pretended
to chase them they ran away. Tatya's mother had great regard
and respect for Baba. She was the woman, as we have seen in
a previous chapter, who went after Baba as he roamed in forests
and fields in his earlier days to feed him and said she would not
eat until she had fed him. When Baba came with the begging
bowl she offered him a seat. When he was seated Tatya would
climb on Baba's back and play with him. His mother pulled
him up and warned him not to be rude to the holy visitor. But
Baba himself was unperturbed. Sometimes Baba begged at
Tatya's house 15 times a day as though to test Tatya's mother's
faith in him. Baba had said she was his sister in a previous birth
and so he was specially attached to her.

Devotees noticed that during the noon arati, in the course
of worship, Baba put two flowers in his nostrils, plugged two
others in his ears and threw one on his head. Although a silver
throne was kept for him in the mosque Baba did not sit on it but
on the sack cloth on the floor. Radhakrishna Ayi decorated the
entrance to the mosque with a garland of bangles. After arati,
Baba sat down for lunch. During the mango season Baba took
one mango daily, just tasted it and gave it to the devotees. Just
before everyone started eating Baba mixed a seer of milk, one
seer of sugar and one seer of roti in a bowl and distributed it
to all his devotees as *prasad*. M. V. Pradhan, describing the
noon meal, wrote :"Baba with his own hands put the food on
our plate and cups in large quantities. Instead of throwing

away such valuable prasad I asked my niece to take away three-fourths of what was served to me and that sufficed to feed my family. What I ate warded off all hunger or appetite for a night meal." Baba almost always gave dessert at the end of the meal. By the time everyone completed their meal many more waiting outside were given the prasad. After the meal Baba was given betel and nuts to chew and he later drank a glass of water.

In the afternoon, after their siesta visitors assembled in the mosque. This was the time for entertainment and there were shows by circus artists, dance and music performances. Baba gave each artist Rs. 2.

As Baba stood at the outer wall of the mosque and talked to people passing that way his words very often were cryptic and strange and it was not easy to understand what he was saying. Sometimes he said :"Ten serpents have gone. Many more will come." Again "people will flock here like ants." "*Vani* (merchants) and *teli* (oil vendors) have troubled me much. I won't stay in Dwaraka Mayi for long. I will go away from here." Sometimes he behaved as though he wanted to leave immediately. On one such occasion Tatya would rush to him and pacify him assuring him that he would punish all those who troubled him and he would not allow Baba to leave Shirdi. Baba would then quietly resume his seat and chat with devotees as if nothing had happened.

Baba had his moments of anger. At times he was in a towering rage and people with him thought it was ungovernable rage. On such occasions his disciples like Mahlsapathy and Prof. Narke even thought Baba was mad. Reading his mind Baba told Narke : "I am not a mad man." But his anger did not prevent him from dealing with his visitors calmly and dispose of their business. He gave suitable replies to their questions and gave them udhi. He followed the principle : rouse up your anger, use it for a time and when you do not want it anymore put it back in the scabbard. He thought this was the proper use of anger. However, he thought anger was the staunch enemy of equanimity so essential for spiritual progress. Baba said : "I get angry with none. Will a mother harm her little one? I love devotees. I am the bond slave of my devotees." One reason given for Baba's occasional burst of anger was that he might be driving away spells of thought or other ethereal waves which might be coming to harm his devotees or the people at large and the anger might be necessary to beat back those waves. His anger was evidently directed at unseen forces.

When Baba came to Shirdi as a young fakir he used to shout in anger, laugh or do other things which appeared to others as crazy. But evidently he was from the beginning dealing with unseen forces and directing his anger and unconventional behaviour at them. When one of his devotees was bitten by a snake and his life was in danger Baba, on seeing the victim, flew into a rage and shouted : "Do not climb up. If you do, take care. Get down, get down." The devotee who had rushed to Baba for relief was puzzled and thought that instead of protecting him Baba was asking him to go away. But a minute later Baba asked the devotee to come up and gave him directions on what to do. He asked him to go home and keep moving about and not go to sleep for 24 hours. Following Baba's instructions the devotee was saved. The angry words of Baba were meant for the poison to come down and to get it out of the devotee's system and not directed against the devotee.

Baba sometimes used expressions which were apparently foul, which abused and cursed persons but which were really curses against the evil influences operating on them.

Baba's method of imparting spiritual benefit was hardly noticeable. He would speak of God only rarely and that too with feeling. His religious practice could hardly be discussed by anyone. But his purity, strength, regularity and self-denial were prominent. He would always go and beg for food even if ill. He would eat only a portion of what he got through alms and the rest was distributed. He was indifferent to comforts.

There were three general or common sittings or durbar during the day. The first was in the morning after breakfast, the second after Baba's return from *lend*i and the third at 5 p.m. During all these sittings Baba spoke to the devotees on how to improve their lives.

Baba's daily routine was well structured and disciplined. He performed no rituals and read no books. Nor did he even write. His instructions were oral. It is said he would wave his arms about, or point his fingers making gestures and saying what he wanted done. Visitors were not permitted to go within 50 feet of him. His attendants would carry out their duties of sweeping the floor and replenishing the dhuni without a word spoken.

Baba had only one long-sleeved kufni or shirt at a time and it was often found to be very old and torn in many places. He personally used to patch it up again and again and wear it. Once in a way he washed it wearing a bright yellow dhoti at that time. He dried the wet kufni holding it over the dhuni and wore it again. All the efforts of devotees to make him put on a new kufni proved futile. Tatya who was the only one to take liberties with him used to tear up the already tattered kufni and throw it in the fire, compelling Baba to go in for a new one. Occasionally Baba himself once in three or four months changed the kufni. Very rarely did he give his discarded kufni to a devotee as a token of grace to be preserved as a sacrament.

The most commonly seen photograph of Baba shows him sitting on a big stone with his right leg thrown over his left knee. This stone is even today found in the front yard of the mosque. Originally it was used for washing clothes by Abdul, Baba's attendant. Once Baba sat on it, it ceased to be a washing stone and became an object of veneration.

Though not a part of his daily routine, yet on a number of occasions Baba left Shirdi to visit neighbouring villages on foot. These were Nimgaon and Rahata. Baba usually left saying he was going to the stream. When he was noticed leaving the mosque it would be reported to Tatya Patil who would rush to Baba and say : "You won't come back if you go. We will not leave you, let us go to Nimgaon tomorrow." Baba would assure him he would surely return to Shirdi, and proceed on his way. At Nimgaon his devotee, Dengle, would receive him with pomp and reverence, worship him and offer him milk. After spending some time with him Baba would return to Shirdi.

Daily he received dakshina amounting to several hundred rupees and he distributed them liberally among bhajan parties, fakirs and beggars. His self-control and equanimity were equally remarkable. His utter disregard of his health was patent. He was accessible at all hours, day and night to whoever wanted to see him. He used to say: "My durbar is always open at all hours." He was just and impartial. He was not obsequious to the rich and highly placed and supercilious and contemptuous of the lowly. Officials of all ranks came to see him, and vagabond, destitutes, beggars and paupers also came in hundreds. He treated them all with perfect equality. Bayyaji Appaji Patel, who massaged Baba, boasted he had the strength of Bhima. He lifted Baba and carrying him in his arms dropped him before the dhuni. One day he tried to lift Baba and discovered he could not. Baba looked at him and laughed. That laughter was a rebuke against pride. Baba's lifestyle was uncompromisingly ascetic save perhaps for his indulgence in tobacco. He would beg for his daily food at five different houses, a fixed number, which never varied. At each house he called out in Marathi : "Mother, give a little bread." Returning to the mosque he would deposit the assorted food he had collected in a mud pot set aside for the purpose in the compound outside the mosque. He would leave it there for some time and meanwhile anyone and anything was allowed to take what he or it liked before he himself partook of this fare. Among those who shared his meal were a sweeper woman, hungry stray dogs and crows. He ate what was left.

The place where Baba sat looked to all outward appearances like an old ramshackle sort of construction. But in that small oblong room Baba sat in the north-east corner. Opposite to him in the corner was the sacred dhuni burning night and day. Near it were the mud pots filled with water for Baba to drink and perform ablutions. The wall had a niche in which were placed a number of clay pipes. On Baba's right were a couple of grinding stones on which he used to grind corn and pulses. There were also a sack of wheat and a sack of country tobacco. When a Muslim visitor came to pay his respects to Baba with flowers and lump sugar and coconuts, fatia was uttered in which Baba joined. The flowers adorned the central niche and the sugar was distributed to all those present. All the while the Hindu devotees present witnessed the fatia and partook of the sugar and pieces of coconut.

A notable ritual in the mosque in the morning was the arrival of Baba's leper devotee, Bhagoji Shinde, who removed the bandage on Baba's hand, applied ghee (or butter) on it and massaged it. He then bandaged it again with a new cloth. This practice was started by Bhagoji ever since Baba suddenly thrust his hand into the dhuni one day to save a devotee's child in a faraway village when it slipped into a furnace from the mother's lap. Even long after the burn in Baba's hand had healed Baba waited every day for Bhagoji to continue his service to him and he did not explain the reason for this to anyone. Bhagoji also prepared the clay pipe for Baba and gave it to him. After having a puff at it he gave it back to Bhagoji for a smoke. Bhagoji thereafter left after the pipe had changed hands five or six times.

Baba went to the lendi (garden) again after lunch and spent about 45 minutes there. The garden as already mentioned had been laid out by him with the help of devotees, rich and poor and was in the middle of the western side touching the Agra Main Road. There is a well in the garden whose water later became well known for its curative properties.

We mentioned about Baba's cryptic remarks and replies. This was the experience of a devotee who wanted to take a photograph of him. Baba said : "No. It is enough if he knocks a wall down." The devotee was perplexed. What did Baba mean? This was the explanation given. A photograph is the likeness of Baba. The wall is the "I am the body" idea which stands between a man and his identity with the spirit. It is enough to destroy that and the true likeness of Baba will appear, not the body, but the spirit.

Baba used to spend time in baking bread and the type of bread he baked, devotees said, was extremely nourishing. The bread was baked in an oven kept outside the mosque. He distributed it to whoever wanted it. A story which was in circulation in Shirdi was that a group of villagers saw Baba lying in a field outside the village with his limbs and head lying detached and separated from his body. Mehr Baba, disciple of Upasani Baba, when asked about this said such a phenomenon could occur but it was absolutely irrelevant to higher development.

At about 8 p.m. daily Baba started distribution of money. There was a large retinue of people who regularly received alms at his hands and they gathered in the front yard of the mosque. Baba would thrust his hand into his pockets to pick the money for each recipient and strangely enough the precise amount he wanted to give each one of them would come into his hands without the need for counting. If it was a new recipient the money he really needed would come into Baba's hands from his pocket. He gave the money gratis and did not expect anything in return. Why he gifted the money no one knew. To newly

married couples who came to receive his blessings he gave one
rupee each. This daily distribution of money continued till
his death. During the Sri Rama Navami festival he gave two
bundles of one rupee currency notes to two of his devotees to
be distributed to the poor after the celebrations. The *naivedya*
offered to him by devotees daily was given away to fakirs and
beggars and bairagis who lived nearby. To each of them Baba
gave a 25 paisa coin daily.

Baba's departure for the chavadi every other evening was
marked by pomp and regal splendour. When Baba was ready
to leave for the chavadi Abdul and Ramakrishni Ayi swept the
road along which Baba walked barefoot. They sprinkled water
on the route and decorated it with rangoli in white. They
spread a cloth over it (this is called red carpet today) all the way
from the mosque to the chavadi. After all these preparations
were completed Tatya Patil came to the mosque and invited
Baba to begin the journey. As Baba stepped down from the
mosque shehnai blared forth music and devotees started singing
bhajans. Shyamakarna, the horse, would lead the procession
and behind it came the palanquin carried by devotees. Baba
refused to sit in the palanquin and always made the journey on
foot behind the palanquin in which were placed Baba's chappals.
The ceremonial umbrella was held over his head. Devotees
carried silver mace and whisks.

Earlier as Baba emerged from the mosque Tatya Patil
adorned him with a gold embroidered shawl. Baba put out one
of the lamps till then burning in the mosque with his right hand
by way of signifying that he had moved out of it. This marked
the start of his night journey. At that moment there was a
crescendo of music and crackers were fired. Volunteers marched
in front clearing the way. Baba walked slowly, holding the
hand of Tatya. Devotees on both sides of Baba held aloft royal
umbrellas and waved ornamental fans. Devotees sang Hari
nama and Baba nama. Women watching the procession from
their houses as it wended its way showered rose petals on Baba.

At the street corner where the chavadi was situated Baba
stood for a while in front of the Maruthi temple and made
gestures with his hands and waved them in all directions. His
face shone brightly all of a sudden and devotees chanted his
name with renewed vigour. During these exciting moments
Mahlsapathy who was holding one of Baba's hands danced in

ecstasy as though possessed. At the entrance to the chavadi Kakasaheb Dixit came out with a silver plate full of flowers which he poured over Baba's head. The chavadi was decorated for the occasion with ornamental mirrors hanging on the walls and the place illuminated by bright lamps.

Tatya entered the chavadi first and prepared Baba's couch and arranged the pillows. He then requested Baba to sit on the couch and lean on a bolster. After Baba sat on the couch comfortably Tatya spread an *angavastram* over Baba's shoulders. Then a crown was placed on his head and garlands and necklaces were put on him. Devotees went to him one after another and anointed him with sandal paste on the forehead. The royal umbrella was held over his head by Nanasaheb Nimonkar. Bapusaheb Jog ceremonially washed Baba's feet which were placed on a silver plate. Betel leaves were offered to him which Baba masticated slowly as though he enjoyed it. Devotees came and prostrated before him one after another. Shama got Baba's pipe ready and gave it to Tatya who lighted it and smoked it for a second to make sure it was fully ignited and then handed it over to Baba. Baba gave the pipe to Mahlsapathy and asked him to smoke. Mahlsapathy after smoking for a while passed it on to other devotees. Bapusaheb Jog gave some more flowers to Baba to smell and enjoy their fragrance.

Before the night arati prayers were held in praise of Tukharam and Jnaneshwar. Arati was taken for Tukharam and Jnaneshwar and Baba joined it in silence and paid his homage to the great saints. Bapusaheb Jog performed the *karpoora* arati by waving a plate with burning camphor before Baba. The devotees again prostrated at his feet and took leave of him. Only one devotee remained, Tatya, who wanted to know if Baba had any instructions for him. He asked: "Baba, may I go?" Baba said : "You may go if you like. But come now and then to guard me during the night". The night durbar, as it was called then, came to an end. Baba stood alone for a while in the room and then prepared his own bed. He spread 50 or 60 cloths one over the other, prepared a soft bed and lay on it. As there were too many mosquitos devotees wanted to fix a mosquito curtain to Baba's bed but he would not permit it. He got angry and threw out the curtain more than once when they forcibly fixed it but he finally gave in and the mosquito curtain stayed. At about 9 p.m. Tatya offered naivedya (food) to Baba, consisting of bread of which Baba took a little. It was at this time that Baba gave Tatya his daily payment of Rs.35.

Early the next morning Baba was taken back to the mosque in a procession in the same way as he was taken to the chavadi with all the paraphernalia and music and bhajan. Khaparde who has recorded his impressions of the processions to and from the chavadi found Baba very weak when he met him. He had to be supported by attendants when he rose and walked to the chavadi and back. His legs seemed to have lost their muscular strength, Khaparde said. When Baba was taken in procession to the chavadi women lining the route chanted : "Deva, deva" and bowed to him. As Baba stepped out of the mosque he was clad in his usual dhoti covered by a loose robe (kufni) with a stout stick in his hand. He also carried a packet of tobacco and a clay pipe. Over his robe he also wore a loose cloth. The piece of white cloth on the head was twisted like a matted hair and flowed down from the left ear on the back.

After returning from the chavadi Baba resumed his daily routine in the mosque. After his first round of begging mission he offered a morsel to the dhuni and took some himself. Then at 9 a.m. he left for the lendi accompanied by his devotees in a procession. It was only when he went to the garden that he wore his chappals. These are now preserved by Sai Sansthan as sacred relics. It was during one of these processions that Baba was photographed along with his devotees and that today adorns thousands of homes all over the country. There was a pit dug up in the garden and a lamp was burning in it. Baba sat before it and asked Abdul, his personal attendant and the only one to be allowed with him in the garden, to keep two pots of water near him. He sprinkled the water in various directions. The devotee who gave these details added that it was not known if Baba uttered any mantra while doing so.

Narasimha Swamiji has written : "With the advent of a flood of visitors a large stream of wealth and materials for pompous display poured in. The former fakir was turned (against his wishes) into a maharaja or prince with a silver palanquin, state umbrella, a chariot and a horse preceded by a procession of bearers of silver mace and all other princely paraphernalia. The money that flowed (chiefly by way of dakshina) was during the last decade of Baba's life many thousands of rupees every month. But all this pomp and all this wealth served only to set off Baba's humility, holy poverty, non-attachment and purity of life. He literally scattered all the money that flowed into his hands among those who gathered round him. Every morning he began and every evening he ended as a pauper fakir. Till the very end of his life Baba's sustenance was the begged bread and vegetable, his raiment was a tattered kufni and a skull cloth and his residence was the bare floor of a dilapidated mosque of two-room dimension where all his devotees came and had his darshan."

In the chavadi, as Baba was preparing to leave for the mosque after an overnight's stay, devotees offered the morning arati which is called kakad arati. In the meanwhile the mosque was swept and cleaned by Madhav Fasle, another attendant of Baba. After the arati Fasle requested Baba to return to the mosque. Baba never moved from the chavadi without Fasle inviting him. Khaparde describing the kakad arati wrote in his diary : "I got up early, attended the kakad arati and was very much struck by the fact that Baba, on leaving the chavadi, made passes with his short stick towards the east, north, and south. Then he proceeded with hard words as usual."

We shall close this chapter with a poem written by Das Ganu Maharaj about Baba. It is as follows :

You are Brahma, Vishnu and Siva
The quintessence of the three gunas
And on this earth you manifest as Sai the powerful
In the early morning you become
Brahma and spiritual knowledge flows from you
And sometimes resorting to the quality of tamas
You assume the terrible form of Siva
Sometimes like Krishna you indulge in childlike pranks
And at times you become the fabled swan in the lake of your
    devotees' minds
Considering your fondness for grantha how can you be called
    Muslim?
And yet if you are a Hindu how do you dwell happily in a
    mosque?
If rich why should you go asking for alms?
And yet how can you be called a fakir when you put Kuber
    to shame with your generosity?

If your house be a mosque why does it have the sacred fire
    of the Hindus burning continuously in the dhuni which
    produces the udhi?
And at arati time on your divine seat you look like Lord
    Vishnu
And at durbar as you sit before the dhuni you appear as
    Sankara
Such lilas of the Trinity manifest in you
Are experienced by us daily, O'Baba Sai!

7

THE APOSTLES

UPASANI BABA

A MONG the apostles of Sai Baba the most prominent was Upasani Baba who at one time was thought to be the successor of Sai Baba and was groomed by him with that purpose in view. As will be seen later in this account Sai Baba went all out to make him an ideal disciple and to bestow on him all his powers. He even went to the extent of asking his devotees to worship him as they worshipped Sai Baba. But Sai Baba's plan did not work and Upasani left Shirdi after three years while Sai Baba wanted him to stay on for four years to get the full benefit of his association with Sai Baba.

Upasani Baba, whose full name is Kasinath Govind Upasani Maharaj, was born in 1870 in an orthodox Brahmin family in Satana village in Maharashtra. His grandfather, Gopal Sastri, was the court adviser on religious and literary matters to the Gaekwad of Baroda. Gopal Sastri was also advisor to many other rulers of petty states. Upasani's father, Govinda Sastri, was a copyist in the civil court of Dhulia. Upasani was one of five sons and he came from a family of village priests. He had little formal education and was married when he was 14 to a girl of eight in 1883 who died a year later. He married again in 1885 and his second wife also passed away shortly thereafter.

Upasani ran away from home and lived away from his family for long intervals. He became interested in yoga, went to a cave and sat in meditation for long periods. He spent many days without food or drink. He went to Sangli and learnt Ayurveda and later set up practice as an ayurvedic doctor in Amaravati in 1896. He started a medical monthly in Marathi

and advertised in it the patent medicines he made. He bought
land in Gwalior in 1907 but found that he had made a mistake
as the land was barren and there was no yield from it. He lost
everything and his health failed; he returned home a broken
man. Then he started on a a pilgrimage in 1910 with his third
wife and visited a number of places. In 1911, a yogi, Kulkarni
in Rahuri advised him to go to Sai Baba. Thinking that Sai Baba
was a Muslim, Upasani said he would not go to see Sai Baba.
Later he met Narayan Maharaj, a Dattatreya devotee who was
said to possess marvellous powers. When Upasani told him of
his poor health Narayan Maharaj made him chew betel and nut
and said he was "finely painted" inside and outside and asked
him to go away.

Upasani again met Yogi Kulkarni who again asked him to
meet Sai Baba. Finally Upasani decided to go to Shirdi and he
met Sai Baba in 1911. After staying for a day Upasani asked
Baba for permission to return home. Baba said: "What! So
soon! When are you returning?" Upasani replied it was not
easy for him to return to Shirdi. Baba said: "Then you had
better stay. Do not go away." Seeing him undecided Baba said:
"Well, go. I shall see what I can do." Upasani thought permission
had been given to him to leave and left Shirdi. While he was
at Kopargaon the priest at the Datta temple there told him to go
back to Shirdi and stay with Baba. Upasani said: "No". As
they were talking some visitors, who said they were going to
Shirdi arrived and the priest told them: "Take this person with
you." But Upasani said: "No, I have been there already." The
visitors said: "That is the best reason. We have not been there.
We want someone to be with us to guide us." So inspite of his
protests Upasani was forced to accompany them to Shirdi.

At Shirdi Baba welcomed Upasani and said: "So you have
come back. You said you would not come back before eight
days." Upasani said: "Baba I cannot understand this. I was
eager to go home and I wonder how I did not. This must be
your doing." Baba said:" Yes, I have been with you all these
days, dogging your heels." Thereafter Upasani continued to
stay in Shirdi. He made efforts to leave and get Baba's permission
through Shama. Baba said: "Let him stay on." Shama wanted
to know what Baba expected Upasani to do. Baba said: "To do
nothing." Upasani did not realise that "doing nothing" meant,

according to Baba, being receptive and receiving everything from him.

The entire operation of moulding, remoulding, raising and reaching the top of the highest spiritual experience is the work of the guru and the guru alone. His great powers moulds everything, internal and external, and the result is that the disciple is turned into the likeness of the guru. This is what Baba meant when he said: "Let him remain doing nothing." Baba asked Upasani to go and live in solitude at the Khandoba temple, not to mix with people but to remain alone doing nothing. Baba wanted him to be free from all shackles and independent of family or other connections. He wanted to make him feel he was entirely dependent on Baba and Baba alone, at least during the period of probation. Therefore, he created a number of problems for Upasani like getting food which became difficult. Baba asked for dakshina and deprived him of his bank account. In this way Baba wanted him to feel that he had no earthly support except the guru. Unable to get proper meals Upasani starved for two or three days. He came to be called "Upavasani". He became a prey to diseases.

Baba expected Upasani to develop nishta and saburi and Upasani was slowly developing them. However, he was not happy. He could not understand what Baba was doing to him. He told a friend that he was being tortured like a dumb brute. He told another that his life was miserable and wasted. He asked a palmist if his future would be bad. Baba had told him he should remain in Shirdi for four years and that he need not do anything at all. Upasani was not able to understand the course sketched out for him by Baba and he had no ambition for God realisation at such cost. He was a total stranger to Shirdi and appeared to many as unworthy of the high honour conferred on him by Baba. Some devotees were jealous and one of them asked Baba: "Baba, we have been attending on you for years and you seem to be conferring a copper plate grant of all your powers to this stranger. Are we all therefore to be neglected? Is it true that you are giving him all your powers?" Baba replied: "Yes. I speak only the truth sitting as I do in this masjid. What I have spoken I have spoken. I have given everything to this person. Whether he be good or bad he is my own. I am fully responsible for him and as for a copper plate grant, why a copper plate grant? I have given him a gold plate grant." Turning to Upasani he said: "Think which is better, copper or gold?" Upasani said :"I do not know, Baba." Baba said: "Copper gets corroded and tarnished. Gold does not. It remains pure always. You are pure Bhagawan."

However this did not make Upasani happy. Baba rarely spoke to him. There was no formal oral instruction and it was only later that Upasani realised that what he got from Baba was his teachings. One of the methods adopted by Baba was to convey his teachings through visions and pictures. Upasani underwent many hardships, mental and physical but these were turned into gains subsequently. When he reported his condition to Baba, the latter said, "I am always with you. You need not fear. The more you suffer now the happier and more excellent will be your future. You are going to be an *avadhuta*. Hundreds will rush to have your darshan."

This prophecy of Baba came true in 1920-35 but at that moment Upasani did not appreciate it. He remarked to a friend that his life was bitter and he did not expect to live long. He would therefore be glad to see his relatives, he said. Thereafter his brother and mother visited him. He began to see visions. Many years after Baba's mahasamadhi Upasani told devotees at Sakori that his guru had rendered him physically impotent and mentally free from sex craving.

One day Upasani had a vision in which Baba came up to him in some mysterious place and sat in front of him. He asked Upasani to come near him saying: "I am going to give you upadesh." As Upasani was trying to approach Baba a dark and dirty person behind Upasani, exactly like him, pulled him back and said: "Do not listen to the guru but listen to me." This interruption took place twice. Then Baba got up, seized that dark person behind Upasani and placed him on a pile of faggots and burnt him. All the time Upasani was shouting: "Baba it is me you are burning." After completely burning the dark person Baba turned to Upasani and said: "Yes. That was you no doubt. But you were in that sin form, namely *papa rupa*. I have destroyed him. You are now free from sin. By our united efforts there are many things to be achieved in the future. How can that be done if sin remains?" Baba told Upasani at one time: "I will take away half of your head and give you half of my own." Upasani then had a vision in which some ruffians cut off his head, scooped the brain and ate the contents and ran away.

In another vision Baba took him to a mysterious place and showed him a heap of silver rupees, 225 feet long, 120 feet wide and four feet high. Over this was a princely bed on which sat a richly dressed and gaily ornamented person. Baba asked Upasani to see that man. "Who is he?" asked Upasani. "It is you," Baba said: "Your body of sin has gone. That *papa purusha* has gone. This is your *punya purusha.*" Then pointing to the hoards of rupees Baba said :"There are hundreds and thousands of houses filled with rupees. All these are ours. You will come to know all this by yourself."

Upasani asked Baba: "If this figure is my punya purusha and the other figure that you destroyed was my papa purusha who am I?" Baba replied: "You are beyond these two, beyond punya and papa. That which constitutes me constitutes you. That is, you are myself. There is no difference between you and me."

Baba declared himself to be the one Iswara, the Antaryami of all and he wanted his disciples to realise he was their Ishta Devata or God and find him and feel him in every creature. One day Upasani was cooking his food at the Khandoba temple, He wanted to take it to Baba and get the prasad from him. While he was cooking a black dog was watching him and it followed him when Upasani left for the mosque with the food. It disappeared after some distance. Upasani thought it was sacrilegious to give food to the dog before Baba had partaken of it. But when he met Baba he was asked: "Why have you come?" "To bring you my naivedya," Upasani said. Baba said: "Why did you come all the way in the sun? I was there." Upasani said: "There was no one there except a black dog." Baba told him: "I was that black dog. So as you refused to give me food there I am not going to take this food." Upasani returned dejected. Next day he was determined not to commit the same mistake. He was looking for a black dog as he was cooking his food but did not find any. However, as he proceeded with his cooking he noticed a sickly person leaning against a wall and watching him. Upasani asked him to go away as it was improper for a low caste man to look on when a Brahmin was preparing his food. The man left. When Upasani met Baba with the food he found him angry. Baba said: "Yesterday you did not give me food and today you told me to go away," Upasani asked: "Where were you, Baba?" Baba said:

"I was leaning against that wall." Surprised Upasani asked: "Could that sickly person be you?" Baba said: "Yes, I am in everything and beyond." It was a problem for Upasani as for many others to understand Baba being in a dog or low caste man. And through Baba's grace Upasani learnt this lesson. When Upasani came to Shirdi in June 1911 he came as a grihasta in such a broken down condition and in such a mood as to warrant his giving up that ashram and developing into a sanyasi or avadhuta, working as a man of God for the benefit of humanity. That was what Sai Baba intended to make of him. He wanted him to be a satguru and asked him to stay in Shirdi for four years. He did not allow him to visit his home in Satana nor permit his third wife to see him in Shirdi. Upasani did not like this restriction as he still thought himself to be a grihasta. His thoughts, ideals and nature had not changed and his views and sentiments at Shirdi were the same as those he had before he came to Shirdi. Baba's attempt was to change these feelings. When he was informed that his wife was seriously ill Upasani sought Baba's permission to go to Satana. Baba held him back saying: "You had better remain here. You can do nothing there." Some days later a letter came to Upasani informing him of his wife's death. He was upset and thought life was useless without his wife. He said: "Now that my wife is dead what is the good of remaining here at Shirdi?" He had hoped that his wife would share the glory and joy of sainthood.

On the midnight of July 25, 1914, Upasani left Shirdi after a stay of three years. He went to Nagpur and then to Kharagpur many hundreds of miles away. Baba accomplished his plan for Upasani only in part. Narasimha Swamiji says: "A tree grew from the seed sown but it did not shoot up in the way in which such a tree should shoot up. On the other hand, it had a bend and a bend of its own. Upasani's older tendencies, idiosyncrasies and ideas though modified by what he picked up in Shirdi were remoulding him and the result was to develop a Upasani Baba working on lines reminiscent of Shirdi but in a direction totally different from Sai Baba's." At one time Baba had an idea that somebody might be found to carry on his work after his death. When some of his devotees asked him:"Are you going to leave the world without entrusting your full powers and possessions to anyone?" Baba replied: "What ! Will there be not some man coming?" This remark coupled with the special treatment of

Upasani by Baba made some people believe that Baba hoped to groom Upasani as his successor.

However, the course prescribed by Baba, namely, thinking only of Sai Baba, was not fully possible for Upasani whose contacts with the outside world could never be obliterated. He kept on pursuing his intellectual studies and wrote 17 poems in Sanskrit in praise of Baba in 1912. He kept up his intellectuality and his learning as important assets. Baba did not want intellectuality. For a disciple it was an obstacle in the pursuit of self-realisation. He had to forget he was learned as it would bolster his egoism. He must begin with himself as a zero and think and work for Baba and nothing else. Baba achieved this with his guru but it was not possible for Upasani at Shirdi. He would not forget his sorrows and think of Baba in such a way as to deaden his feelings towards unhappy events and incidents at Shirdi. In order to help him Baba started Upasani worship in July 1913. He sent Chand Bai Borkar to Khandoba temple to worship Upasani in exactly the same way as she and other devotees worshipped Baba himself. Upasani objected to this and said he did not want to be worshipped. However, the woman devotee went on with the worship and told Upasani that his body did not belong to him but to his devotees.

There was opposition to worship of Upasani from some of Baba's devotees and Upasani felt humiliated. All this culminated in his leaving Shirdi even without informing Baba. Baba did not talk of any successor afterwards. On the other hand he told his devotees: "Think of me, I am there. I am not going away. I shall be active even from my tomb."

After his wanderings Upasani settled down in Sakori not far from Shirdi and collected a large number of devotees through his siddhis and moral tales about Sai Baba. People who felt they were in the presence of a great saint flocked to him and began to worship him. His fame was at one time so great that his devotees found it difficult to get near him. Mahatma Gandhi visited him in 1927. Through him the name of Sai Baba and his teachings spread far and wide and this was his greatest service to the Sai movement. So long as he observed Baba's directions and kept away from women and wealth his influence and power for good was increasing day by day. He reached the pinnacle of his fame in 1927 and 1928. But later, contrary tendencies were noticed and they began to undermine the

foundations laid by Sai Baba. Upasani accumulated wealth in
the form of cash, land and buildings and he began to be seen in
the company of women. Narasimha Swamiji says Upasani had
25 wives, a regular harem with a castle and *anthapuram* (women's
quarters) in it. He was involved in litigation and aroused
antagonisms in many quarters. He went on acquiring women,
first by marrying them to images of Krishna, and when that was
stopped by a law passed by the Bombay Legislative Council, by
marrying them himself. His popularity began to decline
following opposition to him in 1934. Narasimha Swamiji says
Upasani's popularity reached such a low level that people said
they were ashamed to say they had anything to do with him.
Upasani Baba passed away in 1941.

Upasani Baba composed a prayer of several hymns on Baba
the first verse of which is as follows :

Baba is the original sat chit anand swarup, the primordial
cause of original existence and destruction of the universe
Baba has appeared as a human being as the outcome of
the ardent desire of his devotees to see him as such.

In the eight verse Upasani Baba says: "Sai Baba is the unborn,
the veritable Brahman."

MAHLSAPATHY

Among Sai Baba's earliest disciples and the most intimate and
one who stayed with him longest was Mahlsapathy, a goldsmith
by caste and priest of the Khandoba temple in Shirdi. He was
a poor and uncultured villager who, thinking Baba was a Muslim,
objected to his entering the temple and staying there but soon
became his most zealous admirer and ardent worshipper. Baba
found his devotion, dedication and attachment irresistible and
accepted the flowers, sandal and other offerings placed at his
feet in worship by Mahlsapathy, who was the only person
allowed to worship Baba in this way for a long time. In the
goldsmith community to which he belonged Mahlsapathy was
known for his fervent devotion to his tutelary deity, Khandoba
(also known as Mahlsapathy). The Mahlsapathy Purana was his
bible and he read it daily as a ritual.

Every year Mahlsapathy made a pilgrimage to Jejoori, 150
miles from Shirdi, carrying a *kavadi* on his shoulders to worship

the deity in the temple there. On many occasions he went into a trance and at such times it was thought that Khandoba spoke through him. His family consisted of his wife, three daughters and a son who was born very late in his life through the grace of Baba. He was very poor and lived in a mud house and owned some acres of barren land. His association with Baba lasted 50 years. After his first encounter with Baba he developed respect and reverence for him although he was perplexed by his behaviour sometimes which made the rustic folk call him a "mad fakir".

Long after Mahlsapathy started worshipping Baba another devotee, Nana Saheb Engle, was allowed that privilege. Afterwards more people joined in the worship of Baba. As days passed by Mahlsapathy came closer and closer to Baba and became a part of Baba's daily life. He kept Baba company day and night and slept in the mosque with him. He spread his own cloth and on this he and Baba slept, he occupying one half and Baba the other half of the cloth. However Mahlsapathy rarely slept for Baba gave him a task. Baba told him: "You better sit up. Do not go to sleep. Place your hand on my heart. I will be going on with remembrance of Allah nama smaranam, that is, a half conscious trance and during that nama smaranam the heart beat will clearly show you that I am still having nama smaranam. If that suddenly goes away and natural sleep supervenes wake me up." The idea was that the heart beat during natural sleep would be different from the heart beat during meditation. This meant that neither Baba nor Mahlsapathy slept during the night. That also showed that Baba was in meditation to protect his devotees spread far and wide.

Mahlsapathy refused to accept charity or financial assistance although he was desperately poor and even Baba could not persuade him to accept money from him. He always said: "I do not want all this. I want only to worship your feet." He shunned all comforts and would not even lie on a cot as he preferred to sleep on the floor. One night Baba told him:"Tonight we shall be on the watch. The rude Rohilla (death from plague) is wanting to take away the wife of Nigoj Patil. I am praying to Allah to prevent that by namasmaranam. You must see that no one comes and disturbs me." Accordingly Mahlsapathy kept vigil but unfortunately for him in the middle of the night the *nivas mamladar* (village official) and his peon came and wanted darshan of Baba. Mahlsapathy tried to stop them but failed and Baba's meditation was disturbed. Baba rebuked Mahlsapathy and said in anger: "You are a man with a family. Don't you know what is taking place at Nigoj's house? This disturbance has caused a failure in my efforts. That Patil's wife is dead. Let go, what has happened is for the best."

Baba protected Mahlsapathy in many ways and always kept a watch on his life and doings. He warned him even of small trifling things in time to save him from harm. Shirdi was infested with snakes and one evening as Mahlsapathy was leaving the mosque Baba told him he was likely to meet two "thieves" on the way. Mahlsapathy indeed found one snake at his doorstep and the other at the neighbour's house. On another day Baba told him: "When you return come with a lamp for you will find a 'thief' at the gate. Mahlsapathy who came with a lamp found a snake as foretold by Baba and it was killed with the help of neighbours. One day Baba warned him: "Don't put your back against the earth." Ignoring the advice Mahlsapathy who had too much drink slumped to the ground losing consciousness. His back was on the ground. When he became conscious Mahlsapathy found he could not bend his leg and his daughter had to massage his knees and legs. Thereafter he was able to walk and when he met Baba he asked him: "Did I not tell you not to put your back against the earth?" Once Mahlsapathy's wife and children fell ill and other relatives also followed suit. Baba said to Mahlsapathy: "Let the sick people keep to bed." And walking round the mosque with a short stick in hand Baba waved it and threatened someone. "Come, whatever your power may be, let us see. I shall show you what I can do with my *chota* stick if you come out and face me." He warned some unknown object. It was Baba's way of treating a disease. Meanwhile a doctor gave medicines to Mahlsapathy to be given to his family members who were ill. Mahlsapathy consulted Baba who asked him not to give the medicine. As a result all the members of the family got well without the medicines.

In another instance once when Mahlsapathy's wife had gone to her parent's house she developed a tumour in her neck but she did not tell her husband about this. Since nothing is hidden from Baba he informed Mahlsapathy about the tumour and

said: "None can cure it except myself and I shall cure it."
Mahlsapathy who was taken aback by the news simply said:
"Yes, Baba." Soon he got a letter from his wife telling him
about the tumour and that it had been cured. On one occasion
Mahlsapathy who was affectionately called "Bhagat" by Baba
decided to visit his daughter's parents-in-law in a distant
village. While granting permission Baba warned: "You are going
to be insulted there." And so it happened. When Mahlsapathy
arrived at their house he found his daughter's father-in-law
(who had invited him to dine with him) and other members of
the family had taken their meal without waiting for him. He felt
insulted and returned home without taking his meal there and
told Baba what had happened.

Baba forecast to Mahlsapathy that Shirdi would grow up
into a city of many storeyed buildings where big fairs would be
held and where many great men would be coming. He said:
"My Brahmins will gather, and elephants and horses will come
and gurus will be buried." Not many believed Baba at that time
but many decades later all that Baba had predicted had come
true. Shirdi emerged as a town with many tall buildings and
there were annual fairs and festivals and the daily puja of Sai
Baba attracted thousands of people daily from all parts of the
country.

One incident that revealed Baba's love for all creatures was
mentioned by Mahlsapathy. Mahlsapathy used to feed a crippled
dog every night. One night, having fed it, he asked it to go but
it did not leave the place. Mahlsapathy beat it with a stick and
it fled crying out in pain. That night when Mahlsapathy went
to the mosque and massaged Baba's feet Baba said: "There is a
bitch sick like me in the village. Everybody is beating it."
Mahlsapathy repented his action.

As already mentioned Mahlsapathy was with Baba all the
time except when he went home for his meals. When he returned
he would light Baba's pipe and do other odd jobs for him and
at night he prepared his bed. Baba showed his care and
responsibility for Mahlsapathy in many ways and most
noteworthy was what he told him everytime he left the mosque
in the evening: "Go," Baba said, "I go with you" meaning "I will
protect you."

Mahlsapathy continued his nightly puja of Baba after his
death in October 1918 but his own death came four years later.

On September 11, 1922 after completing his puja Mahlsapathy told his family: "Today is my father's *shrada* day, finish cooking soon. Today I close my earthly life and go to heaven." After performing the *shrada* and taking his meal he chewed betel and nut and asked his family to chant Ramachandra nama. He gave his staff to his son and told him: "Spend time piously in *uttama bhakti marga*. All that I told you will happen." He then uttered the word: "Ram!" and breathed his last. His was a dedicated life, a life of love, faith and total surrender. Baba taught Mahlsapathy reverence for all creatures of God and to view them as manifestations of God. He asked him to identify himself with all creatures and to practice ahimsa. Mahlsapathy dictated his memoirs to his son at the fag end of his life.

NARAYAN GOVIND CHANDORKAR

Narayan Govind Chandorkar has been described as the St Paul of Sai Baba. He was greatly responsible for the spread of Sai worship. He was a very learned and influential official of the Bombay government who had a scientific and questioning mind and Baba had to exercise his miraculous powers to convince him of his divinity. He did not come to Baba willingly and was not even aware of his existence. It was Baba who drew him in his own mysterious way.

Chandorkar came of a pious and good Hindu family whose parents were held in high esteem in society. His father was a retired government servant. Chandorkar entered government service at the age of 20 after taking a B.A. degree with philosophy as the main subject. He made a special study of the *Bhagavad Gita* with Sankara Bashya. He quickly rose to the position of a Deputy Collector, which was regarded in those days as a very coveted position. It was at this time that the call came to him from Sai Baba. Chandorkar, who as Personal Assistant to the Collector of Ahmednager was camping at Kopargaon on Jamabandi (revenue collection) work summoned the *karnam* (accountant) of Shirdi, Appa Kulkarni, to Kopargaon. Since it was the practice that no one in Shirdi left the village without securing Baba's permission Kulkarni asked Baba's leave to go to Kopargaon. While permitting Kulkarni to go Baba asked him to invite Chandorkar to visit Shirdi. Kulkarni was taken aback at

Baba's command and pleaded that he was too insignificant a
person in the official hierarchy to think of inviting such a big
official like Chandorkar. Baba insisted Kulkarni should invite
Chandorkar and added he should tell Chankorkar it was Baba
who was inviting him.

When Kulkarni delivered the oral message to Chandorkar
the latter was astonished. He told Kulkarni he did not know the
fakir nor did the fakir know him. Thinking that Kulkarni must
have some axe to grind he sent him away. When Kulkarni
reported the failure of his mission to Baba he was asked to try
again and repeat the invitation. This also ended in failure but
Baba would not give up and Kulkarni was sent back a third
time and this time he was successful. Chandorkar thought there
must be something after all in the invitation from the fakir and
told Kulkarni he would visit Shirdi sometime.

Chandorkar kept his promise and found time to visit Shirdi.
He asked Baba if he had wanted to see him. "Yes," replied Baba.
Chandorkar wanted to know why Baba wanted to see him.
Baba said: "There are thousands of persons in the world and do
I send for them all? Should there not be some special reason
why you alone should be sent for? "Chandorkar said he was
unable to see any special reason. Baba said: "You and I have
been connected with each other in four former births. I now
invite you to come and again have your contact. When leisure
serves you may come." Chandorkar was not impressed and left
with the intention of not returning to Shirdi but he did return
and became an ardent devotee of Baba and later was instrumental
in propagating the Sai faith.

Initially Chandorkar's parents objected to his associating
with a Muslim as they thought Baba to be, but this was overcome
through Baba's control of their minds and Chandorkar's father
finally gave his approval. Baba's first task was to instil faith in
Chandorkar of Baba's divine nature and his personal interest or
attachment to him. He performed many miracles to prove to
Chandorkar of his divinity and his interest in him. Thus on one
occasion when Chandorkar went to a hill shrine, called
Harichandra Hill, 40 miles from Shirdi, for worship, half way
through the journey after a steep climb he felt tired and thirsty.
He asked his companion who was with him to get some water.
But water was nowhere available and Chandorkar became

desperate and prayed to Baba. He said: "If Baba were here he would surely get me water to slake my thirst." His companion said: "Baba is not here. What is the good of thinking of what would happen if he were here?" But Chandorkar felt Baba was there and would help him. Hardly had he spoken than they saw a tribal coming towards them and Chandorkar told him he was dying of thirst and would he help him to get water? The tribal said : "Under the very rock on which you are sitting there is water." He then moved away. Chandorkar and his companion dug under the rock and sure enough there was clean water which they drank to their heart's content. When Chandorkar returned to Shirdi after this experience Baba asked him : "Nana, you were thirsty, I gave you water, did you drink?" Chandorkar also learnt later that at the time when Chandorkar was feeling terribly thirsty Baba had remarked to his devotees in Shirdi : "Nana is very thirsty. Should we not give him a handful of water?"

On another occasion Chandorkar went to a Ganapathi temple in a forest two miles away from the nearest railway station. The train being late by the time he alighted at his destination it was dark and there was no conveyance available to go to the temple. He decided to walk and it was 9 p.m. He still had half the distance to cover and he knew that the *pujari* (priest) would have locked the temple at 9 p.m. and retired for the night. Chandorkar was hungry and tired and he prayed to Baba : " I am not asking for much," he said. "I will be satisfied if at the end of the journey I can get a cup of tea." It was nearly 11 p.m. when he reached the temple and to his surprise the pujari was waiting for him. "Is it Nana?" he asked. Chandorkar confirmed his identity and asked the pujari how he knew he was coming there. The pujari said: "I had an ethereal message from Shri Sai Baba which said: 'My Nana is coming weary, thirsty and hungry. Keep for him a cup of tea.' The pujari added: "Here is a cup of tea ready for you."

Baba showed his concern for his devotees even in the matter of catching trains and meeting official superiors. Chandorkar who was in Shirdi with his companion, Haridas, had to catch a train for Ahmednagar urgently and prepared to leave Shirdi for the railway station. Both of them went to Baba to take leave of him. Baba told them: "You had better take your meal and then leave for the station." While Chandorkar implicitly obeyed Baba his companion feared he would miss the train and left Shirdi in a hurry. When Chandorkar arrived at the railway station very much later he found his companion still on the platform waiting for the train which was late by many hours. It became evident that Baba had known the train was going to be late and so had advised Chandorkar and his companion to take their own time and not be in a hurry.

A similar incident happened a few days later when Chandorkar, who had come to Shirdi, wanted to leave for Kopargaon where he had an appointment to meet the Collector. Baba told him: "Leave tomorrow." "Without another word Chandorkar cancelled his journey. The following day Baba told him: "Now go and meet the Collector." When Chandorkar went to Kopargaon and made enquiries about the Collector he learnt much to his surprise that the Collector who was scheduled to arrive the precious day had postponed his trip and intimated he would be arriving the next day.

In another incident Baba saved Chandorkar's life. A tonga in which Chandorkar and another were travelling from Pune suddenly capsized and both of them were thrown out. In distant Shirdi Baba made a sound like one blowing a conch (indicative of death) and said: "Nana is about to die. Will I let him die?." Chandorkar and his companion got up from the road unscathed.

On another occasion Chandorkar's pregnant daughter was in a serious condition at the moment of delivery. Baba in Shirdi realised that Chandorkar needed help and decided to send a messenger to him with udhi. The messenger complained he did not have enough money to cover the rail and road journey. Baba told him: "Go. Everything will be provided." After he got down from the train which carried him to his destination the messenger wondered how he was going to complete the journey by road as he did not have the money to engage a conveyance. Just then he found a liveried peon shouting his name and when he responded he was told by him that his master had sent him with a tonga to fetch him to the place where Chandorkar stayed. The messenger got into the tonga and reached Chandorkar's place and gave him Baba's udhi which he gratefully received and applied it on his daughter's forehead. Thereafter she delivered a child without any complication. In the meanwhile the messenger had come outside to thank the tonga driver but there was neither the tonga nor the liveried peon to be seen.

They had vanished. The messenger was still more surprised when Chandorkar told him he had not sent the tonga. Both of them then realised it was Baba who had provided the tonga for the messenger.

Chandorkar was convinced more than ever that Baba was God, omnipresent, omnipotent and merciful. He firmly believed Baba had superhuman powers, superhuman love and made superhuman provision of needs for those attached to him and whom he loved. Baba had declared: "My eye of vigilance (supervision) is ever on those who love me. Whatever you may do, wherever you may be, ever bear this in mind—that I am always aware of everything you do." Baba imparted spiritual education to Chandorkar and his effort was to rid him of ego which was manifested in lust, anger, greed, delusions, pride and jealousy and compendiously mentioned as kama, krodha, lobha, moha, madha and matsarya. Baba said: "Restrain lust wholly in respect of others' wives and partly in respect of one's own wife." He said enjoyment of marital bliss was permissible but one should not be enslaved by it. Lust ruined one's mental balance and strength or firmness. *Viveka* (prudence or discrimination) must guide one's mind when tempted by sex. Desire must be controlled and one must not be its slave. So long as the sex urge and anger activated a person there would be no *shanti* or peace, nor buddhi or perfect understanding of things as they were including the self. They were obstructions to spiritual advance.

Baba said lobha (greed) meant violation of social rules and common wisdom. It was good to desire well being but bad to be greedy. To desire under wrong notions was moha (delusion) and this was bad. Madha was pride, conceit and vanity and implied wrong and improper evaluation of oneself and consequently wrong behaviour towards others. Matsarya (jealousy) was the worst of these emotions.

An opportunity occurred to Chandorkar to learn about the evil of lust. One day some Muslim women waiting for darshan of Baba expected Chandorkar who was present to move away since they were in purdah. When Chandorkar got up to go Baba asked him to stay and said: "Let these people come if they care." The Muslim women thereupon came, unveiled their faces and touched Baba's feet in reverence. Among them was a young beautiful girl and Chandorkar was smitten by her beauty. He said to himself: "Shall I have another opportunity to see this angelic face?" It was then that Baba slapped Chandorkar's thigh and after the women had left he asked him: "Do you know why I slapped you?" Chandorkar knew his thoughts were low and unfit for one who was in the presence of Baba. He asked Baba: "How is that even when I am near you such low thoughts sway my mind?" Baba replied: "You are a man after all and the body being full of desires these spring up as sense objects approach." He added: "Are there not lovely temples with well coloured exteriors? When we go there do we admire the exterior beauty or the God within? When you see the God within do you ever care for the outside beauty of the building? Similarly, remember God is not only in temples. He is found in every creature. Therefore when you see a beautiful face remember it is a temple and the image of the God within is the jiva, pre-eminent part of the universal soul. So think at once of God or the universal soul in objects beautiful or ugly."

In another instance Baba intervened at the nick of time when one of his disciples was about to go to bed with a prostitute. He flung open the door, and signalled to H.V. Sathe of his presence. Baba seemed to say, "You have come all the way to your guru and now you are descending to hell." Sathe was ashamed and immediately left the place never to go there again.

An incident occurred which showed that Chandorkar, through Baba's grace, had conquered the sex urge. Bannu Mayi, a 20-year-old Muslim woman was highly spiritually developed and she wandered in the streets of her village, Bodegaon, naked, immersed in spiritual ecstasy. People thought she was mad but some believed she was a saint. Chandorkar wanted to have darshan of her and with Baba's permission he went to see her taking with him presents for her and food. But he could not find her and nobody was able to tell him where she was. Chandorkar prayed to Baba and Bannu Mayi suddenly appeared before him. He prostrated before her and with a feeling of reverence he pulled out the thorns on her body which she might have encountered during her wanderings in the forests. But she did not seem to be bothered and she went away. Chandorkar wanted to see her again and desired she should wear the clothes and ornaments he had brought her and the naivedya he had prepared for her. But she did not come. Chandorkar again prayed to Baba when again she suddenly appeared in front of him. Chandorkar fell at her feet and she vanished. Chandorkar could not suppress his desire to see her once again and spent his time in a temple praying within closed doors and Bannu Mayi gave him darshan again.

Baba advised Chandorkar on charity. He said almsgiving should be straightforward. No one should utter falsehood when asked for alms and say he did not have the money and give some other excuse when in fact he had it and was unwilling to give. The beggar, Baba said, was not to be treated as a nuisance or as a contemptible individual. According to the tenets of Hinduism a beggar is God himself. Therefore, the gift to the beggar must be with due respect and not with contempt or insolence.

Chandorkar's family suffered some calamities. He lost his grandchild and his son-in-law and the family was in great distress. Baba told them: "If you are grieving for the child and the son-in-law and have come to tell me that you are mistaken, you should not come to me for these. They are not in my power. The birth of a child and death of relatives are dependent on *purva karma*. Even Parameshwara, the great God who has created this world, cannot alter this. Do you think He can tell the sun and the moon, 'Rise some two yards further from your usual or appointed place'? No, he cannot and will not do that. That would produce disorder and chaos." Chandorkar asked Baba: " If that is so how is it you tell someone 'You will have a son, and he gets a son and you tell another, You will get employment, and he gets it?" Baba replied: "I do not do any chamatkar. You have your village astrologers. They work for three or four days or see your palm and give out their predictions, some of which come true. I just look further ahead. What I say happens. My art also is a sort of astrology. But you do not understand this. To you my words look like chamatkar because you do not know the future. So you regard events as proof of my miracle working power and you turn your reverence to me. I, in turn, turn your reverence on to God and see that you are really benefited."

Baba revealed his knowledge of the scriptures when he put to test Chandorkar on his understanding of the *Bhagavad Gita.* One day he found Chandorkar mumbling a *sloka* while massaging his feet and asked him what it was. Chandorkar said he was reciting a verse from the *Gita.* Baba asked him to recite it loudly. The verse dealt with guru-sishya relationship. Baba asked him to give a word for word translation and particulars about the gender, case, tense etc. Chandorkar could not believe that Baba was so well versed in Sanskrit grammar. Baba asked him about the points made in the verse and it became a regular cross examination. Also Baba went into the character of Krishna as a *jnani*. He asked why a jnani like Krishna should refer Arjuna to other jnanis instead of himself giving Arjuna jnana. He asked: "Is not Arjuna a soul of the nature of *chaitanya* that is knowledge? Then why should knowledge be given to that which is already knowledge?" Chandorkar was dumbstruck and could not answer. He realised he was before a giant whose knowledge of the scriptures was astounding. Baba proceeded to ask: "Is not jnana that which is beyond mind and speech? Therefore what the guru says through his mouth is not jnana and what is not jnana is *ajnana*." Baba further explained: "What the guru teaches is primarily ajnana which tends to result in jnana. Jnana is not created but is there and is not uttered. The uttered word like an optician's instrument simply removes the cataract from the eye of the pupil who thereafter sees and recognises himself in a state of pure knowledge."

Baba then went on to explain the meaning of the whole stanza in the *Gita* and referred to the duties of the sishya. He said : "*Seva* is not any ordinary message. You must surrender *tan, man, dhan* (body, mind and possessions). You must not feel you are rendering service to the master. Your body already surrendered to the master is his property and you must feel 'No merit is in me. I am merely making the body which is yours to serve you'."

In another instance Chandorkar felt he could not strictly follow the injunction in the scriptures that he should wait for an *athiti* (guest) before taking his meal. He complained to Baba he found it difficult to find an athiti and he asked himself how could the vedas set down such an impossible task. Baba read his thoughts and said : "Yes, the devil, they would come. You think athiti will come wherever you go. But you do not look at the athitis when they do come. The mistake is not in the veda. The mistake is in your interpretation. An athiti is not necessarily a person who is a Brahmin by birth who would come to your quarters to sit at a meal with you. After your puja is over take some food in your hand and leave it in some corner and thousands of athitis will be coming one after another, each in its own due course and partake it. They are the dogs, crows, flies, ants, etc. To you they do not look like athitis but they are athitis, for God is in them all. If you do this the vedic injunction is fulfilled and you obtain the punya you deserve".

Narasimha Swamiji says, because of his familiarity and intimate contact with Baba, Chandorkar failed to see the divinity in Baba and also that his divinity was not confined to his body but extended to all creatures as Baba was their antaryami or soul or self. Baba said : "I am not at Shirdi alone. I am inside every creature, ants, flies, etc." Chandorkar did not realise this and Baba wanted to make him realise it. One day he asked Chandorkar to prepare eight cakes for naivedya and then take his food. When Chandorkar prepared the cakes as instructed and placed them before Baba he did not touch them, but some flies sat on them. Baba then asked Chandorkar to take the prasad away (that is, the remnants of the food which the guru had first tasted). Chandorkar insisted that Baba should eat some of the cakes and Baba said he had already taken it. Chandorkar asked :"When? All the cakes are there." Chandorkar went away disappointed and Baba called him back and said:" You have been living with me for 18 years now. Is this all your appraisal of me? Does Baba mean to you only the 3.5 cubits height of this body? Am I not in the fly and the ant that settled on the cakes?"

Chandorkar said he knew it but could not realise it. If Baba could make him realise it, he said he would eat the cake as prasad. Then Baba lifted his hand and made a gesture. Narasimha Swamiji says Baba thereby revealed a secret which Chandorkar was hiding deep in his heart and Chandorkar discovered Baba knew the secret. The explanation was that Baba was the antharyami or his inner soul in his heart. If Baba was his antaryami he must be the antaryami of the fly and ant also, Chandorkar thought, and he agreed to take the cake as prasad. It was evident that what Baba wanted was not intellect or the keenness of intellect. Chandorkar's vast learning had all to be unlearnt before Baba could impart anything to him. What counted with Baba was humility, receptivity and a readiness to receive all that Baba gave. Mahlsapathy was not at a disadvantage in this respect. Perhaps he had more humility and receptivity than Chandorkar. For instance, Chandorkar thought that Baba did not understand the *Gita* and could not throw light on the *Upanishads*. So long as these false ideas remained in his mind he could not make any progress. That was why Baba punctured his conceit by his severe cross examination in regard to the verse from the *Gita* which he recited. Chandorkar realised that knowledge was not to be had by mere study of books alone but by openness of mind and approach to the source of all light. Baba taught that before one learnt what was valuable one must unlearn what was harmful.

The approaches to Baba by Mahlsapathy and Chandorkar were different. There was complete surrender on the part of Mahlsapathy who was very humble and very poor and had to depend on Baba for guidance, guardianship and for all that he wanted. He therefore regarded Baba as being on the same level as his deity Khandoba. Mahlsapathy would not think of philosophical or scientific explanations for Baba's lilas and never troubled himself about them. On the other hand Chandorkar who derived the fullest benefit by contact with Baba constantly tried to find out how Baba functioned, what was the meaning of his lilas and words and whether Baba's siddhis fitted with the religious ideas which Chandorkar already had. Baba dissuaded Chandorkar and other educated devotees like him who came to Shirdi from going into such disquisitions and told them there was no use in doing so. Narasimha Swamiji says, to the last Chandorkar and others like him were "wobbling" and never attained that complete surrender which Mahlsapathy achieved so effortlessly. Baba was a university in himself and his methods were strange and infinite in variety. He suited himself to each pupil and provided special courses peculiar to each disciple. All the siddhis were at his command and he utilised them as and when the occasion required for every purpose he had in view. Narasimha Swamiji says, by drawing thousands of devotees to him and making them hold on to him and draw more and more benefits from him Baba had to make them happy by the use of his extraordinary powers. The display of his weird knowledge and weird powers were the best means for drawing people and holding them on to him and lifting them step by step up the ladder of spirituality. Baba had to draw Chandorkar to him by reason of his association with him in previous births and make him the most prominent and notable among his early apostles. Chandorkar working with

Das Ganu Maharaj was responsible for building up the big world of Sai bhaktas which spread like wildfire later.

DAS GANU MAHARAJ

Das Ganu Maharaj, one of the close associates of Baba, was responsible for the spread of his name and fame in Maharashtra through his ballads and discourses. His full name is Ganapat Rao Dattatreya Sahasrabuddhe. He was a constable orderly attached to Chandorkar and had the opportunity to visit Shirdi with Chandorkar and meet Baba. Narasimha Swamiji says that for a long time though Ganu had high regard for Baba, he could not accept him as God or as his guru. Baba brought about a great transformation of his mind although at first it was unwilling submission to Baba's charisma on Ganu's part. When Ganu arrived in Shirdi in 1890 he had little education and was employed as an actor in village dramas in which he played female roles, dancing and singing. His ambition was to go up the official ladder and became a sub-inspector in the police department. Baba, however, had other plans for him. He was determined that Ganu's character, calling and work should be totally changed.

When Baba told Ganu he must give up his post in the police department Ganu pleaded with him :"Baba, let me become a sub-inspector for which I have passed the departmental examination and hold the appointment for at least a year and thereafter I will give it up." Baba told him he would not become a sub-inspector and he would see to it he did not get the job. From then on Ganu found himself in a number of difficult situations in his official work and it was Baba who got him out of trouble every time. Baba continued to press him to leave the service and Ganu continued to ask for time. On one occasion Ganu went to a place of pilgrimage outside his jurisdiction without the permission of his superiors. His fellow constables who were envious of him were about to betray him. Seeing himself in grave trouble Ganu went to the Godavari river and taking some water in his hand called upon Baba to save him. He prayed :"Baba, let me escape this time. I swear I shall certainly give up my police service." Shortly after, a village official told him that some dacoits had been found in the village sharing their spoils and he wanted Ganu to arrest them. Ganu went to the village, arrested the dacoits and seized the booty and returned to his station, much relieved. When his superior asked him why he had left the station without permission Ganu got away by saying he had gone to the village to arrest the dacoits and seize the booty.

On another occasion, Ganu was sent along with others to capture a notorious dacoit. Unfortunately before tackling the dacoit, the dacoit caught hold of him and was about to strangle him. Ganu prayed to Baba :"Save me, save me, I will give up the police service." Suddenly the dacoit let go his hold on Ganu and released him with a warning.

In another incident Ganu was falsely implicated in a misappropriation case and there was danger of his going to prison. He sent a prayer to Baba again, as usual promising to resign from the service if he was saved. He told the official who enquired into the charge that he would make up the missing amount and resign from the service. This was agreed to by the official. Baba thus achieved his aim of getting Ganu out of the police department which he thought stood in the way of Ganu's spiritual progress. Ganu told Baba :"I have now left government service and I and my wife have to stand in the street as we have no property or income." Baba said :"I shall provide for you and your family," and he did. In later years he became a rich man acquiring land and property and he was never in want. Baba advised him to concentrate on his ballads and discourses. Ganu was good in singing kirtans. He had a metallic voice and held big audiences spellbound with his singing which sometimes went on for eight hours. As he sang and spoke Ganu would keep a picture of Baba by his side and even though his discourse might be on Tukharam, Namdev or Jananeshwar he would find opportunity to mention Baba and hail him as a saint, or a Satpurusha whose darshan would be a blessing to anyone who sought it. This resulted in hundreds of people rushing to Shirdi to receive Baba's blessings.

Baba developed Ganu's character and purified it by making him spend his time whenever he went to Shirdi in reciting Vishnu Sahasranamam in the temple there. Baba advised all his devotees to recite Vishnu Sahasranama which is the chanting of the 1,000 names of God. It is believed that this chanting will enable a person to get a male issue if he has no issues, wealth if he has no wealth, power, fame, glory and success if he is without these. It will also wash away the sins of ages. It is also said that the repetition of one name contained in the Sahasranama, namely, Ram, will be equivalent to the merit of chanting all the 1,000 namas. Baba told a woman devotee :"Say Rajaram, Rajaram constantly, that would remove all troubles and take you to the Lord." He told another devotee to repeat "Sri Rama, Jaya Rama, Jaya Jaya Rama".

Baba told H. S. Dixit that he had been practising Hari nama japa constantly as a result of which Hari appeared before him and thereafter he stopped giving medicines to the sick and gave them udhi instead with remembrance of Hari which was enough to cure all diseases. He said he had had a heart disease (Baba said this probably metaphorically) and he had kept the Vishnu Sahasranama close to his heart and Hari had descended from the Sahasranama and cured his disease. It should be mentioned here that Baba's great disciple, Radhakrishna Swamiji, also made it a point to impress upon his devotees to chant the Sahasranama regularly and said it would bring them happiness and prosperity and solve all their problems.

To return to Das Ganu Maharaj, he became greatly attached to Baba who made him understand things which others normally could not understand. Baba helped him on special occasions when Ganu wanted to write a Marathi commentary on *Amritanubhava*, a famous Marathi religious treatise. He had been told this was not possible but he prayed to Baba and got his blessings. He wrote and completed the commentary. It was so good that it was praised even by his critics. He then wanted to translate the *Isavasya Upanishad* into Marathi but was again discouraged by some people who told him the *Upanishad* was very difficult to translate. He went to Baba who said there could be no difficulty and asked him to go to Kaka Dixit's residence where the servantmaid, Malkarni, would give him the meaning (of the *Upanishad*). Ganu went to Dixit's house as directed and in the morning heard a girl singing in great ecstasy. She was singing about the beauty of an orange-coloured silk sari and going into raptures about its floral embroidery and borders. To his surprise he found the girl was wearing a rag and there was no silk sari on her body. Taking pity on her Ganu asked a friend to buy her a cheap sari. Malkarni wore it for a day and threw it away the next day and Ganu found her again in a tattered dress and singing in ecstasy the song of the silk sari.

Ganu then understood the meaning of the *Upanishad*. He realised the girl's happiness lay not in the external sari which she had thrown away but in herself. And the *Upanishad* said the same thing. "All the world", says the first verse of the *Upanishad*, "is covered by the maya of Iswara. So enjoy bliss not by having the externals but by rejecting the externals." The girl, Ganu saw, was happy as she was and contented. Thus Baba taught him the *Upanishad* through a servantmaid.

Baba saw that Ganu did not believe that he was God; he was sceptical and his belief was not deep. He made him realise his divinity through the exercise of his superhuman powers. On one occasion Ganu expressed a desire to go to the Godavari (which was also usually referred to as Ganga) four miles away from Shirdi. Baba said :"Why go there? Is Ganga not here?" And Ganu saw water flowing from Baba's toes. He took the water in his palm and sprinkled it on his head but did not drink it as devotees usually do with holy water. This had a sequel as we shall see later in this narrative.

Baba asked Ganu to complete the reading of the *Bhagavatham* within seven days (this is called *saptaka*). Ganu said he would do so but Baba must see to it that he got *sakshatkar* as a result. Baba said if there was intense concentration, that sakshatkar could be had. Ganu went through the saptaka but there was no sakshatkar. He asked Baba :"When will you give me sakshatkar?" Baba said :"You see me. This is sakshatkar. I am God." Ganu said :"I expected you to say that, but I am not satisfied with it." Ganu considered Vithal of Pandharpur alone as God and not Sai Baba. Many years later after Baba's mahasamadhi Ganu went to see a saint who was a great spiritual leader. This saint at first refused to see him and when Ganu persisted allowed him in. He told Ganu :"You call yourself a kirtankar (ballad singer), why then have you ahamkar (egoism)?" Ganu said everyone had his ego and it was impossible to avoid it. The saint said: "Shall I tell you what kind of ahamkar you have? Is not Sai Baba your guru and shall I say what you have done to him? Did not Baba produce water from his feet and what did you do with it? You sprinkled it on your head but would not drink it because you are a Brahmin and the Ganga was coming from the feet of Baba dwelling in a mosque. Is it not akamkar?" Ganu fell at the feet of the saint and said what he said was true.

Ganu was well known not only as a ballad singer and a storyteller but also as a poet with literary skill. His poems on Shivaji were such as to rouse the patriotic spirit which, he being a government servant, embarrassed the alien government. Some of his writings were prescribed as textbooks by the Bombay University. He wrote a number of books on Marathi saints. In these books he devoted a chapter or two to the life and teachings of Baba. To him has been credited the discovery of the early life of Baba and his discipleship under Venkusa in Selu which he later published in a book. He went to Selu, contacted Srinivasa Rao, subedar of Selu, in 1903 and discovered the ballads and family papers referring to his grandfather's grandfather, Gopal Rao Deshmukh who took care of Baba when he was left with him by the fakir's wife. The book was published in 1906. The arati performed at Shirdi today includes several of Ganu's verses about Baba which have touched the hearts of devotees.

Among the books on Baba written by Das Ganu the first was *Santakathamritha* published in 1903. Then came *Bhakti Lilamritha* (1906) and the last book *Bhakthi Saramritha* was published in 1925. Two chapters of a book relating to Baba were placed in Baba's hand who said: "All right." None of the books was read to Baba nor was he asked for information before they were written about himself. What Baba said of his own accord was picked up. Baba talked of his Selu antecedents and Das Ganu made enquiries at Selu about Baba's antecedents. As each book was placed in his hands Baba said: "That is all right." Das Ganu said he did not know if Baba knew to write, read or even to sign his name.

He mentioned in one of his books that Baba gave him this advice on how to dress as a *kirtankar* (ballad singer) : "Why do you go dressed as a bridegroom to perform kirtana? Take away all that above the waist (including lace pagadi, etc.). Narada inaugurated the *kirtan padathi* (procedure). Hence Narada's dress should be adopted, bare above the waist, dress below the waist, *chipla* and tanpura in hand."

H. S. DIXIT

Hari Sitaram Dixit, a well known solicitor of Bombay, was an intimate associate of Sai Baba and he was largely responsible for the establishment of Sai Sansthan and its progress after the mahasamadhi of Baba. He managed the affairs of the Shirdi Sansthan as its honorary Secretary till his death in 1926. He started *Sai Lila Masik*, the monthly organ of Sai Sansthan in which Baba's devotees recorded their experiences.

Dixit was a high-caste Brahmin and had a brilliant scholastic career. He became a leading solicitor of Bombay and his name figured prominently in the press as he defended the accused in sedition cases, especially those involving B. G. Tilak. He was active in social and political work and was elected to the Bombay Legislative Council in 1901. He resigned his membership later in order to pursue his spiritual path. During a visit to England he met with an accident and his leg was injured. In spite of best efforts it could not be set right. He continued to limp and he was depressed. In 1909 Chandorkar advised him to see Sai Baba who might remove his handicap. Madhava Rao Deshpande, familiarly known as Shama, took him to Baba in 1909. Dixit was so impressed with Baba that he began to make frequent visits to Shirdi. In 1910 he decided to build a house in Shirdi which came to be known as Kaka wada. Kaka is the affectionate name given to him by Baba. Soon Dixit gave up the idea of treatment for his lame leg and said: "Lameness of the body does not matter much" and he wanted Baba to cure the lameness of the soul.

Baba took great interest in Dixit and told him: "I will take my Kaka in a *vimana*," meaning that he would ensure his *sadgati* (Salvation). Dixit who was then 48 abandoned a lucrative practice and luxurious life and decided to embark on a spiritual career under Baba's guidance. Baba said he would care for Dixit and his family. He told him: "Why should you have any anxiety or care? All care and responsibilities are mine." When Baba gave this pledge it so happened that Dixit's eight-year-old daughter met with an accident in Bombay when an almirah filled with dolls fell on her and she escaped without any injury. Dixit came to know about this accident later and realised that Baba had saved his daughter's life.

Dixit's life in Shirdi from 1912 onwards took on the character of a *vanaprasatha* ashrama. Baba directed him to stay upstairs in his house and not to leave it. Dixit obeyed this injunction strictly. He was kept in solitude by Baba for nine months. When his wife rushed from Bombay to meet him Baba told her: "Have no fears at all about Kaka. I will look after him myself." Dixit read the scriptures during his enforced solitude as directed by Baba. When his daughter died, a copy of the *Bhavartha Ramayana* came to him by post and he gave it to Baba. Baba holding the book upside down flipped the pages and gave a page to Dixit to read. The page contained a passage in which Rama consoles Tara, Vali's wife, after her husband's death at the hands of Rama.

At the end of the nine months' seclusion Baba allowed Dixit to visit Bombay. In the early days when he was still in practice he one day placed a trunk full of currency notes and coins before Baba and said: "All this is yours." Baba dipped his hands into the trunk and taking a handful of notes and coins distributed them to people who had flocked to him and very soon the trunk was empty. On one occasion Dixit was down with fever. Baba advised him to go to his house in Bombay. "The fever will last four days," he told him, "but have no fears, it will pass away and you will be all right. Do not allow yourself to be bedridden. You can go on eating *sira* (semolina pudding) as usual." In Bombay the doctor who examined him asked him to stay in bed and take the prescribed medicines. But Dixit sat up and began eating sira which fever patients usually avoid. His temprature shot up and doctors warned him it would take a serious turn if their advice was not followed. However, to everyone's surprise Dixit's condition which went from bed to worse suddengly took a turn for the better and in a few days he was his normal self again.

Baba's promise to Dixit that he would take care of his family was exemplified in the case of his brother. Dixit one day received information that his younger brother in Nagpur was ill. He said to Baba he was sorry he could not be of service to his brother. Baba said cryptically: "I am of service." Dixit could not understand what Baba meant but at that very moment in Nagpur a sadhu had called on his brother and used the very words Baba had used: "I am of service," and cured his illness. Dixit had developed so much faith in Baba that he would not take any decision or undertake anything without going to Baba whose orders he obeyed to the letter althought sometimes it must have been against his better judgement.

To test him Baba one day directed that a sick goat which was in a pitiable condition and near death should be put out of pain with a knife. While all devotees present excused themselves from executing this task Dixit alone was ready to carry out Baba's orders. He took the knife and as he was about to kill the goat Baba stopped him and said: "Let the creature remain. I will kill it myself but not at the mosque." Baba carried the goat a few yards away from the mosque where it died.

Baba emphasised the need for a guru or guide for self-realisation. When someone asked him: "Baba, where to go?" Baba replied: "Up," meaning, to heaven or God. He was asked: "What is the way?" Baba said: "There are many ways from many places. From this place (Shirdi) there is a way but the way is full of obstacles. There are tigers and bears on the way. If one is careless there is a deep pit into which one may fall." Dixit asked: "But if there is a guide?" Baba said: "In that case there is no danger or difficulty. The tigers and bears will move aside."

There were some cases in which Baba found himself prevented from doing anything. This happened in the case of Dixit's daughter, Vatsali, whom he had saved once when an alimirah had fallen on her. When she was in Shirdi she fell ill and Dixit was hoping that Baba could cure her. Instaed Baba appeared before Vatsali in a dream and said: "Why should you be down here, come and be lying under the margosa tree." This sounded ominous and was confirmed when Baba asked Shama: "Is Kaka's girl dead?" Shama was shocked and said: "Why are you speaking so inauspiciously?" Baba merely said: "She will die in the afternoon." This happened exactly as Baba foretold.

On another occasion when Dixit pleaded with Baba to revive the son of an old man who had died of snake bite Baba said: "Do not get entangled in this. What has happened is for good. He has entered a new body. In that body he will do good work which cannot be accomplished in this body which is seen here. If I draw him back into this body then the new body he has taken will die and this body will live. I will do this for your sake. Have you considered the consequences? Have you any idea of the responsibility and are you prepared to take it up?" Dixit did not press his request.

Before he came under Baba's influence Dixit was well known for his short temper. But he conquered it throught Baba's grace. He was transformed into a man of self-control, suave and agreeable. After Baba's mahasamadhi, on one occasion Dixit was in need of Rs.30,000 to be paid to a marwari and the deadline for payment was drawing near. He did not know how he was going to meet his obligation in time. Then he had a dream in which the creditor was pressing him for repayment. He told Dixit he had a friend who would provide him with the money. On waking up he cursed himself for not consulting Baba (through draw of lots) and he sat in his chair and waited till the last day for something to turn up but nothing happened. Then at the last minute a young man appeared at the doorstep who was the son of an old friend. He told Dixit that after his father's death he was managing his father's property and wanted an investment for his money. He said he had brought with him Rs. 30,000 which he wanted to invest and he asked for Dixit's advice. Dixit told him he needed the money and struck a deal with him and got freed from a difficult situation.

Dixit had a number of cats and dogs which he reared. Even in Shirdi cats would come and he would feed them with rice and ghee, remembering Baba's words that he was in every creature. Once he asked Baba if serpents could be killed as they were the cause of many human deaths. Baba said: "No. You should not kill them. The serpent will not kill us unless it is ordered by God and if God so orders we cannot escape it." And so Dixit did not kill snakes and scorpions which infested Shirdi. Once a black scorpion was spotted by Dixit and people nearby wanted to kill it but Dixit brought a long stick and made the scorpion climb it. He then carried it and left it at a safe distance. He would not kill ants or bugs and flies. Bugs were all over the place in his house in Shirdi but they never disturbed his sleep. He used to say: "My sleep is not disturbed by them. At best they drink only half an ounce of blood and my body can easily make up that loss. Is not God also in bugs?"

After Baba's mahasamadhi Dixit continued to seek Baba's guidance through casting chits after prayer and asking a child to pick a chit at random. He said he always received instructions from Baba to questions referred to him. On one occasion acting on Baba's instructions in this way he brought his brother to Bombay from Nagpur where he did not have much practice as an advocate. He did not do much better in Bombay either and Dixit wondered how Baba could be wrong in his directions. Shortly after, the Administrator of Kutch, a native state, consulted Dixit for a suitable candidate for appointment as Dewan of Kutch and Dixit suggested his brother's name. This was accepted and his brother became the Dewan of Kutch.

Dixit did not treat Muslims differently from Hindus. This was seen in an incident after Baba's passing away. At that time Bade Baba or Fakir Baba, a Muslim devotee, wished to live in Shirdi but since the house there mostly belonged to Hindus no one was prepared to rent a room to a Muslim. Dixit came forward to accommodate him in his house in spite of protests by Hindu pilgrims.

Dixit died on an ekadasi day, considered auspicious, and in the way Baba had predicted for him. He had come to the railway station with his friends for the journey to Bombay where he had to meet a friend. Although they were late they succeeded in getting on the train as it was also late. Dixit said: "See, how merciful Baba is. He has given us this train this minute. He has not made us wait even for a minute. Baba had made the train come late and enabled us to catch it or else we would have been stranded here." He said this while sitting opposite to his friends and then appeared to fall asleep. Dabolkar, his friend, thought Dixit was sleeping and going near him shook him and asked: "Are you sleeping?" But there was no answer, for Dixit was dead. As Baba promised Dixit had been taken away in a vimana to heaven.

ANNA SAHEB DABOLKAR

The mantle of H. S. Dixit fell on Govind Raghunath Dabolkar (called Anna Saheb Dabolkar) and also known as Hemadpant. Dabolkar was a government servant and a good friend of Dixit who told him about Sai Baba. He was a self-made man who rose from the position of a village official to that of a first class magistrate. He did not believe in having a guru and he was strengthened in this belief when a friend of his lost his son even though his guru was at his bedside.

However, he was prevailed upon to visit Shirdi where Dixit presented him to Baba. Baba told Dabolkar: "Kaka is a good man. Go on listening to him." Dabolkar's faith and fervour grew with his contacts with Dixit. A friend of Dabolkar told Baba of his desire to write a biography of Baba. He said: "Anna Saheb wishes to write a book on your life. Don't say that you are a poor begging fakir and there is no necessity to write about your life. But if you agree and help him he will write or rather your grace will accomplish this work. Without your blessing and consent nothing can be done successfully." Baba blessed the venture by giving udhi to Dabolkar and placing his hand on his head. He said: "Let him make a collection of stories and experiences, keeping notes and memos. I will help him. He is only an outside instrument. I should myself write about myself and satisfy the wishes of my devotees. He should get rid of his ego, surrender it at my feet. He who acts like this in life, him I will help most. I serve him in his house in all possible ways when his ego is annihilated and there is not a trace left of it. I myself shall enter into him and write my life. Hearing my stories and teachings will create faith in my devotees and they will easily get self-realisation and bliss. But let there be no insistence on establishing one's own view and no attempt at reducing others' opinions of any sort."

Dabolkar promised he would follow Baba's advice and surrender to him. Baba's permission for the book's *Sai Satcharita* was given in 1916 but two years later when Baba passed away Dabolkar had written hardly two or three chapters and most of the book was completed after 1918. He wrote 52 chapters and passed away in 1929. What he had written was first published in *Sai Lila Masik*, the official organ of Sai Sansthan. After Dabolkar's death the 53rd chapter was added to the book and the complete book was published later. It was a monumental work which ranks him as one of the great apostles of Baba. Written in verse in Marathi the book runs to 1,000 pages and in the homes of Maharashtra it enjoys the same religious and spiritual significance as the *Ramayana*. It has been the cause of thousands of people becoming Sai bhaktas. The book narrates the stories about Baba collected from Sai devotees and their experiences are recorded. Dabolkar said Baba's hand was "visible in moulding my fate even from the beginning."

The writing of the book completely changed Dabolkar's outlook and thinking. He became totally devoted to Baba's service. He said: "The moment I touched Baba's feet I began a new lease of life. I felt much obliged to those who took me to Baba and I consider them my real relations. I cannot repay my debt to them. A peculiarity of Baba's darshan I find is that by his darshan our thoughts are changed, the force of previous actions (karma) is abated and gradually non-attachment or dispassion towards worldly objects grows. It is by the merit of actions in many past births that such a darshan is got. If only you see Baba really all the world assumes the form of Sai Baba."

In a conversation with Shama Dabolkar heard the story of Radhabai Deshmukh who came to Baba and asked for immediate mantra upadesa. She went on a fast for three days insisting that Baba should give her upadesa. Shama said he intervened on her behalf with Baba who told the woman: "Mother, why are you subjecting yourself to unnecessary tortures and inviting death? You are my mother and I am your child. Pity me. I will tell you my story. If you listen to it, it will do you good.

"I had a guru. He was a very great saint and most merciful. I served him very long indeed. Still he did not whisper any mantra into my ear. I was anxious never to leave him but to stay with him and receive instructions from him. But he had his own method. He just had my head shaved and asked me to give two paise as dakshina. I gave the same at once. If you ask how a perfect guru could ask for dakshina and yet be called desireless I shall explain to you. What he had asked for was not coins. The first paisa he asked for was nishta or firm faith and the second paise he wanted was for saburi or patience or perseverance. These two I gave him and he was pleased. I served my guru for 12 years. He brought me up. There was no lack of food or clothing. He was full of love. He was love incarnate. His love was indescribable. Rare is such a guru. My mind was always fixed on him. That was the first paisa — nishta. The second paise was saburi, that is, my waiting patiently and for long on my guru and serving him. This saburi will take you across *samsara*. Saburi is manliness in man. It removes all sins and afflictions, gets rid of calamities in various ways, removes all fear and ultimately gives you success. Saburi is a mine of virtues and is the consort of good thought. Nishta and saburi go together. My guru never expected anything else from me, but he never neglected me. He always protected me. I lived with him and sometimes away from him. Still I never felt the want or absence of his love. He protected me by his glance as a tortoise feeds its young ones.

"Oh! Mother, my guru never taught me any mantra. How can I give you any? Do not try to get mantra or upadesa from anybody. Make me the sole object of your thought and actions and you will undoubtedly attain paramartha, the spiritual goal of life. Look at me wholeheartedly and I shall do the same, that is, look at you wholeheartedly. Sitting in this masjid I speak the truth and nothing but the truth. No sadhanas, no proficiency in sastras is necessary. Have faith and confidence in your guru. Believe fully that the guru is the sole actor or doer. Blessed is he who knows the greatness of the guru and worships him as Hari, Hara and Brahma, trimurthi incarnate."

The woman bowed to Baba's advice and gave up the fast. When Dabolkar went to Baba and related the story as given out by Shama Baba said: "Wonderful is the story. Did you catch its significance?" Dabolkar said: "Yes, the restlessness of my mind has vanished. I have got true peace and come to know the true path." Baba said: "My method is quite unique. To get knowledge of the self *dhyana* (meditation) is necessary. If you practise it continuously the *vrittis* (thoughts) will be pacified. Being quite desireless you should meditate on the Lord who is in all creatures and when the mind is concentrated the goal will be achieved. Meditate always on my formless nature which is knowledge incarnate, consciousness and bliss. If you cannot do this meditate on my form from top to toe as you see here night and day. As you go on doing this your vrittis will be one pointed and the distinction between the meditator, dhyana and the thing meditated upon will be lost and the meditator will be one with consciousness and be merged with Brahman. The mother tortoise is on one bank of the river and her young ones on the other bank. She gives neither milk nor warmth to them. Her mere glance gives them nutrition. The young ones do nothing but remember (meditate upon) the mother. The tortoise glance is to the young ones a downpour of nectar, the only source of sustenance and happiness. Similarly is the relation between the guru and the disciple."

Dabolkar mentions that Baba used to grind wheat on a stone grinder. He described the two grinding stones as karma and bhakti and the handle with which Baba ground the wheat as jnana. With it Baba was grinding and destroying the sins and miseries of his numerous devotees. It was the firm conviction of Baba that knowledge of the self or *atman* was not possible unless we grind and destroy our sins caused by the three gunas, *sattva, rajas* and *tamas.*   It is recorded that one day as Baba was grinding wheat four women devotees appeared before him and took over the grinding themselves, in spite of Baba's protests. Then Baba told them: "The wheat belongs to me. Don't take away the wheat flour but take it in heaps and throw it in the air on the street." It was noted that there was then danger of a cholera epidemic in Shirdi. Baba might have used this method to ward off the epidemic.

Dabolkar gave this description of Baba: "When one gazes upon Baba's face all hunger and thirst are gone. What other joy can compare with this? One forgets all miseries of earthly existence. Gazing into his eyes one loses one's sense of individuality. Bliss gushes out from within and the mind sinks into an expanse of sweetness."

Dabolkar took over as secretary of Sai Sansthan and as editor of *Sai Lila Masik* after the death of Dixit and he retained these posts until his own death.

G. S. KHAPARDE

Among Sai Baba's intimate devotees was a politician of Madhya Pradesh (called Central Provinces under British rule) who has left a diary which gives us interesting glimpses of Baba and also his meeting with the Indian patriot and nationalist leader, Bal Gangadhar Tilak. He is G. S. Khaparde whose full name is Dewan Bahadur Ganesh Sri Krishna Khaparde. He was an advocate practising in Amroati. He was a notable figure in Indian politics and in the law courts of Madhya Pradesh and in the provincial Legislative Council. He belonged to the extremist group of B. G. Tilak with whom he was closely associated and he was always in danger of being arrested and prosecuted by the alien rulers. Having heard of Sai Baba he wanted to meet him for his temporal and spiritual welfare.

He visited Shirdi in December 1910 and saw Baba surrounded by devotees, many of whom were government officials — high and low. He heard Baba speak in parables and was told that he protected people in difficulties. For instance, he was informed that a head constable who was charged with extortion was acquitted through Baba's grace. Khaparde left Shirdi after staying there for a week and when he went back to Amroati his troubles began. He had a roaring practice and he feared that his arrest which he expected any moment would affect his livelihood. This anxiety and stress affected his health and he was not able to work as before and this meant a decline in practice. He went to Shirdi again in 1911 and Baba told him: "This is your house. Why should anybody fear when I am here?" Khaparde went on postponing his return home on Baba's advice although his relatives were pressing him to return.

Baba wanted to be certain that Khaparde would not be prosecuted. He said: "My eye of vigilant supervision is ever on those who love me." He revealed to Mrs Khaparde that he was watching the minds of the Governor and the Home Member of the Central Provinces Government. It was evident they were thinking of proceeding against him for sedition in respect of many of his speeches. Khaparde stayed with Baba for three months and rumours were set afloat that Khaparde had given up practice and that he preferred the company of a fakir. This finally influenced the government in its decision not to proceed against him. Khaparde noted in his diary: "Baba told my wife that the Governor came with a lance, that Sai Maharaj had a tussle with him and drove him out and that he finally conciliated the Governor." Khaparde added: "The language is highly figurative and therefore difficult to interpret."

Khaparde who wrote his diary in English recorded what happened in Shirdi during his stay there and gave vivid pictures of Baba's visitors and the stories that Baba narrated. His diary is a valuable source of information on Baba and Narasimha Swamiji calls him the "Pepys of Shirdi." Among several things mentioned in the diary is one about Baba's glances which transformed the lives of his devotees. Khaparde said it was a "yogic glance" which transported the recipient to an ocean of bliss for hours on end. Khaparde wrote in his diary on January 12, 1912: "Baba gave me a yogic glance. I was in ecstasy of bliss the whole day." He wrote on January 17: "Baba smiled benignly. It is worthwhile spending years here (Shirdi) to see it even once. I was overjoyed and stood gazing like mad." In another entry Khaparde said Baba made him understand things and solved his problems merely by giving him his pipe to smoke.

Narasimha Swamiji says that Baba's glances were part of the inducement to pull Khaparde away from worldliness and external attachments and to make him lead a life of surrender and detachment. On one occasion when Khaparde's son was stricken with plague Mrs Khaparde went to Baba and pleaded with him to save her son. Baba told her that he had taken the plague on himself and showed her buboes on his person. Khaparde recorded an instance in which a woman devotee from Pune with a long standing eye trouble came to Baba and sat before him. Baba cast a glance at her eyes and the eyes stopped watering and giving pain. On the other hand, she saw Baba's eyes watering, indicating that she was cured of her trouble.

It was Khaparde who brought B. G. Tilak to Shirdi on May 19, 1917 to meet Baba. Khaparde did not give any details about the meeting between the spiritual and political giants but it was learnt from other sources that Tilak, during his talks with Baba, wanted to know if he approved the lines on which he was working for India's freedom. Baba did not reply directly to his question but said: "You are getting old. You require rest. Why don't you take rest?" This was later considered significant since Tilak passed away in January 1920.

Baba tried to make Khaparde understand the pettiness of men who were hankering after wealth of the world which never lasted. How was Khaparde to get his wealth? Only by seeking the favour of innumerable persons and avoiding the displeasure of others. All this required, Baba said, that his time and attention be wasted upon petty creatures. Baba told him that he must serve God alone. "What God gives lasts for ever, what man gives does not," Baba said to him.

Narasimha Swamiji says: "Unfortunately the very high degree of attachment to the world that persisted in Khaparde despite his great leaning in sacred books and his daily prayers, attendance at a good number of discourses and bhajans and kirtans, prevented him from receiving adequate benefits from Sai Maharaj." Khaparde left Shirdi in March 1912 and never visited it again till May 19, 1917 when he accompanied B. G. Tilak for his meeting with Baba when he spent a few hours there. Khaparde was not fully dedicated to Baba like H. S. Dixit. He was too much in worldly affairs, in politics and in accumulating wealth and fame. His son, after a successful career as a lawyer, became a minister and Khaparde himself became a member of the Council of State (Upper House of the Central Legislature). He lived long and passed away full of honours and fame.

G. G. NARKE

Prof G. G. Narke, geology professor of Pune, who was an ardent devotee of Sai Baba, has left us details of some of the miracles performed by Baba and of his mysterious travels in worlds beyond our own. Narke, a talented scientist who had studied in England, had been unemployed for some time and did not get the job suited to his qualifications and had to be satisfied with temporary appointments. Baba told him: "Go to Pune." Narke wondered what that meant for he had nothing to do with Pune. But one day when he was travelling in a train he heard there was a vacancy for a geology professor in a Pune college and he at once went there, applied for the job and got it. He then understood that Baba had foreseen his appointment.

Narke wrote in his memoirs that Baba was living and operating in other worlds besides this and that he also functioned in an invisible body. His words were highly cryptic, symbolic, allegorical and not something which everyone could understand. But if one followed his words carefully, Narke said, the meaning would be clear. Baba was often misunderstood when he spoke in his mysterious ways. Narke gave an example. When a devotee reported to Baba that a relative of his was dead from tuberculosis Baba said: "How can he die? In the morning he will come back to life." The dead man's relatives lighted lamps round his body and waited for him to come back to life. But nothing happened and they were all angry with Baba for giving them false hopes.

After many days Baba appeared in a dream to a relative with the dead man's head on his own and said: "The man's lungs were in a rotten condition. From the torture of all this I saved him." The meaning of what Baba said thus became clear to the relatives. What Baba said referred not to this life but to the survival of human personality which takes new forms of life.

Narke said Baba used to sleep either at the mosque or at the chavadi and while sitting in front of the dhuni in the mosque he would often refer to the distant places he had visited overnight and what he had done. People sleeping by his side and seeing his body would wonder how he could have travelled when his body was there. Baba often described scenes in other worlds. For instance the relatives of a marwari boy were returning after the boy's funeral and they heard Baba say: "He must be nearing the river now, just crossing it." Narke said the reference should have been to Vaitarani which dead souls had to cross.

Narke said Baba had a peculiar way of giving information to particular individuals in the midst of a group which only those concerned alone could understand and not the others. Baba told Narke that he controlled the destiny of departed souls. That was an important function of his.

According to Narke Baba thought he did not have anyone in Shirdi to serve him as he served his guru. "I would tremble to come in the presence of my guru," he once said. Baba asked: "Who dares to call himself my disciple? Who can serve me adequately and satisfactorily?" Narke said Baba's was the power that controlled our fate here and now as well as our experience and fate in the future in this world and many unseen worlds. The duty of a disciple of Baba is only to keep himself fit for the guru's grace."

Narke said: "Though Baba is God from the devotees' point of view yet he is a man seen in flesh and blood and with limitations to which an individual embodied soul is subject. The two co-exist and both are true, each in its own way." Once some devotees complained to Baba that Narke did not believe in the *Puranas* and asked him: "Are the *Puranas* true?" Baba said: "Yes." He said Rama and Krishna were great souls because they were avatars. The devotees said Narke was saying that Baba was not God. Baba said: "What he says is true. But I am your father and you should not speak like that. You have to get your benefit and everything from me."

Narke said Baba followed the bhakti path. Its features were : Guru Bhakti, serving and loving the guru and God. Baba stressed the importance of devotion to one's guru and treating him as God. It was seeing God in, through and as the guru and identifying the guru with God that marked the Bhakti path shown by Baba. Baba's method of teaching varied. He would simply touch with his palm the head of a devotee and that would have one kind of influence. Sometimes he pressed his hands heavily on the devotee's head as though he was crushing out some of the lower impulses. On occasions he would pat on the back of the devotee or would press his palm over his hand. Each had its own effect affecting the sensations and feelings of the person concerned. Apart from touch he effected an invisible operation on the devotee which brought about a great change in him.

Narke relates that Baba gave to one of his devotees, Kusa Bhav Baba, a boon. "Henceforth," he said, "you will have the power to produce udhi, that is, udhi from the Dhuni Mayi of Shirdi by merely remembering me and holding forth your hands. Give this udhi freely. It will help all people and you will get punya." Kusa Bhav gave this udhi to Narasimha Swamiji when he met him in Pune. Kusa Bhav closed his eyes and stretched his hands with uplifted face and suddenly his palm was full of udhi and he said: "Hold your hands and receive the udhi." Narasimha Swamiji found the udhi to be warm coming as it did fresh from the Dhuni Mayi in Shirdi on a cold day.

Narke narrates an incident which showed that Baba could command the elements. On one occasion when a devotee was preparing to leave Shirdi after darshan of Baba there was a storm and rain and he was afraid he would not be able to get back to Bombay. He went to Baba to seek his advice. Baba looked at the sky and said: "Arre, Allah, enough. Stop the rain. My children have to go back home. Let them go back without difficulty." As Baba spoke the rain began to abate and became a drizzle and the devotee had no difficulty in starting on his journey.

Baba advised a woman devotee who was short-tempered: "If anyone talks 10 words at us let us reply with one word. Do not quarrel or battle with anyone."

Narke told Narasimha Swamiji that he was introduced to Baba in 1913 after he returned from England. Baba said: "You introduce him to me! I have known him for 30 generations." Narke said: "At arati, Baba was in a towering rage. He fumed, cursed and threatened for no visible cause. I doubted if he was not mad. That was a passing thought. In the afternoon he stroked my head and said: 'I am not mad.' Nothing is concealed from him. Nothing was beyond him, or concealed from him, past, present, future." He added: "One day in 1914, Baba had got ready a number of kufnis (robes which are worn by fakirs) and presented them to a number of people. I was watching the distribution from a distance and hoped that one might be given to me. Baba beckoned to me and said: 'Don't blame me for not giving you a kufni. That fakir (evidently meaning God) has not permitted me to give you one.'"

Narke's relatives asked Baba what was to become of Narke. Baba said: "I will settle him at Pune." Four years later in 1917, Narke was appointed Professor of Geology in the Engineering College of Pune.

Narke gave this impression of Baba: "Anyone who judged Baba from the outside was very far out in his appraisal. He was adapting himself to the capacity for understanding of the people who came to him for help. Most of them were superficial and sought only material benefits and to them he did not reveal his inner nature. But when anyone capable of diving deeper came to him he revealed more of himself and his true powers. He had the peculiar art of giving information to particular individuals in the midst of a group in a way that they alone could understand and not the other members of the group. Strangely enough at one and the same time he could and did benefit many people by a few words or action. To one deeply observing him the startling fact came through in greater and greater prominence that Baba was living and operating in other worlds besides this world and in an invisible body. Remarks made by him openly would be treated as meaningless ranting by those who did not know him. Baba never spoke untruth, never spoke meaningless jargon but only those who were familiar with his ways could make out the meaning of what he said or did, that is, when it was intended for their understanding."

M. B. REGE

M. B. Rege, Judge of the Indore High Court, was one of the favoured devotees of Sai Baba. He related his reminiscences of Baba to Narasimha Swamiji. He said: "I look upon Sai Baba as the Creator, Preserver and Destroyer. I said so before his samadhi in 1918 and I say it now. To me he had no limitations. I thought of him as a mental or spiritual image in which the finite and the infinite blended perfectly, — yet allowing the finite to appear before us at times. Now that the body has been cast off the infinite alone remains as Sai Baba."

When Rege first met Baba as a student Baba embraced him and said: "You are my child." Baba sent him to Radhakrishna Ayi, a dedicated disciple of Baba who spent all her life in the service of Baba. It was said she lived only for Baba and her happiness lay in doing anything he wanted or what was needed for him. He sent to her his devotees and she took care of them during their stay in Shirdi, treating them as her own children. Being an advanced sadhaka she had developed certain powers in addition to her bhakti. Her concentration was helped by her proficiency in music and she could also play on the sitar. She and Rege decided to do japa and they adopted Sai nama for their japa.

When Baba asked Rege what he was doing in the morning Rege replied: "Japa."

"Japa of what name," asked Baba.

"Of my God," Rege said.

Baba: "Who is your God?"

Rege: "You Know it."

Baba: "That is all right."

Baba once told Rege: "These people want to find God, that is, Brahman, in these books. Do not read books but keep me in your heart and if you unify or harmonise head and heart, that is enough". Baba did not, however, rule out study of religious books like the *Ramayana*, the *Bhagavad Gita* and the *Bhagavatham*. Baba said to Rege once: "Ask me anything you want, I will give it to you." After much coaxing and persuasion by Baba Rege said: "Baba, I want this. In this and in any future birth that may befall me you should never part from me, you should always be with me." Baba said: "Yes, I shall be with you, inside you, outside you, whatever you may be or do."

Rege said there were three ways in which Baba communicated with his devotees. The first was the active waking state: When the devotee was in difficulties or if Baba wanted him to take a particular course the devotee got an inspiration on what course should be adopted and the feeling that the inspiration came from Baba. This happened in Rege's case. When he was in Radhakrishna Ayi's house he would feel that Baba called him and would go to the mosque and find that Baba was in fact waiting for him. The second method related to the sleeping or trance state. Baba would appear in a dream or a trance. This was called sakshatkara and considered most impressive and unmistakable. In the third method Baba asked his devotee to go to some other person who would not even know why the devotee was sent to him but who nevertheless helped the devotee in accordance with Baba's internal and unperceived guidance. Sometimes the person to whom the devotee was sent was totally unfit to help him, as for instance, in the case of the rustic girl to whom Das Ganu was sent for interpreting the *Isa Upanishad.*

Rege said Baba was conservative and impartial in his religious views asking all devotees to keep to their own religion and not to interfere with others' religions. He discouraged intolerance in every form. To him Vithal and Allah were the same as also all saints. Baba said once: "Untruth I have never uttered before nor will I utter it at anytime." Baba could change the mind of any person at will. In one instance a devotee who was charged with a number of others in a criminal case the magistrate acquitted him and others even without hearing the prosecution or examination of the connected papers. Baba had acted on the magistrate's mind. It is called *manasthambam.*

Ramakrishna Ayi stayed in Shirdi for eight or nine years and died at the age of 35. She was a great organiser and in her service to Baba she never spared herself to add worldly grandeur to the daily occupations of a saint. She was a woman of resolute will and assertive temperament. It was she who introduced the night *shej* (devotional prayers before sleep) arati and the kakad (devotional prayers in the morning) arati at the *chavadi.* She was a person of strange ways. She would break into laughter suddenly or melt into tears while singing and either continue slowly with her singing in a choked voice or stop singing altogether while continuing to sob.

R. B. PURANDHARE

R. B. Purandhare was a petty clerk on a salary of Rs. 35 per month who had to support a family of five, including his mother, brother, wife and child. Sai Baba directed his life at every stage and Purandhare acted on his instructions although they might seem unreasonable and even risky. But Baba always proved right. For instance Purandhare was told to stay one day at Nashik and leave the place the next day. When he went to Nashik he found some members of his family were suffering from cholera and he was advised to get away. But Purandhare followed Baba's instruction and stayed with his family. He took them with him the next day to his home in Bombay safely.

Purandhare was a man who was very emotional and he frequently lost his temper and quarrelled with people. Baba reformed him with his love. He wanted Purandhare to have a house of his own and although Purandhare told him he had no money or resources to build or buy a house Baba insisted he should have one and never ceased to tell him so. At one stage Baba said: "Ask that man (Purandhare) whether he thinks me to be a man or a beast. Why does he not act on my words?"

In the end Purandhare did purchase a site through the help of a friend who gave him the money without asking to sign any document. And Baba asked him to build a house on it. Purandhare did not know where to go for the money and worrying about it got a terrific headache. Baba said the headache would go only after he built the house. Finally he got a loan from his office and started to build the house.

Narasimha Swamiji says: "Here is an instance of Baba's love, forcing a man to get a house when he could hardly afford it." Purandhare had a lot of financial difficulties and Baba, anticipating every little difficulty gave him warnings through dreams and visions and helped him to overcome them. Purandhare was so much attached to Baba that he wanted to be near him all the time ignoring his official duties. On one occasion

he was anxious to go to Shirdi but during the night Baba appeared
in his dream and told him : "Beware! If you come I will hit you.
Do not come. Why should you come so often? I am not away
from you. I am with you. Do not play the fool." As he was
wondering why Baba had asked him not to come to Shirdi there
was a strike in his office and he realised that if he had left
Bombay he would have been considered as supporting the strike
and had gone away to hide the fact.

In 1915 Baba was seriously ill. He could not move about
without being helped by others. He suffered from exhaustion
and endured physical suffering. At that time Purandhare who
was leaving with his family for his village suddenly felt impelled
to go to Shirdi. He asked his family to go to the village and
rushed to Shirdi where he found Baba expecting him. Baba told
him: "I feel exhausted. Do not leave me. I have been expecting
you for the last three or four days." Purandhare wept seeing
Baba's condition. Baba said: "Do not cry. In two or three days
I will be all right. Allah has put me to pain which I must
endure."

Out of his love for Baba Purandhare did not even mind
going against Baba's wishes when he wanted to provide a garage
for the silver palanquin intended to take Baba in procession but
which he never used. He dug holes in the mosque to insert the
wooden poles and when Baba protested and said: "You want to
break my mosque wall," Purandhare told him the wall would
be safe and proceeded with the work.

8

ABOVE ALL RELIGIONS

BABA was above all religions. He is God and God is beyond religion. To describe him as a Muslim is contrary to established facts. It has been proved beyond doubt and he himself had said so on several occasions that he was born of Brahmin parents and there is no evidence to show that he changed his faith in the course of his saintly life. His fakir garb, his frequent chanting of the name of Allah and his residence in a dilapidated mosque led innocent villagers of Shirdi to believe he was a Muslim but they none the less worshipped him as they would a saint of their own faith. In any case this issue is irrelevant so far as Baba was concerned for he functioned in a wider plane where there was only God without any colour or creed or symbols or rituals and with compassion and love. He was greatly attached to his foster-father, the Muslim fakir who brought him up and he had great reverence for him. He was his first guru and it was as a sign of respect for him that he frequently invoked the name of Allah and fakir to indicate God or guru. For him Allah, Ram, Rahim were the same and he made no distinction between one religion and another. He was the universal spirit which permeated all things, creatures and beings who provided security and protection to all those who approached him irrespective of their religion, creed or caste. His love and compassion encompassed all and to him they were all children of God whose agent he said he was on earth.

His was a spotless and blameless moral life which placed before all a wonderful model of ethical perfection. By his personal example he showed himself to be a great unifying factor and a universal force. He taught people to overcome meaningless barriers of separation between man and man and made them realise the brotherhood of humanity. His tolerance, equal vision and universality are a unique and unparalleled phenomenon. He showed people how to recognise the presence of God in all beings. Very few understood his true worth while he was alive. He was rightly described by a contemporary saint as "a diamond upon a dung heap."

Baba preached no cult. He was not the founder of any sect. He did not set up any spiritual hierarchy. He showed a way of life. In a subtle but very effective way he chiselled into men's hearts the truth that the supreme mission of life is to sense God, see God, live in the proximity of God, grow like unto God and become one with God.

Baba held all religions in reverence. He pronounced the fatiya and listened to the Quran from Muslims and uttered Rama mantra to the Hindus and taught them the *Bhagavad Gita*. He discouraged conversions and asked his devotees to stick to their faith. His mosque contained the *nimbar* towards which Muslims turn for prayer, a fire which Hindus and Parsis worshipped and the sacred Tulsi brindavan was there for the Hindus. He called the mosque Dwarakamayi or Brahmin Mosque. A devotee has said: "The eminence of Baba as a saint is not in his striking out a new line of thought or expounding a new philosophy or religious system. His greatness consists in drawing to himself men without any faith or adequate faith in their own ancient systems."

While dissuading people from changing their religion Baba said what was important was not mere external conversion but conversion of the heart which made a man lose his sinful and bestial nature and climb up to Godhood. His vision was that all people should be really converted and should have God in their hearts; get firmly attached to God so that all of them will be soaked through and through with the idea of God; and in consequence there will be no friction between one person soaked in God and another person also soaked in God.

Baba said: "God is great. He is the Supreme Master (the phrase Allah Malik which is the Arabic equivalent of God was frequently on Baba's lips). How great is God? No one can compare with Him. God creates, supports and destroys. His lila (sport) is inscrutable. Let us be content to remain as He makes us, to submit our wills to His. Take what comes. Be

Sri SAINATH MAHARAJ at the DWARAKAMAYI

H.H. SRI NARASIMHA SWAMIJI ,
Founder-President of All India Sai Samaj, Madras.

H.H. ŚRI SAIPADANANDA RADHAKRISHNA SWAMIJI,
Founder-Patron, Sri Sai Spiritual Centre, Bangalore.

SRI SIVANESAN SWAMY,
an ardent Sai devotee blessing the visiting Sai devotees.

contented and cheerful. Never worry. Not a leaf moves but by His consent and will. We should be honest, upright and virtuous. We must distinguish right from wrong. We must each attend to his own duty. But we must not be obsessed by egoism and fancy that we are the independent causes of action. God is that actor. We must recognise His independence and our own dependence on Him and see all acts as His. If we do so we shall be unattached and be free from karmic bondage."

Baba pleaded for love of all creations. He said: "Love all creatures. Do not fight with any. Do not retaliate nor scandalise any. When anyone talks of you, that is, against you, pass on unperturbed His words cannot pierce your body. Others' acts will effect them alone and not you. Do not be idle, work, utter God's name. Read scriptures." Baba told a devotee: "We should not harbour envy, rivalry or combative disposition towards others. If others hate us let us simply take to nama japa and avoid their company." He told a child: "Listen to the words of your parents. Help your mother in her tasks. Speak the truth and truth alone."

Baba preached industry and patience. He said: "Life is lived in vain if no yoga, tapas, or jnana is achieved." He gave this advice to his devotees: "If any man or creature comes to you do not discourteously drive them away but receive them well and treat them with due respect. Sri Hari will be certainly pleased if you give water to the thirsty, bread to the hungry, clothes to the naked and the courtyards of your houses for strangers to sit and rest. If anybody wants any money from you and you are not inclined to give, do not give but do not bark at him like a dog. Let anyone say hundreds of things against you. Do not show your resentment by giving bitter replies. If you always tolerate such things you will certainly be happy. Let the world go topsy turvy, you remain where you are and look on calmly at the show of all things passing before you. Demolish the wall of difference that separates you from me. And then the road for our meeting will be clear and open. The sense of difference, such as I and you, is the barrier that keeps away the disciple from the master and unless that is destroyed the state of union or atonement is not possible. Allah Malik or God is the sole protector, nobody else is our protector. His method of work is extraordinary, invaluable and inscrutable. His will be done and He will show us the way and satisfy our hearts' desires. It is on account of rinanubanda (relationship from former births) that we have come together. Let us love and serve each other and be happy. He who attains the supreme goal of life is immortal and happy, all others merely exist and merely breathe."

A rich man once went to Baba and asked him: "What is God like?" Instead of answering his question Baba sent some devotees who were present to various people and ask for dakshina. They all returned empty-handed. But Chandorkar got the money from the same persons whom they had asked. It was then explained to the rich man that the answer to his question was that a man must be qualified to ask the question, 'Who is God?' and only a deserving man would get the answer.

Baba said: "I want surrender of five senses, the five pranas, manas, buddhi and ahamkar (mind, intellect and ego) all of which involve vairagya, that is, detachment. The road to Brahmajnana is hard to tread. All cannot tread it. When it dawns there will be light. One who feels unattached to things terrestrial and celestial is alone competent to have Brahmajnana." He added: "To get atmajnana dhyana is needed, that is, the atma *anushtana* (practice) that pacifies and carries the mind into samadhi. So give up all desires and dwell in your mind on God. If the mind is thus concentrated the goal is achieved."

Baba said: "For dyana meditate on me either as with form or as formless which will give more ananda. If such formless contemplation is hard then think of my form just as you see me here. With such meditation the mind dissolves into unity (that is, it attains *laya*). The difference between subject and object (me and you) and the act of contemplation will be lost." He added: "The guru's glance is bread and milk to the pupil."

To those who wanted to get away from samsara Baba said: "The idea that the sorrows of life can be avoided by man by running away from society into the forest is absurd. Wherever you go you have your body and your mind and these will give you your joys and sorrows in any place and every place. The body, as long as it lasts, must produce its *pararabdha* karma of sorrow and joy. Therefore the proper course would be to face facts and lead the proper life."

Baba never disliked family ties and did not condemn them as hopeless fetters. He mentioned that he had various relations, father, sister, brothers, cousins and he maintained a high level of duty towards them in every janma or birth. This must be a reference to his previous birth for Baba is not known to have revealed any relative in this birth except his parents.

Das Ganu Maharaj, Baba's intimate devotee, once told Baba: "You ask me to read the whole of *Bhagavatha* in seven days and I shall do so but I must have appearance of God at the end of it." Baba said, "Yes, Vithal will appear but there must be sufficient *bhava*, that is, intensity of concentration on God." He added, "If you are unable to think of *nirankara* concentrate upon my form (that is, think of me as God"). H. S. Dixit who was a devotee of Vithal, felt His presence very elusive and momentary and in order to confirm that it was real and it was Vithal that he saw he went to Baba who assured him his experience was real for Baba knew the mind of each of his devotees and what happened to them. However Baba added: "Vithal is a very elusive person, tie him fast, else he will elude."

Khaparde has written: "Baba fulfilled my idea of God on earth." The moment I touched his feet all the load of my worldly cares disappeared though a few minutes earlier those cares were so oppressive as to excite disgust for life. Such an experience is not only my personal experience but also the experience of thousands of devotees whom I met at Shirdi during my protracted stay there in 1911-12. The whole of the countryside worshipped him. Each visitor of Sai Baba went away satisfied. Each was anxious to repeat his or her visit to the saint as often as it could be managed. It was a sight to see and enjoy."

Prof. Narka wrote: "I have placed Sai Baba among the household gods we worship daily at home. Sai Baba is God, not an ordinary satpurusha. The divine gleam in Sai's eyes denotes he is the satpurusha. His powers and actions are wonderful. In 1916 when Prof. Narke went to Shirdi he was told that Vama Rao Patel, an advocate, was doing service to Baba by begging for food in the village on behalf of Baba. It occurred to Prof. Narke he should also do the same service to Baba and he thought: "Why should I not be given that work?" When dressed in western style he met Baba (he had no time to change), Baba was being asked for permission to send Vaman Rao for begging. Baba pointed to Narke and said: "Let this man go and beg for food with that bowl today." Narke then took the bowl and went and begged in the same dress. He continued to do this service for four months. He said the honour of begging on Baba's behalf was reserved only to a few people.

Baba seldom gave any long discourses to his devotees especially after their number began to swell in hundreds, after 1908. Some of his rare discourses are referred to in Das Ganu's book. Baba did not subscribe to any particular school of philosophy but what he said seemed to be a mixture of various schools of thought. As Narasimha Swamiji points out, the people who came to seek Baba's blessing were hardly of the kind to understand any high philosophy. In his talks to devotees Baba referred to the inner nature of various problems, for instance, property. He said the sadhaka in his progress had to analyse "I" and all its derivations like "mine", etc. "Mine" meant property. Property and egotism, both warped the real vision which would enable a person to understand what he really was. Self was distinguished from "I" by understanding that "I" was the egoistic aspect of the self. Too much identification with the body and its nature was involved in the "I". The real self was more inward and was the true basis of "I". That self was regarded as the one that underlay all selves. It was the same as the Paramatma, the Parabrahmam. It was God.

Baba taught that it was ruinous for anyone who desired his true welfare to go on dwelling over and over again upon "I" and "mine". The most important thing for a sadhaka was to dissociate himself from the body idea. "I" and "mine" represented the body idea.

Baba referred to all manifestations through the power of God or Brahman as the work of maya and the highest goal of spiritual endeavour was to go back to God crossing this world of appearances which kept us away from Him. Baba was never concerned with maintaining philosophical conclusions, never debating various conflicting philosophical theories. He was a guru intent on practical guidance of those who sought it from him. Khaparde writes in his diary that Baba told him: "This world is funny. All are my subjects. I look upon all equally but some become thieves and what can I do for them? People who are themselves very near death desire and make preparations for the death of others. They offend me a great deal, but I say nothing. I keep quiet. God is great and has His officers everywhere. They are all very powerful. I am also very powerful. I was here eight or ten thousand years ago."

Baba applied the law of karma even to dogs and other creatures. Explaining the law of karma Narasimha Swamiji says it is a theory of cause producing effect. Every action done with a certain attitude of mind tends to strengthen that attitude and produces not merely the results worked for but also a tendency to continue that mentality further and further with greater and greater strength. As an example, the story of Veerabadrappa and Basappa is quoted. These two bowed to Baba in a previous birth. They had bitter differences. Veerabadrappa by reason of his greed for money and with considerable power and personality was furious with Basappa for claiming the property which came to Gowri, wife of Veerabadrappa. Basappa, also greedy, sought that property but was also a coward. Veerabadrappa vowed to drink the blood of Basappa who sought refuge with Baba. But before the revenge could seeking his protection take place both Veerabadrappa and Basappa died. Veerabadrappa was born a cobra and Basappa a frog, in the present birth. It was when the cobra was about to swallow the frog that Baba intervened and told the cobra (Veerabadrappa): "Cease your hatred. Give up your attempt to harass your enemy, Basappa." Veerabadrappa the snake then surrendered to Basappa the frog. Baba said: "One's evil karma will continue till one's contact with a satpurusha who will save one from further consequences."

The law of karma for good and virtuous persons promotes good and for evil persons it promotes evil. Baba has said: "If one puts his foot on Shirdi soil his karma is abolished!" There are certain events and happenings which are the result of previous karma and cannot be altered. However Baba was able to mould these and shape them at certain stages and modify them for the benefit of the concerned devotees. This was seen in two instances. In the first case a South Indian devotee suffered intensely from guinea worms and requested Baba to hold up his suffering for 10 later births and leave him free in this birth. Baba told him: "What! You want janmas? What has to be endured in ten janmas can be crushed into ten days by the power of satpurushas." Baba asked him to remain with his legs outstretched at Dwarakamayi. He said a crow would come and peck at his wound and cure him. In a few days Abdul, Baba's attendant, accidentally put his foot on the devotee's wound and crushed all the guinea worms in it. Baba said Abdul was the crow and no other crow was required to peck at the devotee's wound. The devotee was then asked to go home and in ten days he was completely cured and his sufferings ended.

In the second instance a devotee, Bhimaji, who had contracted tuberculosis came to Baba. Baba said: "In bringing this chap to me what a load of responsibility you are placing on me." Baba meant that the tuberculosis from which the devotee was suffering was the result of his previous karma when he had committed a theft. Baba told him: "The fakir is merciful and your disease will be cured." He was sent to stay and sleep in a wet verandah of a house. He did so and had two dreadful dreams. In one he was mercilessly beaten by a schoolmaster. He felt the pain and cried. In the second dream he felt someone was placing a stoneroller on his chest. He suffered all the pangs of approaching death. Baba thus changed the punishment which the devotee had earned by his previous karma. The devotee recovered his health.

Baba has said in his previous births he was full of vairagya, self-denial and was working for the benefit of others. He had conquered all desires. He always sacrificed his own interest to promote that of other people, a brother, stepmother and a neighbour. In all these cases he acted without expectation of any reward and purely out of regard and compassion for them. These features of his past lives must have been so deeply ingrained in his soul that from his very birth he must have had these characteristics which later had the chance for growth and fruition. Deserted by parents at a very early age Baba was brought up by a begging fakir who appeared to be a highly advanced sufi. After his death his wife left Baba in the care of Gopal Rao Deshmukh, the Selu zamindar. All these were stepping stones for Baba to develop trust, faith, purity, vairagya and Godliness. He fed on bhakti alone and by means of that became all that he was. He cultivated love and his soul was nothing but the fullness of love—love that neutralised and chilled the fire of enmity hurled at it. When he came to Shirdi mischievous boys threw stones at him. He forgave them and in the tiny hands which had cast the stones he placed sugar candy. Love unifies, synthesises and strengthens one's self or moral nature, especially by the perception of unity of one's self with other selves. In the case of Baba there were rules of conduct, principles, and practice of secrecy, self-suppression and concealment which prevented the beholder from guessing the existence or the extent of the internal love. It has been said that a sadhaka or saint should not betray his fullest development and though wise should behave like a child, though clever should behave like an ignorant man, though learned should talk like a crazy or insane person and though versed in the scriptures should act like brutes for thus his concentration will remain undisturbed by others.

Baba once told Shama, that for 72 janmas or births he had been with him. That meant that Baba had looked after this devotee through all his previous births for over 2000 years. Shama in this birth was a poor villager who was obliged to depend on Baba. Baba provided him and his children with means of subsistence, comforts and safety as he did in the case of so many others. When another disciple, Prof. Narke, was introduced to him Baba said he had known him for 30 janmas.

Baba recognised in his accounts of his previous births and the present one that he had parents and that he had to help and support them and his brothers and sisters. He said his sister in former birth gave him support and in the present birth continued to support him. He recalled that Tatya's mother whom he recognised as his sister in a previous birth made it certain that he had his food and did not starve. Baba would not forget even the slightest service done to him in previous or present births. He said Dada Kolkar, G. S. Khaparde, Bapusaheb Jog, H. S. Dixit, Shama and he were all students of a common guru in a previous birth and therefore he had brought them together in the present birth to renew contacts. He helped each one of them in a remarkable way.

Baba recognised even playmates of previous births and said he found a tomb where a girl who had been his playmate was buried. He spent sometime there. He recognised his rinanubhanda to animals in the past or present births. He said Mrs Khaparde was a cow in a previous birth and gave him plenty of milk. He recognised two goats as having been his human companions in a former birth who by their misfortune had been degraded to the level of animals. He bought them, fed them and then freed them (as we have seen in a previous chapter). We have also mentioned the story of Veerabadrappa, who was born as a snake and Basappa as a frog and were saved by Baba from carrying on their enmity from an earlier birth.

Baba was very human at times and lapsed into sentimental tears. This happened when a favourite devotee of his, Megha, died in 1912. Recalling the occasion Khaparde says: "Baba did not show his face clear and did not appear to open his eyes. He never threw glances spreading grace. Baba came just as Megha's body was being brought out and loudly lamented his death. His voice was so touching that it brought tears in everyone's eyes. Baba followed the body upto the bend in the main road near the village and then went his usual way. Megha's body was confined to flames under the banyan tree and Baba could be distinctly heard crying even at that distance. He was seen waving his hand and swaying as if he was saying good-bye to the departed soul."

There were controversies over whether Baba was a Vaishnavite or a Shavaite. This started because some of his devotees put on the vibhuti on his forehead and the Vaishnavaites asked why Baba did not have the namam. To all of them Baba replied: "What am I to do? This worshipper believes that I am his guru and puts on me marks which he put on his guru." The truth was that Baba was neither a Vaishnavite nor a Shavaite either in his views or in his external observances although he took interest in all these groups. He did not belong to any of them but submitted to the wishes of his devotees in order not to offend them. Left to himself he would not have any marks on his forehead. He did not believe there was a separate Shiva and a separate Vishnu. To him there was only one God who might be called Shiva or Vishnu or Vithal or Rama or Allah or Hari. He believed God had to be approached with love from the heart while the external marks and observances or names might vary.

Another objection that was raised had to do with the worship of Baba. It was said that Baba had no right to allow his worship by Hindus or by anybody else. A Christian missionary said: "This worship shows that he puts himself on a level with God and this is a mortal sin." The orthodox Hindus raised the same objection. They said by allowing himself to be worshipped Baba had ceased to be respected. The answer to these critics is that gurus like Baba agree to be worshipped to carry out the divine plan that the vast masses of people should approach God through a guru or god-man and derive therefrom all the benefits which they wish to attain—temporal and spiritual. Baba did not object to the ceremonies and rituals followed by Hindus, especially after death. He, in fact, believed that certain benefits could be derived by the recently departed soul by the observance of these ceremonies. He had the remarkable power of guiding and directing the departing souls at the moment of death and thereafter. Baba said: "If a devotee should die even a thousand miles away I draw the spirit to myself and see that it is helped." In course of time opposition from the orthodox Hindus to Sai worship became less and less with a number of them in eminent positions joining the Sai movement and treating Baba as their great divine guru.

His devotees swear Baba is God and why not? Baba, although a human being, had all the attributes of God. He was omniscient, he was aware of everything that happened anywhere and everywhere including what passed through the minds of human beings and creatures. He would read the past and future of his devotees. He was omnipresent. He was simultaneously present in a number of places to the utter surprise and delight of his devotees and this has been vouched for by devotees who saw him in Bombay at the puja room of a devotee and in Shirdi. Baba had said often that he was not confined to his body at Shirdi but was everywhere and in everything. He controlled the elements and he shaped events to happen differently from what they would have in the normal course. He read men's thoughts hundreds and thousands of miles away and no one who came to Dwaraka Mayi could have thoughts without Baba being aware of them the moment they originate. He proved his oneness with all Gods and saints. And more than anything else his love and compassion for all creations of God were so deep and all embracing that only God could shower them in such abundance. What devotees prayed to the deities they worshipped in their homes or in temples they received by the mere glance of this living God who assured them protection and security, fulfilled all their desires and made them happy. Is it then any wonder that they came to believe that he was God walking on earth? It did not matter to them that he appeared to belong to another religion (and he was supremely indifferent and did not think it necessary to reveal his true self to them) but he was God all the same to them and some called him "Muslim Vishnu". Everything about him was mysterious and his thoughts and ways were unfathomable and inscrutable, the true marks of

God. It was not only the illiterate and simple folk of Shirdi and the neighbourhood who worshipped him as God but intellectuals and men and women with power and influence and in high positions of life who accepted him as a divine being who for them was God. One of them in fact said : "In Baba I found my conception of God."

Das Ganu Maharaj described Baba's family thus : courage was his father, pity his sister, discrimination and judgement his brothers. The earth was his cot. Gangaji, a sadhu, once met Baba who told him : "If we want to give people heavenly nectar they beg us to give them poison. Faith in or esteem for truth is gone. Untruth is hailed, cheered and esteemed." Gangaji said his experience was more or less the same. "I tried converting a few to good faith but was in turn deceived. So it is that I have now given up all attempts in this direction."

A sadhu living on the banks of the Godavari near Rajahmundry, whose name was Vasudevananda, once gave to a devotee who said he was going to Shirdi for darshan of Sai Baba a coconut to be presented to Baba with his greetings. However, on the way the devotee and his friends made use of the coconut, while preparing a meal. And whey they reached Shirdi and had darshan of Baba he asked them : "Fetch my coconut where is it ? Give it to me immediately. I am anxious to receive my brother's coconut." Baba knew what the devotee and his friends had done with the coconut and said : "My property which you held in trust for me was lost by reason of the evil company you had." The devotee admitted his guilt and said he would get another coconut. Baba stopped him and said : "That (another coconut) has not the same value or merit as the one given by Vasudeva. Well water cannot stand comparison with Godavari water. Well, what has happened has happened. You are my children. So there is no reason for getting angry."

Narasimha Swamiji says Baba was the living emblem of Hindu-Muslim unity. His life and teachings were the strongest and most forcible expression of the underlying unity of all communities and creeds in India. Till the last breath of his life no one could be quite sure whether Baba was a Hindu or Muslim by birth or breeding. He professed no religion. There were elements of both Hinduism and Islam so closely intermixed in him that a conclusion was not easy. People nevertheless drew their conclusions and Baba laughed at them. At one stage in his life in a fit of anger he threw away his clothes and standing naked called out : "You worthless fellows, try and find out whether I am a Hindu or Muslim." His intimate devotee Chandorkar, thought Baba was not circumcised but some others thought he was. Having been brought up by a Muslim fakir, Narasimha Swamiji says, the probability is that Baba was circumcised. But whether he was circumcised or not was irrelevant to Baba and an insignificant matter. Similarly, some devotees noticed that Baba had his ears bored, an indication that he was a Hindu. Till the end of his life Baba did not care to give any information about his birth and early life. Narasimha Swamiji says Baba had perfect and clear consciousness of himself, not the body but as the spirit, merely using the body for certain purposes. Baba said :"Main (I am) Allah hum. I am Lakshminarayan." He said this to impress particular devotees that he was the divine spirit in the particular forms they recognised as God. The doctrine of love pervaded the atmosphere in the mosque or Dwaraka Mayi. It was a doctrine which could unite not only all religions but all groups. Baba was the creator of inter-communal unity and he was its emblem, says Narasimha Swamiji.

Baba's effort was to unite Hindus and Muslims into one community with a common religion, spiritual and worldly interest. In order to guide his Muslim followers initiation into Islamic scriptures by a maulana became essential. So he accepted a second guru besides Gopal Rao Deshmukh. He was Jawar Ali Maulana who came to Shirdi and found Baba being worshipped by Hindus at the mosque. He asked Baba if he knew the *Quran* and the *Shariat*. Baba had learned neither. The maulana took him to his village where Baba stayed with him for two months and was initiated into the mysteries of Islamic spiritual literature. He underwent all the discipline and work of a disciple, like doing hard physical work for the guru. The people of Shirdi, not being able to bear the separation of Baba, went in deputation led by Mahlsapathy to the Maulana and appealed to him to release Baba. The Maulana agreed to release Baba on condition that the maulana was also allowed to go with Baba to Shirdi. This was agreed to and the Maulana stayed with Baba in the mosque for some days. But he left the mosque after sometime following a quarrel with a devotee who got the better of him in an argument.

Baba realised the difficulties in bringing the Hindus and Muslims together. The only factor that could bring them together was a saintly personality acting as a God or guru, absolutely neutral, allowing all sects, religions and creeds to have their own ways yet bringing them all under one platform, namely, devotion to that saintly personality and enabling them to see that the differences were petty and ridiculous—unworthy of serious men of jnana or realisation. Baba was that saintly personality. Hindus, Muslims, Christians and others who came to know about him felt they were before a higher influence and they could all approach him and realise God through him. They willingly made him their guru and protector.

By allowing his worship to be done at the mosque by people of various faiths Baba built up by a slow process a united community engaged in common worship. Sai devotion came to mean tolerance to all faiths and the acceptance of the basic principles found in all religions. Baba once said that in a former birth he was Kabir who brought under his leadership Hindus and Muslims. They were called Kabir Panthis. Baba allowed Hindus to treat him as an avatar or an ishta devata or guru as they liked. He permitted Muslims approaching him to read the *Quran* and *Shariat,* treating him merely as an avalia or saint with remarkable powers. All alike felt that Baba was the soul of love and purity and a storehouse of superhuman powers and superhuman enlightenment. The Muslims did not interfere with the day-long rituals of Hindu worship and the Hindus did not interfere when on Idga day Muslims held their prayers in the mosque. During the day Hindu Puranas and scriptures were read while at night the *Quran* or *Shariat* was read. Though Baba did not perform *namaz* he encouraged Muslims to do so five times daily as required by their religion at the mosque. He showed his displeasure and was angry if there was any religious intolerance.

Baba's message was : "Love one another, even as I love you all." Through his message of love and tolerance he preserved communal amity in Shirdi. While there were communal riots in other places during Hindu or Muslim festivals there was absolute peace in Shirdi. There was no book or fixed doctrine to which he wanted all to subscribe and no specific observance was forced on anyone. The majority of his devotees were Hindus and they worshipped him at the mosque with rituals based on those followed at Pandarpur. Everyone of them saw in Baba the very form of the deity he wanted to worship. A South African devotee's personal deity was Rama and he hesitated to bow to Baba when he came to the mosque. He thought Baba was a Muslim and he remained outside the mosque. But a few minutes later he rushed into the mosque and fell at Baba's feet. He said: "I saw that Baba's form was really the wonderful form of Sri Rama. As I found my Rama in Baba I worshipped him." A police official who venerated Hanuman said that Baba appeared to his eyes exactly like Hanuman. Another devotee who worshipped Dattatreya similarly saw his ishta devatha in Baba. Baba exercised this remarkable power to induce faith in persons who came to him.

In the daily noon arati at Shirdi it is said in the prayer : "In principle there is no difference between Hindus and Muslims. To show this you (God) came into the world with a human body. You look upon both Hindus and Muslims with equal affection. This Sai shows himself all pervading as atman or soul of all."

Baba's objective was to remove hatred and spread mutual love between religions and groups. He wanted to bring Hindus and Muslims together by showing them that they were all working under one common loving father and that their differences were immaterial and not deserving of being given importance. His main work was that of a samartha satguru who had to diffuse religion and help the good and remove the evil that oppressed the good.

Baba had very few Muslim devotees as compared to Hindus. The Muslims who came to him were lured by the monetary benefits they got from him and by his supernatural powers. They were not motivated to learn from his spiritual teachings. From the very beginning, as we have noted, Baba's aim was to bring the two communities together and remove their mutual suspicions and distrust and enable them to work together for the common good. According to Baba's own statement he had a Hindu birth and this was confirmed by his bored ears. No Muslim child has his ears bored. The fakir who adopted Baba lived in a place near Patri, where Baba was born. The fakir must have been of a highly pious disposition and full of vairagya.

These qualities must have been imbibed by Baba in his infancy and he must have learnt to look upon the fakir as his guru God. Baba used the word fakir to denote God or guru God who was constantly watching him and guiding him. Narasimha Swamiji surmises that the fakir must have been a Sufi. Sufis frequently go into a trance and in that condition use the words "Anal Haq" to express their state of mind. "Anal Haq" was occasionally used by Baba but this has been denied by some devotees. Baba while referring to God or guru used with equal facility the word Allah, fakir or Hari. He called nama japa as Allahsmaran or Hari nama smaran.

Baba once said Hari descended from Vishnu Sahasranama (thousand names of God) which he placed upon his chest and that thereafter he got relief. He told Dixit that he went on saying, Hari, Hari, and Hari appeared before him. Thereafter he stopped giving medicines to the sick who came to him and gave only udhi. For Baba, Hari and Allah were the same. Narasimha Swamiji says that when Baba left his guru Venkusa and settled down in Shirdi he had reached a condition in which the fusion of Allah and Hari was perfect. He appeared to be a Muslim fakir but Hindus supported him and Hindu sadhus appreciated him. Baba's appearance as a Muslim in dress or in language (Hindustani or Urdu) he used or his references to Allah did not prevent the Hindus from worshipping him as their God or guru. The Muslims, as we have already seen, regarded him as an avalia, a person with numerous siddhis, and as one who devoted himself to the service of God and humanity. Along with Ramanavami celebrations the Muslim ceremony of Sandal also went on in the mosque. The Muslims applied sandal paste with their palms to various objects. On this occasion a procession was taken out in honour of great Muslim saints. Sandal paste and scrapings were put in flat dishes and with incense burning were carried in the procession to the accompaniment of music through the streets of Shirdi. After returning from the village the contents of the dishes were thrown over the walls of the mosque. One day on Sri Ramanavami day the Hindu and the Muslim processions coincided and were taken side by side and thereafter this practice continued without any hitch.

Hindu devotees poured in hundreds and thousands at the mosque which Baba called a "Brahmin mosque" and also named it as Dwarakamayi. Narasimha Swamiji says the Muslims' attitude to Baba could never reach the level of devotion of Hindu devotees. A good number of Muslims gathered round Baba because of the money he distributed and the supernatural powers he displayed but he could not find a single person among them who got into spiritual contact with him. But there was a devoted Muslim attendant of Baba, Abdul, who served him till the end and who continued to live in Shirdi even after Baba's samadhi. Abdul was attached to Baba for 30 years and continued to be his devotee for 36 years after Baba's death. Abdul passed away in 1954. He was a native of Nanded on the banks of the Tapti in Gujarat. He had been under the care of a fakir, Amiruddin. Baba asked the fakir to send Abdul to him. Abdul came to serve Baba at the age of 20. Baba welcomed him to Shirdi with these words: "My crow has come." Abdul was entirely in Baba's service. He fed the perpetually burning oil lamps at the mosque and the chavadi with oil. Like Baba he also sought alms in the village. He lived in a stable near the mosque. He read the *Quran* sitting near Baba in the mosque. Baba occasionally opened the pages of the book and asked him to read particular passages. He even quoted some passages from the *Quran*. Abdul kept a notebook in which he recorded Baba's utterances. The notebook was Abdul's *Quran*. He did all the menial work in the mosque, even scavenging. Abdul has written: "Baba's blessings to me were strange and sometimes concealed in abuse and violence. He has beaten me and Jog (another attendant) many times. By Baba's blessings I have full faith in what he has said, guiding me and everyone else aright." When Baba passed away Abdul was the only Muslim in the establishment and his work was to decorate Baba's samadhi and receive the first prasad for his sustenance. He got the gift of prophecy by Baba's grace. About this Abdul wrote in his notebook: "When anyone wishes to know about the future or other unseen or unknown matter he comes to me and states the problem. Then I reverently consult this book of Baba's utterances and the answer that comes out of the page that is opened will be the correct answer. This has been tried and proved many times. This gift of prophecy is due to Baba's grace."

Narasimha Swamiji examined Abdul's notebook which was in Marathi. In it there were prayers to Maruthi by Baba. There were recitals of avatars of Gods devotailing Prophet Mohammed with the ten avatars of Vishnu. Abdul, like Baba, revered Maruthi and prayed to the avatars of Vishnu. He gave udhi to Baba's devotees and helped them to achieve their desires. Baba used to advice Abdul: "Eat very little. Do not go in for a variety of eatables. One sort of dish will suffice. Do not sleep much." Abdul's notebook threw a hint that Baba treated himself as one of the avatars. It was also stated there that Baba prophesied that the British empire in India would have only nine rulers. In 1947 when the ninth British monarch was ruling India the country became independent.

From Abdul's unpublished works it is clear that Baba had a profound knowledge of Islam. Just as he was able to explain and comment on Hindu scriptures he was equally at ease with Muslim religious tenets and traditions. He was a unique blend of all faiths.

Mrs Kashibai Kanikar, a scholar of Pune, who wrote in *Sai Leela* of her experiences said: "On hearing of Baba's miracles we were discussing according to our theosophic convention and fashion whether Sai Baba belonged to white or black lodge. When once I went to Shirdi I was thinking seriously about this in my mind. As soon as I approached the steps of the masjid Baba came to the front and pointing to his chest and staring at me spoke rather vehemently: "This is a Brahmin, poor Brahmin. He has nothing to do with black things. No Mussalman dare step here. He dare not." Again pointing to his breast he said: 'This Brahmin can bring lakhs of men on the white path and take them to their destination. This is a Brahmin's masjid and I won't allow any black Mussalman to cast his shadow here.'"

According to one biographer, a few hours before he breathed his last, Baba told Tatya Patil that Brahmins alone would take care of his tomb. Prof. Narke, an ardent devotee of Baba, has written that Baba once told him his guru was a Brahmin. It is obvious that the Brahmin guru would not have adopted Baba as a disciple if he was a Muslim by birth. Baba was a vegetarian like his Hindu followers. He wished to convince his devotee, if he was a Hindu, that he was Vishnu, Lakshminarayan, Vithal and he made sacred water flow from his feet as Ganga flowed from Shiva's head. So great was the prejudice of ages that a devotee who thought he was Vishnu chose to call him "Muslim Vishnu". There were differences (sometimes poles apart) between the various notions which people had about Baba and this made it difficult to present the real Baba as distinguished from the popular distortions of him. His devotees and strangers alike said he could not be understood and nobody could know the secrets of Sai Baba.

Sai Baba remained mostly in the possession of Hindus and it is the Hindus who are managing Sai Sansthan at Shirdi. The books and journals about Baba are all written by Hindus.

Here is an assessment of Sai Baba by Radhakrishna Swamiji: "Sai Baba is a rare phenomenon and his service to humanity if judged calmly would be found great enough to require a special corner for him in our pantheon. Baba was a superman, a guru or God himself for Sai devotees. He was a man of complete effacement, master of the highest renunciation, possessed of supreme wisdom and the very incarnation of love and motherly compassion. He is an avataric saint who, even while he dropped his mortal coil 44 years ago (this was written in 1962), lives today in the hearts of his devotees to remind them and the world at large of his divine message of tolerance, truth and absolute surrender to the supreme will of the Lord. To a world plagued by personal, group, national and international rivalries and by bigoted fanaticism no message can have more vital meaning than this message of mutual forbearance and understanding. Baba is unique among the great saints of India. He did not remain aloof as a lofty yogi in his ivory tower, nor did he remain lost in ecstasy. He was not an impersonal man but one who was most approachable and one who showed his sympathy for all men. He exhibited powers not easily discovered in men. He commanded the elements, discarnated spirits and brute creations, nay, controlled the minds of thousands of men and women near or remote. The thoughts of men could never be hidden from him and he exercised this remarkable power only for the benefit of humanity."

9

"WHY FEAR WHILE I AM HERE?"

"**W**HY fear while I am here," Sai Baba told hundreds of thousands of his devotees all over India while alive and after his mahasamadhi. His words of wisdom and advice extended to every aspect of day to day life and its problems. He often spoke in parables and they had deep meanings and significance which were not lost on his devotees. This chapter is exclusively devoted to his sayings and parables. We begin with Baba's selected sayings.

Dwaraka Mayi wards off all dangers and anxieties from her children. Highly merciful is this Masjit Ayi. She is the mother of those who place their entire faith in her. If they are in danger she will save them. Once a person climbs into her lap all his travails will be over. He who sleeps in her shade attains bliss.

As soon as one climbs the steps of Dwaraka Mayi sufferings due to karma are at an end and joy begins. That Fakir (God) is very kind and will relieve your troubles.

My eye of vigilance and supervision is ever on those who love me.

Whatever you do, wherever you may be ever, bear this in mind — that I am always aware of everything you do.

If one ever meditates on me, repeats my name, sings my deeds and is thus transformed into me, one's karma is destroyed. I stay by his side always.

You should have truth always with you. Then I shall always be with you wherever you are and at all times.

If one ever dwells on me in his mind and will not even taste food before offering it to me I am his slave. So also if he hungers and thirsts after me and treats all else as unimportant.

Look to me and I will look to you.

Trust the Guru fully. That is the only sadhana. Guru is all the gods.

Simply say "Sai Sai" with heart overflowing. I care not for show of respect and forms. I rest in such devotees.

I am formless and everywhere.

If anyone casts his burden on me and thinks of me I look after all his concerns.

In this abode of my devotees there will be no dearth of food and clothing.

Why should anyone fear when I am here?

If a devotee is about to fall I stretch out my hands to support him. I will not let him fall.

I get angry with none. Will a mother get angry with her children? Will the ocean send back the waters to the several rivers? I love devotion. I am the slave of my devotees.

People come and say, Baba give. I tell them to take. No on takes.

My tomb will speak and move with those who make me their refuge.

As soon as a devotee calls me with love I will appear. I require no train to travel.

All that is seen is my form: ant, fly, prince, pauper. Sometimes I come as a dog, sometimes as a pig.

I look equally on all. Not a leaf moves except by my grace. I look at all with equal eyes.

God has agents everywhere; they have vast powers. I have very great powers.

I draw my devotee to me at the time of his death even though he may die a thousand miles away (from Shirdi).

Without God's permission nothing can be done by me.

I am the progenitor of God. Meditate on me as pure Ananda Nirakara but if you cannot do so meditate on this Sai body exactly as it is.

To know me constantly think "Who am I?" by *sravana* and *manana*. Who are we? What are we? Where are you? Where is all this world? Think and think. In reality you are not different from God.

Do not say of anyone that he is inimical. Who is whose enemy? Do not entertain ill-feeling towards anyone. All are one and the same.

I am you. You are me. There is no difference between you and me. That which constitutes me constitutes you.

Joy and sorrow are mere delusions. Mere appearance of worldly joy is not true happiness. Whenever any idea of joy or sorrow arises in your mind resist it. Do not give room to it. It is pure delusion.

Mukti (release) is true joy or happiness. Going through births and deaths is unhappiness. All joys and sorrows of samsara are unreal.

God is everywhere. There is no place from which He is absent.

Till the mind is conquered one is reborn. But among births human birth is most precious.

Worship God in form, in His images, to make the mind steady and concentrated. When an image is worshipped with deep devotion the mind attains concentration without which there is no steadiness of mind.

Live a moral life. Then you will be pure even at death. At the time of death have no desire at all. Concentrate on God, your Ishta Devata. If death comes when your mind merges in the Ishta Devata mukti is attained.

Every pot coming to me comes with its mouth downwards (that is, in an unreceptive fashion).

The times are degenerating. People mostly think ill and talk ill of others. But I do not retaliate, I do not care to listen to such talks. People become more and more sceptical, they are disposed to look more at the evil side of things.

One should not stay in any place where saints or one's guru are ill spoken of.

Ajnana is the seed of samsara. If the guru *kripa* paint is put on the eye the maya screen lifts and jnana survives. Jnana is not an effect. It is ever self-existent. On the other hand ajnana has a cause and an end. God is one, the devotee is another. This is the root of ignorance. Remove it. Jnana remains. Ignorance finds a snake in the rope. Remove the ignorance, then the rope is known for what it is.

A person who has not overcome lust cannot see God, that is, get God-realisation.

If anyone is angry with another he wounds me to the quick. If anyone abuses another I feel the pain. If anyone bravely endures the abuse I feel highly pleased.

Never accept gratis the labour (and property) of others. This should be the rule of your life. (Baba said this as he paid Rs. 2 to a man who brought him a ladder to get down from the top of a house.)

What God gives us is never exhausted. What man gives never lasts.

Love all creatures. Do not fight with any or retaliate or scandalise any. When anyone talks of you (against you) pass on unperturbed. His words cannot pierce your body. Others' acts will affect them alone, not you. It is only your own acts that will affect you.

Do not be idle. Work, utter God's name, read scriptures.

If anyone talks 10 words at us if we reply at all, let us reply with one word. Do not quarrel, retaliate or bandy words with anyone, giving tit for tat.

If you avoid rivalries and bickerings God will protect you.

Return not evil for evil. Return good for evil.

What you sow you reap. What you give you get.

Sat sangh, that is, moving with the good, is good. Dusangha, that is, moving with evil-minded people, is evil and should be avoided.

Enjoyment of marital pleasure is permissible. But be not, enslaved by it. Mukti is impossible to persons addicted to lust. Lust ruins mental balance, strength and firmness.

Death and life are manifestations of God's activity. You cannot separate the two. God permeates all. See with your inner eye. Then you will realise you are God and not different from Him. Like worn-out garment this body is cast away.

Gain and loss, birth and death are in the hands of God. Look after life just so long as it lasts. When death arrives do not be grieved. The wise ones do not grieve for death, the fools do.

The five pranas were lent for us till now. Now the lender claims back his own and they are returned. Air goes back to air, fire to fire. Every one of the five elements goes back to its place. The body is made up of earth. Therefore its return to earth is not a thing to bemoan.

So do not be jubilant over a birth. This is the process of creation. Be not be moved by it.

The earth bears seeds. Clouds drop their rain on them. The sun sends its rays and makes them sprout. Earth, clouds and sun keep on their sport and happy course in all directions. But they neither exult at the growth nor deplore the destruction of the sprout. You should be unaffected like these. If you are, whence can sorrow come to you? Mukti is the absence of sorrow.

Karma is the cause of joy and sorrow. Therefore put up with whatever comes to you. God is the all controller and the all protector. Think of Him always. He will look after you. Surrender completely to Him and you will see what He does.

What we do in our past lives we reap the fruit of it now. Why cry out now against fate?

All gods are one. There is no difference between a Hindu and a Muslim. Mosques and temples are the same.

I speak things here. Things take place there (in accordance with my words). This is all God's sport (lila).

God is, and there is nothing higher than Him. He is perfect, infinite and eternal. He is omnipresent, omnipotent and omniscient. He is the creator, sustainer and destroyer. Surrender voluntarily and totally to His will. Not a blade of grass moves without His will. Trust in Him and do the right. Let the inner light (enlightened conscience) guide all your actions.

Perform your duty conscientiously and with detachment regarding yourself, not as the doer but only as an instrument in His hands.

Surrender the fruit of action to Him so that action will not harm or bind you. Let your love and compassion flow to all creatures of God.

God is the Lord and Master. There is no other Truth. His ways are unique, inscrutable and mysterious. There is no one higher than God. How He will protect and sustain is known only to Him.

Herculean effort is necessary for the attainment of God. Who says He is out of reach? He is there in the tabernacle of our heart, nearer to us than the fingernail to the finger. Without unflinching faith and patience you will not see Him. One who has both these will undoubtedly see Him.

It needs insight to recognise God. His will will be done. He will show the way and all your heart's desires will be fulfilled.

One who has received His grace is silent but he who falls from His grace talks too much. His grace must be earned by merit.

All are equal in my eyes. Men of all sorts, good and bad, come to my durbar. I have to care for them equally.

He who lays his hand on a devotee of God will suffer for it.

Members in a family are bound to have differences, but do not quarrel.

One who means well will do well. Great is the reward of virtue. The vicious suffer.

It is rinanubanda (ties of previous birth) which brings human beings, birds and animals to each other. Therefore do not drive away anyone, even the meekest.

Be hospitable to anyone who comes to you. Give water to the thirsty, bread to the hungry, clothing to the naked and shelter to the homeless, and God will bless you.

Whatever you give me will come back to you redoubled.

Why are you anxious? I take all cares from you.

Sit quiet. I will do the needful. I will take you to the end.

My business is to give blessings.

I will not allow my devotee to be lost. I will account to God for all those that have been given to me.

We should be honest, upright and virtuous.

We must distinguish right from wrong.

We must each attend to our own duty.

Once I had heart palpitation and my life was in great danger. I put *Vishnu Sahasranama* over my chest. God descended from it into my body and the disease left me and I was safe.

Whatever you do, do it thoroughly, else do not undertake it.

Always take your meal before you start on a journey.

My name will speak. My dust will reply. I will never leave anyone in the middle.

I will not allow my men to get away from me.

Stick to your own guru with unabated faith, whatever the merits of other gurus and however little the merits of your own guru.

Do not borrow for celebrating a feast or festival, for a pilgrimage or any other journey.

God is afraid of evil and evil is afraid of God.

Money says : if you use me well I shall serve you well. Meal (food) says : cook me well and I shall serve you well.

A Yogi is always better than a *bhogi.*

He who, being a king, wears a beggar's robe is good.

The fruit of good is great; that of evil very little.

I have to go thousands of kas (about three miles) to protect thousands of people. Once the strings are entrusted to the satguru there is no cause for grief.

There is a low, born one (Mahar) in the body. He should be evicted.

There shall be no want in the house of my devotee.

Do not deceive or do harm to people at any time.

Give alms and charity to the extent of your power.

Fortune disappears like one's shadow at midday.

Do not tease and oppress people in your arrogance of wealth without any cause.

To carry on worldly life we require means (wealth). Just as biles is necessary for the body so is wealth necessary for carrying on affairs in this world. Though wealth is necessary do not get entangled in wealth alone (that is, do not get over absorbed in it.). Never be miserly, be liberal. But excess of munificence will not do. If all wealth is exhausted none thereafter will care for you. The union of munificence or generosity with extravagance will be a great misfortune.

If one has power or authority that should not be abused. When seated in the judicial chair no bribes should be accepted.

Whatever is your appointed duty do that as well as you can with great care.

As long as life continues protect it. When death has occurred do not indulge in vain sorrow and lamentation.

Associate with the good. Be in their group. Let not the shadow of the evil, the wicked and callous men bereft of faith fall upon you.

Do not taste proscribed ˙ood.

Do not indulge in senseless disputations. Speak no falsehood at any time.

While the body is strong (and produces lust) let your pleasure be with your own wife. Do not let the mind be tainted with lust at the sight of other women.

If desire you must have the desire for liberation. If you must be passionate be passionate in the love of God Listening to accounts of saints will make the heart pure. Parents must be respected. The mother is equal to 1,000 *Thirtas.* The father is a God to be worshipped. So prostrate before him. Love your brothers. Do not abandon your sisters if you have power to help them.

Do not cut jokes with your children or get into the habit of exchanging witty sallies, for that is the privilege of friends, not parents.

Do not make yourself cheap or become familiar with your servants.

Do not sell your daughter (in marriage). Let not an old man's wealth or land induce you to bestow your daughter on him. The bridegroom has to be handsome and qualified as will befit your daughter.

The husband is God, the Pandarinath of the wife. Let her have pure love and faith in the husband and rejoice. When the husband is angry she ought to be submissive and humble. She should help him in his affairs. Such a woman is blessed and is a *grihalakshmi,* the goddess of the home.

A woman should so conduct herself that she becomes a model for others to copy. She must never go against her husband's wishes even in matters of vow and penance she may undertake.

The mind is naturally fickle but do not permit it to be impetuous. Even if the senses are agitated the body should be restrained.

The senses are untrustworthy; so do not hanker after desires. By constant practice (and dispassion) fickle-mindedness will disappear.

Baba loved to speak in parables which were intended to convey spiritual messages and also the foibles and follies of men. Here are some from the hundreds which have been recorded.

There was a traveller who was accosted in the morning by a demon. The traveller looked upon it as a bad omen but on proceeding further be saw two wells, the sweet water of which slacked his thirst. When he felt hungry he met a farmer who, on the suggestion of his wife, supplied him with food. He saw a field ripe with corn and wished to have *harda.* The owner of the field gave it to him. So the traveller felt happy and proceeded, merrily smoking. In the forest through which he was passing he saw a tiger,lost courage and hid himself in a cave. The tiger was very big and came near him. Baba who happened to pass that way instilled courage in him, got him out and put him on his way saying: "the tiger would not hurt you unless you hurt him in some way."

(The meaning of the parable is : individual self, ego or jiva is the treavaller, agnana — conscience — is the demon. Thirst for perfection is his hunger. Spiritual teaching is the food he got. The two wells stand for viveka or right discrimination and vairagya or dispassion. Harda stands for devotional surrender. The mysterious depths of consciousness of a sadaka or a seeker is the forest. The tiger stands for the dangers that confront a seeker, the mystical powers which drive him off the true path to perfection. A satguru can restore him to the true path to spiritual perfection).

Baba had four brothers one of whom would go out, beg and bring cooked food, bread and corn. His wife used to give out just enough for their mother and father but starved all the brothers. Baba then got a contract, brought the money home and everyone was supplied with food including the well-to-do brother. Later that brother got leprosy. Everyone shunned him. The father turned him out. Baba used to feed him and to see to his comforts. Ultimately the brother died.

(Meaning : The parable teaches us that irrespective of the attitude of others to him a seeker should remember that his relations with others as a result of karma, links of the past continue and he should be loving and considerate to them.)

Baba said he used to sit in a corner and desired to exchange the lower part of his body with that of a parrot. The exchange came and he did not realise for a year that he had lost a lakh of rupees. Then he began to sit near a post and then a great serpent woke up and was very angry. It used to jump and fall down.

(Meaning: parrot is a bird characterised by excess of lust in popular belief. Baba exchanging the lower portion of his body with that of the parrot indicates that Baba had succumbed to the demands of the flesh. The lakh of rupees he lost indicates he had lost all the spiritual powers he had accumulated by earlier sadhanas. The pillar or post stands for the spine and sitting near it symbolises meditation on the base of the spine or *muladhara.* The jumping snake is the awakened *kundalini* or the serpent power.)

Baba said he visited a place and the patil there would not let him go unless he made a plantation and hard footpath through it. He said he completed both.

(Meaning : God is the landlord or the patil. Raising the plantation signifies the establishment of a spiritual centre. The footpath stands for the spiritual path which Baba had to lay for his devotees. The parable indicated that God had ordered Baba to play the role of a guru.)

A man has a very beautiful horse which, in spite of his best efforts, would not be yoked to a carriage. It was given the usual training but to no purpose. At last a learned man suggested it should be taken back to the original place where it was bought. This was done and the horse became all right in the harness and made itself useful.

(Meaning : The horse stands for mind which is difficult to harness and unite with a chosen subject of meditation. Taking it to its original place signifies investigating the source of mind when it naturally gets stilled.)

Baba said many people came to take his money. He did not resist but let them take it away. He only noted their names and followed them. When they stopped for their meals he killed them and brought his money back.

(Meaning : The parable describes the attentive watching of the mental processes which leads to quietening of the mind and regaining a calm meditation. One pointedness of mind, dispassion, control of senses, are the wealth. Desires born of various modes like rajas and tamas are the thieves.)

There was a blind man who lived in Shirdi. A man enticed his wife and murdered the blind man. Four hundred people assembled at the chavadi and condemned him. They ordered that he be executed. This order was carried out by the village hangman who did this out of some motive and not merely as a part of his duty. The murdered man was reborn as the son of the hangman.

Baba told a woman devotee : "The sky is cloudy. It will rain. The crops will grow and ripen. Then the clouds will disperse. Why are you afraid?"

(Meaning : The overclouded sky is her present state of gloom and ignorance. The rain is the hardship and discomfort that she will undergo but it is also the divine grace that will ripen the seeds of spirituality in her heart unknown to her during the dark night of the soul. The dispersal of the clouds is the attainment of light and bliss when the seed has ripened.)

10

BABA'S LILAS

B ABA helped his devotees in hundreds of ways to remove
anxiety, fears, ward off disease and misfortune and to
bring hope and cheer into their lives. He granted their prayers
readily and was ever at their beck and call to attend to their
needs and aspirations. All he asked from them in return was
absolute faith and surrender to him. We had a glimpse of the
service he rendered to his devotees in the previous chapters.
In this chapter we shall relate more experiences of devotees as
narrated in Hemadpant's *Sai Sat Charita* and from other sources.
These experiences relate to what happened during Baba's lifetime
and those which occurred after his samadhi. Some of these are
quite extraordinary and incredible but they cannot be doubted
since they come from the lips of the very people who experienced
them.

We have taken the following from *Sai Sat Charita*.

A devotee by name Bala Ganpat Shimpi suffered from a
malignant type of malaria. He tried all sorts of cures but without
effect. The fever did not abate a bit. He went to Shirdi and fell
at Baba's feet. Baba told him: "Give a black dog some morsels
of rice mixed with curds in front of the Lakshmi temple."
After Shimpi returned home he mixed rice and curds and brought
it to the Lakshmi temple in front of which he found a black dog
wagging its tail. He gave it the curd rice which it ate greedily.
The devotee was cured of his malaria.

Dattopant hailing from Harda (Madhya Pradesh) suffered
from severe stomach-ache for 14 years. He did not get any
relief from any of the remedies suggested to him. Then hearing
about Baba he came to Shirdi and sought Baba's help. Baba
looked at him kindly and placed his hand on his head. He then

gave him udhi with his blessings. The man felt relieved and his stomach-ache was gone.

Nana Chandorkar, an intimate devotee of Baba, suffered from stomach pain and could not be cured by doctors. Baba asked him to eat *burfi* (sweetmeat) mixed with ghee. The strange unconventional medicine gave complete relief to Chandorkar.

Harischandra Pitale of Bombay had a son who suffered from epilepsy. Attempts to cure him through allopathy and ayurvedic medicines proved futile. Pitale heard Das Ganu's kirtans about Baba in 1910 and went to Shirdi with his family. No sooner, Baba saw the boy than the boy fell down unconscious, foamed in the mouth and began to sweat. His parents thought his end was near and the mother began to sob. Baba consoled her and said: "Do not wail like this, wait a bit, have patience. Take the boy to your lodge, he will regain consciousness in half an hour." The parents took the boy to their lodge as directed and the boy regained consciousness as foretold by Baba. He fully recovered and the parents were very happy. They went to Baba and thanked him. Baba said: "Are not all your thoughts, doubts and apprehensions calmed down now ? Hari will protect him who has got faith and patience." When Pitale and his wife later went to Baba to take leave of him Baba said to Pitale: "Babu, I had given you before Rs. 2, now I give you Rs. 3. Keep this in your shrine for worship and you will be benefited". Pitale accepted the money but wondered what Baba meant when he said he had given him Rs. 2 previously since it was his first visit to Shirdi. Baba however did not enlighten him. When Pitale returned to Bombay he narrated the incident to his old mother who recalled that Pitale's father had taken him to a Hindu saint at Akkalkot for darshan many years ago when he was a child. The saint had given the father Rs. 2 for being kept in the shrine and worshipped. The father worshipped it till his death but thereafter the worship was neglected and everyone had forgotten about the sacred two rupees. Pitale's mother said: "The Akkalkotkar Maharaj has appeared to you in the form of Sai Baba just to remind you of your duties and to worship." Pitale now understood Baba's remarks and action.

Gopal Narayan Ambadekar of Pune was a devotee of Baba. He was in straitened circumstances and suffered other calamities for seven long years. He visited Shirdi every year and apprised Baba of his condition. In 1916 his plight became worse and he decided to commit suicide in Shirdi. He came to Shirdi with his wife and stayed there for two months. One night he decided to jump into a well near Dixit's *wada*. Nearby was a hotel and its owner, Sagun, also a devotee of Baba, came and talked to him, "Did you ever read Akkalkotkar Maharaj's life"? he asked him and gave him a book. On reading the book Ambadekar came across a story which told of a devotee who suffered from an incurable disease and in desperation threw himself into a well. Immediately the Maharaj came there, lifted him from the well and advised him: "You must enjoy the fruit—good or bad—of your past actions. If the enjoyment is incomplete suicide will not help you. You have to take another birth and suffer again. So instead of killing yourself why not suffer for sometime and finish the store of the fruit of your past deeds and be done with it once and for all?" Ambadekar was moved by the story and he took it as Baba's way of telling him not to take his life. He became a stauncher devotee of Baba.

A man working in a press in Bombay saw in a dream an old man with a beard standing and surrounded by his devotees. Some days later he went to the house of a friend to hear kirtans by Das Ganu. It was always the practice of Das Ganu to keep a picture of Baba before the audience. Lakshmichand, the man, recognised the picture as that of the old man he had seen in his dream and he decided to go to Shirdi for Baba's darshan. As he and a friend reached Kopargaon on the way to Shirdi he wanted to buy some good mangoes for offering to Baba but he was so immersed in the beauty of the scenery and sights that he forgot about his intention. He, however, remembered it as they were nearing Shirdi and just then an old woman stopped the cart in which they were travelling and offered mangoes which she carried in a basket on her head. The woman said: "Take all these mangoes and offer them to Baba on my behalf." Later Lakshmichand had darshan of Baba who said: "Cunning fellow! He does bhajan on the way and enquires from others. Why ask others? Just think for yourself whether the dream is true or not. Where was the necessity of darshan by taking a loan from a marwari? Is the heart's desire now satisfied?" Lakshmichand was struck with wonder. How did Baba know all that had happened before his visit to Shirdi? The point to be noted in this incident is that Baba never liked people to run into debt to seek his darshan or celebrate any festival or for a pilgrimage.

Lakshmichand had another experience of Baba's powers. One night he witnessed Baba going in procession to the chavadi. Baba had then a bout of cough and Lakshmichand thought this suffering of Baba might be due to somebody's evil eye. Next morning when he went to the mosque Baba said to Shama: "I suffered yesterday night from cough. Is it due to some evil eye? I think that somebody's evil eye had worked on me and so I am suffering." Baba was only relating Lakshmichand's unspoken thought.

A bhajan party from Madras on its way to Varanasi stopped at Shirdi having heard of Sai Baba and how he distributed money to needy persons. The party consisted of a man, his wife, daughter and sister-in-law. The party did good bhajan and sang well. All the members of the party except the wife inwardly craved for money. The wife had love and regard for Baba. As arati was being performed Baba was so pleased with her devotion and faith that he gave her darshan of her favourite deity, Rama, in his own person. To her Baba appeared as Rama while to others Baba remained as Baba. The woman was so much moved that tears trickled down her eyes and she clapped her hands in joy. The other members of her party could not understand the reason for her behaviour. Later she disclosed to her husband how she saw Rama in Baba. Her husband would not believe her and dismissed it as hallucination. One night the husband had a dream in which he was arrested in a big city and locked up in a police station. He saw Baba standing outside the police station and he asked him why this should happen to him. Baba said: "You must suffer the consequences of your action." The man said he had not done anything to invite this punishment on him. Baba said: "If not in this life you must have committed some sin in your previous life." The man said, assuming that he had committed a sin then why should it not be burnt and destroyed in Baba's presence? Baba asked :"Have you got such faith?" The man said: "Yes." Baba asked him to close his eyes. No sooner did he do so than he heard something falling down and opening his eyes found he was free and the policemen guarding him had fallen bleeding. As he became frightened Baba said: "Now you are well caught. Officers will now come and arrest you." The man begged Baba to save him and Baba again asked him to close his eyes. He did so and when he opened them again he was free and out of the lock-up. Baba was at his side and the man fell at his feet. Baba asked him :"Is there any difference between this namaskar and your previous ones?" The man said, "There is a lot of difference. My former namaskars were offered with the object of getting money from you but the present namaskar is offered to you as God." The man desired in his mind he should have darshan of his guru, Ramdas. Baba asked him to turn back and see. And when the man turned he saw Ramdas in front of him and he fell at his feet. Ramdas vanished. Then he woke up. Next morning when he went to the mosque Baba gave him two rupees as prasad and a packet of sweets and blessed him. He said: "Allah will give you plenty and He will do all of you good." The bhajan party thereafter earned plenty of money and their pilgrimage was successful. (Hemadpant says the story illustrates one of the methods followed by Baba—which is being followed even now—in some cases to improve and reform his devotees.)

The Tendulkar family of Bandra in Bombay were staunch devotees of Baba. Mrs Savithri Bai Tendulkar had published a book describing Baba's lilas. Her son Babu was studying hard for the medical examination but he was discouraged by astrologers who told him he would not be successful but should appear for the examination only in the following year. Babu was dejected and seeing his condition his mother went to Shirdi and sought Baba's help. Baba said : "Tell your son to believe in me and not get disappointed. Ask him to throw away the horoscope and predictions of astrologers and palmists and get on with his studies. Let him appear for the examination with a calm mind, he is sure to pass. Let him have trust in me." Babu was encouraged by Baba's message and continued his studies vigorously and appeared for the written examination in which he did well. But he was still worried he might not pass it and decided not to go for the oral examination. However the examiner sent word to him through a fellow student that he had indeed passed the written examination and should come for the oral examination. Babu did so and passed both examinations with credit and Baba's prediction came true.

Babu's father, Raghunathan, who was employed in a company, was getting old and in poor health. The management decided to retire him and give him a monthly pension of Rs. 75. His wife was worried that this might not be sufficient to run the household. Fifteen days before the final settlement Baba appeared in Mrs Tendulkar's dream and said: "I wish that Rs. 100 should be paid as pension, will this satisfy you?" The lady said: "Baba, why ask me this? We fully trust you." Though Baba specified Rs. 100 as pension Raghunathan actually got Rs.110 as pension as a special case.

Waman Narvekar once gave Baba a rupee coin. On one side of it was engraved the figures of Rama, Sita and Lakshman. On the other side there was the figure of Maruthi. With folded hands the devotee handed it over to Baba in the hope that he would bless it and return it to him. But Baba pocketed it. Shama who was nearby told Baba of the devotee's intention to worship the coin consecrated by Baba and requested it be returned to the devotee. Baba said: "Why should it be returned to him? We should keep it ourselves, if he gives Rs. 25 it would be returned to him." When this amount was placed before Baba he said: "The value of this rupee far exceeds that of Rs. 25. Let us have the rupee in our store." Baba told Shama: "Keep this in your shrine and worship it." No one had the courage to ask Baba why he did what he did.

Kakaji Vaidya, a temple priest of Vani in Nashik district of Maharashtra, was faced with adversity and calamities and lost his peace of mind. He prayed to the goddess of the temple to give him peace of mind and rid him of anxiety. The goddess appeared to him in a dream and told him :"You go to Sai Baba and then your mind will become calm and composed." Kakaji wanted to know who the Baba she mentioned was and before he could get a reply he woke up. He thought the Baba mentioned by the goddess might be the Tryambakeshwar (Shiva) and went to Tryambak and stayed there for 10 days worshipping the God there. However he remained restless and returned home and again prayed to the Goddess. The goddess again appearing in a dream chided him :"Why did you go to Tryambakeshwar in vain? I mean by Baba Sri Sai Samarth of Shirdi." As Kakaji was thinking of going to Shirdi a guest came to his house in the form of Shama, a very intimate devotee of Baba. Shama had come to Vani to fulfil a vow his mother had taken when he was ill as a child that she would bring him to the goddess at Vani and pray at her feet. Then after some years his mother fell ill and she took another vow that if she was cured she would offer the goddess two silver breasts. At her death-bed the mother reminded Shama of her vow. Shama forgot about the vow until he was reminded of them by an astrologer who had come to Shirdi. Shama had two silver breasts prepared and placed them before Baba. He requested him to accept them and free him of the vows as Baba was to him the goddess. Baba, however, insisted Shama should go to Vani and offer the breasts to the goddess in person. That was how Shama came to Vani and while searching for the temple landed at Kakaji's house. Kakaji was overjoyed to know Shama was an intimate devotee of Baba and after Shama fulfilled his vows before the goddess the two left for Shirdi. As soon as Kakaji prostrated before Baba at the mosque his mind became calm and peaceful. A mere darshan of Baba brought him mental peace and happiness and his heart was so full of joy that he could hardly speak a word. Baba gave him udhi and Kakaji returned home happy.

Narayan Motiram Jani of Nashik was a devotee of Baba. He served under another Baba devotee, Ramachandra Vaman Modak. Jani went to Shirdi with his mother. Baba told the mother her son should no longer work under anyone but start his own business. His prophecy came true some days later when Jani left his employer's service and started a boarding lodge which did well. Once a friend of Jani was stung by a scorpion and he was crying with pain. Jani knew that if he applied udhi in the affected part the pain would subside but he could not find udhi. His stock had been exhausted. Then he stood before Baba's picture and invoked his help. Taking a pinch of the ashes of the joss stick burning in front of the picture and viewing it as Baba's udhi he applied it on the painful spot of his friend's body and the pain vanished.

A sadhu of Bombay, Balabuva Sutar, came to Shirdi for the first time in 1917. When he bowed before Baba he said: "I know this man since four years." The sadhu wondered how that could be since that was his first trip to Shirdi. But later while thinking about Baba's remark he remembered that he had prostrated before Baba's portrait four years previously. He thought: "I merely bowed before his photo but this act of mine has been noticed by Baba and he has made me realise that seeing his photo is the same thing as seeing him in person."

In a similar instance Appasaheb Kulkarni of Bombay worshipped a portrait of Baba presented to him by Babasaheb Bhate. He performed puja and offered naivedya to the picture daily and longed to see him in person. One day while he was on a tour a fakir came to his house. His features resembled those of Baba in the picture and Mrs Kulkarni and her children asked him if he was Sai Baba. The fakir replied: "No," but added that he was an obedient servant of Baba and had come there on his instructions to enquire about the welfare of the family. Then he asked for dakshina. The lady gave him a rupee. He gave her a small packet and asked her to keep it in the puja room along with the picture of Baba. Then he left. When Kulkarni returned and heard from his wife about the fakir's visit he cursed himself for not seeing the fakir. He thought the dakshina of one rupee given to him was too low. Had he been present he would have given him Rs. 10. He searched in vain for the fakir. When he went for a walk after taking food he met a man who he thought was the fakir. When he accosted the man he put out his hand and asked for dakshina. Kulkarni gave him a rupee. He demanded again and again and got nine rupees from Kulkarni. The fakir was still unsatisfied and demanded again. Then Kulkarni gave him a 10-rupee note which the fakir took and returned the nine rupees he had earlier received. Kulkarni then realised that Baba had taken from him what he had promised to give him. Kulkarni took the nine rupees sanctified by Baba's fingers and placed them in his shrine for worship.

In 1917, Haribhau Karnik of Dahanu (Thane district) came to Shirdi on Guru Poornima day and worshipped Baba. He offered clothes and dakshina and after taking leave of Baba through Shama came down the steps of the mosque. Then he thought he should offer one more rupee to Baba and was about to turn and climb back when Shama signalled to him he should not return since he had received permission from Baba to leave. On his way back home Karnik went to the temple of Kala Rama in Nashik for darshan. Narsing Maharaj, in the garb of a sadhu, came to him and said: "Give me one rupee." Karnik was surprised but paid the money most willingly. He thought that Baba had recovered the rupee which he had wanted to give him through the sadhu.

An old gentleman of Horda (Madhya Pradesh) was suffering from a stone in his kidney. His friends recommended surgery to remove the stone. But he was too old and weak and lacked the strength of mind to undergo surgery. The *inamadar* (city official) of the town where he lived happened to visit the old man. He was a devotee of Baba and always had a stock of Baba's udhi with him. He mixed the udhi with water and gave it to the patient. Within five minutes the udhi was assimilated, the stone was dissolved and came out with his urine. The old man heaved a sigh of relief.

Baba's udhi also cured the daughter of an Irani gentleman who suffered from epilepsy. When the convulsions came she lost her power of speech, her limbs became paralysed and she fell down unconscious. Her father got Baba's udhi from Kaka Dixit and gave it to his daughter mixed with water daily. In the beginning the convulsions which were occurring hourly began to slow down to once in seven hours and after a few days stopped completely.

Here is yet another instance of the power of Baba's udhi. A man belonging to Bandra (Bombay) suffered from insomnia. When he did sleep his diseased father appeared in the dream, abused and spoke ill of him and tortured his mind. He consulted a devotee of Baba who gave him Baba's udhi and asked him to apply it on his forehead before going to bed and keep the udhi packet under his pillow. To his great joy and relief the man got sound sleep and there was no disturbance of any kind.

Balaji Patil Newasker was a great devotee of Baba. Every day he swept and kept clean the streets of Shirdi through which Baba passed. Once on the anniversary of his death a feast was arranged and the guests who came in hordes were more than those expected, by three times. Mrs Newaskar was worried. She thought the food prepared would be insufficient to feed them all. Her mother-in-law comforted her saying: "Don't worry. It is not ours but Sai's food. Cover every vessel with a cloth containing udhi. Serve from the vessel without opening the cloth. Sai will save us from ignominy." The woman did as she was advised and she found to her great surprise and joy that not only was the food sufficient to feed all the guests but plenty of it remained after use. Hemadpant's comment is: "As one feels Sai intensely so he realises accordingly."

There was a ceremony at the house of B. V. Deo, a village official of Dahanu which included feeding of 100 or 200 Brahmins. He requested Baba through a letter to attend the ceremony. Baba asked Jog to reply that three of them, himself, Jog and another, would attend the function. A few days before the ceremony a sadhu met Deo and said he was opening a

subscription list for the cause of protection of cows. Deo told
him it was not the time for a subscription list as one had already
been opened in the village for another cause. He asked the
sadhu to visit the place after two or three months. A month
later at the time of the ceremony the sadhu came to Deo's house
in a tonga. Deo thought he had come for subscription. The
sadhu divining his mind told him he had not come for money
but for meals. Deo welcomed him and said the house was his.
The sadhu said he would come with two others and Deo said
they were welcome too. Two hours later the sadhu came with
two others and took part in the feast and went away. After the
ceremony Deo wrote a letter to Jog regretting Baba's absence at
the function and complaining of breach of promise. Before Jog
opened the letter Baba said: "Ah! He says that I promised to
come but deceived him. Inform him that I did attend the dinner
with two others but he failed to recognise me. Then why did
he call me at all? To keep my words I would sacrifice my life.
I would never be untrue to my words." When Deo got Jog's
reply conveying Baba's remarks he blamed himself for being
misled by the sadhu's first appearance for subscription and for
missing the significance of the sadhu's words when he said he
would come for the dinner with two others.

In 1917 Baba appeared in a dream to Hemadpant and said
he would come to his house for meals that day. Hemadpant
was delighted and told his wife to prepare food for an extra
guest. As the family was preparing to sit for dinner with a
special seat reserved for Baba no one turned up. Disappointed,
as they were about to commence eating there was a knock at the
door and Hemadpant found two Muslims waiting to see him.
One of them gave him a packet which he opened. He found a
beautiful picture of Baba. He placed the picture of Baba
reverently in the seat reserved for him at dinner and offered
naivedya to him. This was how Baba fulfilled his promise to
Hemadpant in the dream.

How did the picture of Baba come into the hands of the
Muslim, Ali Mohammed? This is the story behind it. While
wandering in the streets of Bombay one day Ali saw a hawker
selling a picture of Baba, bought it, framed it and hung it on the
wall in his house. As he fell ill and underwent an operation he
moved to a relative's house where he stayed for many months.
His house in Bandra was closed and the pictures of Muslim

saints and also that of Baba were damaged for lack of care. Later one of the Muslim saints who did not like image worship threw away a picture of a Muslim saint offered to him. He asked Ali to throw away all pictures into the sea and was told his sufferings would then end. Ali sent his agent to the house and had all the pictures removed and thrown into the sea. When Ali returned home he found to his great surprise that Baba's picture was still there as he had left it before he went to his relative's place. Fearing his relatives' disapproval he thought of a way of disposing it and decided it should be given to Hemadpant who would take good care of it. And this was how Baba's portrait came to Hemadpant at a very appropriate time.

This is the story of Baba accusing a devotee of "stealing rags"when what he meant was entirely different. B. V. Deo, Mamaladar of Dahana, had a desire to read *Jnaneshwari,* a well known Marathi commentary on the *Bhagavad Gita* by Jananeshwar. However he was not able to make headway in reading the book. Try as he might he was not able to read a few lines without being distracted by evil thoughts. He thought Baba would set matters right and went to Shirdi. Jog to whom he related his problem advised him to present the book to Baba and take it back after it was blessed by him. Deo met Baba and offered him one rupee as dakshina. Baba asked for Rs.20 which was given. In the night Deo met another devotee, Balaram and asked him how he secured Baba's grace. Balaram said he would tell him after arati the next day. When Deo went for Baba's darshan the next day he asked for Rs. 20 as dakshina which was given. Then after the noon arati Deo again met Balaram and asked about Baba's method of teaching and what Baba told him. When Balaram was about to reply Baba sent someone to call Deo. When Deo came Baba asked him with whom he was talking and what was it about. Deo said he had been talking to Balaram and heard from him about Baba's fame. Baba again asked for Rs. 25 as dakshina which Deo gladly gave. Then Baba took him aside and said: "You stole away my rags without my knowledge." Deo denied any knowledge of the rags but Baba asked him to make a search. Deo searched and found nothing. Baba got angry and said: "There is nobody here and you are the only thief. So gray haired and old you come here for stealing." Baba lost his temper and began abusing him. Deo was afraid he might be beaten also. After about an hour Baba asked him to return to his lodge. On returning to his lodge Deo told Jog and Balaram all that had happened. Baba sent for them in the afternoon and said his words might have pained the old man (Deo) but as he had committed the theft he could not but speak out. Baba again asked Deo for Rs.12 as dakshina. Deo collected the amount from those near him, paid it and prostrated at Baba's feet. Baba said: "Go on daily reading the pothi (*Jnaneshwari*). Go and sit in the wada, read something regularly every day and while reading explain the portion read to all with devotion and love. I am sitting here ready to give you the whole gold embroidered *shella* (valuable cloth), then why go to others and steal rags and why should you get into the habit of stealing?" Deo then realised what Baba meant by "stealing rags". What he asked Balan constituted "the rags" and Baba did not like his behaviour in this respect. As Baba was ready to answer any question he did not like Deo to ask others and make unnecessary enquiries. That was the reason why he had scolded Deo. However Deo took the scolding as flowers and blessings and went home satisfied and contented. Baba did not stop there. Within a year he went to Deo and enquired about his progress. One night in 1914 Deo had a dream in which Baba appeared and asked him if he understood the pothi. Deo said: "No. Unless you shower your grace I will not be able to understand". Baba said :"Read it before me, in my presence." Deo asked: "What shall I read?" Baba said: "Read Adyatma"(Spiritualism). Deo went back to bring the book and open the chapter indicated, but then he woke up. His joy knew no bounds.

Sapatnekar was a pleader practising in Akkalkot. In 1913 he lost his only son and sought solace by visiting holy places and shrines. But he had no peace of mind. Then he remembered what a law college student had told him about Baba while he was studying there and decided to go to Shirdi. He saw Baba from a distance in the mosque. When he went near and fell at his feet Baba asked him to get out. Sapatnekar left Shirdi with a heavy heart and much dejected. After a year his wife had a dream in which, as she was going to a well to fetch water, she saw a fakir sitting under a neem tree. He came to her and said: "Why get exhausted for nothing? I shall get you a pitcher filled with pure water." She got afraid and ran away with the empty pitcher with the fakir following her. Then she woke up. She told her husband of the dream and they decided to visit Shirdi. At

Shirdi the wife recognised Baba as the fakir of her dream and reverentially prostrated before him. Blessing her Baba said: "My arms, abdomen, and waist are paining for a long term. I took many medicines but the pain did not abate. I got sick of the medicines as they gave me no relief but I am surprised to see now that all the pains have disappeared." Though no name was mentioned Mrs Sapatnekar understood Baba had been relating her own troubles and she was now cured of her pains. But Sapatnekar was not so fortunate. Baba still asked him to get out but Sapatnekar fell at his feet and asked for pardon for all his past actions. Baba relented and placed his hand on his head and in his characteristic way began telling the story of Sapatnekar in his own way, how he lost his son and how he suffered. Baba said: "The fellow blames me and charges me with the killing of his son. Do I kill people's children? Why does this fellow come to the masjid and cry? Now I will do this. I will again bring that very child back in his wife's womb." He placed his hand again on Sapatnekar's head and said: "You are care free now. Place entire faith in me and you will soon get your object." In course of time the couple got a son as promised by Baba and they took the child to him and Baba blessed it.

Here is a story of a man who did not believe in Baba and wanted to test him. His name was Hari Kanoba. He wore a lace-bordered turban and had a new pair of sandals. He went to Shirdi and had darshan of Baba. When he started to leave the mosque and searched for his new sandals he found they had disappeared. He returned to his lodge disappointed and even when he offered puja and naivedya before his meals he could think only of his missing sandals. Then after finishing his meals he came with some others to the portico of the house. They saw a boy with a stick on which was tied up a pair of sandals. He was calling out the name of Hari Kanoba and giving a description of him and the name of his father and asking him to claim his sandals. Hari stopped the boy and told him he was the man he was looking for. The boy told him he had been sent by Baba to hand over the sandals to him. Hari wondered how Baba knew his name and that of his father and also about the lace turban and other features of his dress given out by the boy. He no longer disbelieved Baba's miraculous powers. Baba had passed his test.

Here is another story of one who came to scoff but remained to pray. He was a sadhu who was on his way to Shirdi to see Baba. When he approached the mosque he saw two flags flying over it and wondered why a saint should take a liking for the flags. This did not denote sainthood, he thought and decided to turn back. His fellow travllers told him that Baba did not care a fig for the flag and other paraphernalia, like horse, palanquin which his devotees had provided him and persuaded the sadhu to continue his journey.

The sadhu reluctantly agreed and arriving at the mosque he saw Baba at a distance and was very much moved by his presence. He approached Baba for his blessings when Baba got into a temper and shouted: "Let our humbug (paraphernalia) be with us. You go back to your home. Beware if you come back to the masjid. Why take the darshan of one who flies a flag over his masjid? Is it a sign of sainthood? Remain here not a moment." The sadhu was taken aback by Baba's outburst. Baba had read his thoughts and his doubts. His faith in Baba was confirmed and he became a staunch devotee.

Here are some more accounts of Baba's lilas from other sources.

Lakshman Govind Munge, living in Nashik, wanted to marry but he had no money. He went to Rahata village to seek financial help from an uncle. Most unexpectedly he had darshan of Sai Baba there. Baba had come there from Shirdi and was sitting alone in front of the Maruthi temple. Munge had not heard or seen Baba before and took no notice of him. But Baba on his own accosted him and said: "Listen, I was thinking of you yesterday and you are walking in front of me today. Why have you come to Rahata?" Munga said: "My marriage is settled but I have no money with me now." He said that he wanted to ask his uncle who lived there if he could help him. Baba asked him to sit for a while in the temple and gave him a fruit to eat. He said "if you need money for your marriage I can give you one or two thousand rupees." Munge wondered how the fakir in rags could give him so much money. Baba said: "Go back to Nashik. Do not worry." Munge returned to Nashik and began to ask people known to him for help. He came across a marwari moneylender who lent him the money he wanted. Munge got married and then went to Shirdi and told Baba how he had got the money for his marriage. Baba blessed him and gave him udhi. He asked him to visit him whenever he had any problem.

Babu, a young man, was an employee in the Land Survey Department. He was introduced to Baba by H. V. Sathe. Babu immersed himself in the service of Baba and he sometimes even forgot his official duties. Baba assigned him work which kept him in Shirdi and away from his official work. It later transpired that the reason why Baba showed so much concern and attention to Babu was the fact that he knew that Babu would die shortly. Baba wanted him to spend his last days peacefully in Shirdi and keep him by his side. Babu fell ill in 1910 and died in Sathe Wada. H. V. Sathe said Baba's grace enabled Babu to attain satgathi (salvation).

Bhivpuri is a small railway station near Bombay. Keshavarao Pradhan lived there. Two years before Baba's samadhi Pradhan went to Shirdi and had darshan and blessings of Baba. He prayed to Baba to come to Bhivpuri. Baba gave him an idol of himself and said: "You may now return to Bhivpuri with this idol. You may install it in a temple. You need not come to Shirdi to see me." Pradhan kept the idol in a room in his house. Some months later he again visited Shirdi and Baba said: "I have gone to your place. Why have you come to Shirdi? Your own place is Bhivpuri. You should know that I am there." Pradhan constructed a temple in a nearby village, Ukrool, installed Baba's idol there and carried on daily puja. He could see the temple from his residence. Then strange things began to happen. Pradhan saw Baba walking round the temple. During nights the temple doors would be locked by the priest and still on some nights the temple doors opened and shut automatically and Pradhan saw this happen with his own eyes. He and his family were mystified and they believed that Baba lived both in Shirdi and Bhivpuri. After Baba's samadhi Pradhan visited Shirdi and prayed to Baba: "When will you make your Bhivpuri mandir attain as much grandeur as your samadhi mandhir in Shirdi?" Baba granted his prayer. For soon devotees began to throng Bhivpuri in hundreds and the temple premises was expanded to accommodate the pilgrims coming from far and near.

R. A. Tarkhad of Bombay was without a job for a long time after he gave up a mill manager's post. He came and stayed in Shirdi with his wife. After some days he asked Baba's permission to return home. Baba asked him to return to Bombay via Pune and avoid the Manmad route. The wife grumbled as it was a longer route and would cost more. But Tarkhad decided to obey Baba knowing full well that he would not have asked them to take a longer route without purpose. In Pune the couple stayed with a friend for the night. Learning that Tarkhad was in search of a job the friend told him that a local mill owner was badly in need of a manager. Tarkhad went and saw the mill owner who was so impressed with him that he appointed him manager on the spot. Tarkhad's problem was solved through the grace of Baba.

Sankarlal Keshavram Bhatt, a shopkeeper of Bombay, was lame in one leg. Hearing of Baba's magical powers he came to Shirdi in 1911 and prostrated before Baba who blessed him. Later as he walked a few steps in the river sands to reach the ferry the jammed nerves in his leg loosened and to his surprise he was able to walk erect and his lameness had gone for ever.

Janardan Moreshwar Fanse stopped at Shirdi on his way to Rameshwaram on pilgrimage. He had darshan of Baba who advised him to return home since his mother had abstained from taking food since the day he left home and if he failed to return she might die. Fanse returned home as advised by Baba and his mother was greatly pleased to see him.

The story does not end there. A resident of the area where he lived was attacked by cholera and came to Fanse and he gave him Baba's udhi and he was cured. This resulted in more patients coming to him and soon the stock of Baba's udhi was exhausted. When he went to a neighbouring village he was asked to treat a patient whose condition was serious. Fanse did bhajan and the patient who came and sat there was seen concentrating on Baba's picture kept there. The patient's father asked Fanse to treat his son. To get out of the awkward situation Fanse demanded a high fee of Rs. 200 and this was agreed to. That night Baba appeared in Fanse's dream and instructed him what medicine to give to the patient. Fanse prescribed the medicine and the patient recovered. He was given the stipulated fee but he refused to accept it and left. The father feeling that Fanse should receive some recognition of his help left a shawl worth Rs. 200 at his house. Fanse thought that the shawl should be sent to Baba but he was pennyless and also in the meanwhile Baba had attained samadhi. Baba appeared in his dream and advised him to sell the shawl and with the money purchase rice and distribute a part of it to the poor and to start business with the rest of the rice selling it at a profit. Following Baba's advice Fanse built up a flourishing business and was happy.

Baba has continued to protect and bless his devotees from his samadhi. He has proved he is a living God as the following accounts of his devotees show. We begin with two incidents among many mentioned by Narasimha Swamiji.

This happened in Coimbatore in Tamil Nadu in January 1943. Sai bhajan was going on in the Sai Mandir one evening. Suddenly a snake appeared and moving towards the installed picture of Baba lay before it and listened to the bhajan. It continued to be there frightening none, harming none and neither frightened nor harmed by anyone. After 9 p.m. the devotees dispersed and when they returned the next morning they were surprised to see the cobra still there near Baba's picture. They chanted verses in praise of Baba and showered rose petals on the snake which quietly accepted their adoration and did not budge from the place. Then a photographer came and took a picture of the cobra with the heap of flowers on it. It was only at midday that the cobra, which had come there the previous evening, left the mandir. The devotees had no doubt that it was Baba who had come there in the form of the snake to bless them.

At Ramachandrapuram in Andhra Pradesh Sai devotees found on day that flowers and plantains that were offered during worship of Baba's picture contained inscriptions. When a big garland of 1,000 roses was placed on Baba's picture thousands of the word "Sai" were found inscribed on the rose petals in Telugu as also the words "Om Sai". More surprising still, the naivedya placed before Baba's picture was accepted by Baba. This became evident when a part of the offering was found missing.

Mani Aiyer of Kumbakonam in Tamil Nadu had a daughter, Rajalakshmi who was dumb. He took her to Shirdi in 1942 and both of them sat in the samadhi mandir and prayed to Baba. At that moment Das Ganu Maharaj, the great devotee of Baba, entered the mandir for darshan and he heard Rajalakshmi's story. Das Ganu asked her to utter three words: "Sai Baba Bolo." Rajalakshmi at once uttered the words "Sai Baba" but could not make out "Bolo". Father and daughter stayed there for a few days and Rajalakshmi regained her power of speech. Mani Aiyer brought her back to Kumbakonam and she was duly admitted to school and she became a normal child.

Arthur Osborne in his book, *The Incredible Sai Baba,* narrated an incident which reveals the mysterious ways of Baba.

Miss Dutton, a British woman and a Catholic, had long been a nun. She found that because of her feeble health she was not able to stand the strain of work imposed on her as a novice in a convent near Calcutta. She appealed to the Pope to allow her to leave the Convent and live independently in Calcutta. The Pope's permission was received and Miss Dutton was packing up to leave the convent. She did not know anyone in Calcutta and did not know where to go. While she sat in the room very much worried she saw a Muslim fakir standing before her. She was alarmed. The door of the room had been bolted from inside and she could not understand how the fakir had entered the room and how he could have gained admittance into the convent. He spoke to her in English and said: "You should not worry so much. When you go to Calcutta everything will be all right." The fakir then asked her for a few rupees as dakshina. Miss Dutton said she had no money. He said :"You have got Rs.35 in the cupboard over there." Miss Dutton had forgotten she had kept the money there. She opened the cupboard and took out the money (which was Rs. 35 as stated by the fakir) and turned to give it to the fakir. But he was not there. He had disappeared as mysteriously as he had entered the room. The remarkable thing was that Miss Dutton was now at peace with herself. Her worries vanished. She felt that the reassuring words of the fakir had given her strength of mind. Some days later she left the convent and travelled to Calcutta where most unexpectedly she met her nephew who took charge of her and helped her to secure a convenient flat for her residence. She told Arthur Osborne who lived in an adjacent flat of her experience. Osborne showed her a picture of Baba and asked her if she could recognise him. Miss Dutton recognised Baba as the fakir who had been in her room. She exclaimed: "Yes, this is the fakir who helped me and gave me his blessings. I have been thinking of him since then. I have been praying to him day and night."

Here are some more stories of Baba's lilas after samadhi, gathered from other sources.

In 1927 a couple was returning to Bombay by train after taking part in the Sri Rama Navami festival in Shirdi. The wife alighted at Thane to fetch water and as she was getting into the carriage with a jug of water the train started and she fell down under the carriage. The husband and others shouted to the guard to stop the train but the train stopped only after it had gone some distance. The husband and the other passengers feared the woman must have been crushed under the wheels. When they reached the spot of incident to their great wonder they saw the woman standing on the platform unscathed and smiling. She told them that as she fell she remembered Baba and he suddenly appeared and pushed her to the edge of the platform and held her tight there till the train passed. What was mysterious was that there was hardly room for two persons between the wheels of the train and the platform so how could anybody have saved her?

An ardent devotee of Baba embarked on an ambitious plan to write a book on Dattatreya and he prayed for Baba's help and assistance. Sitting in his room in Hyderabad in Andhra Pradesh he began his task one night. Very soon he found he had a visitor in the room and it was Baba who had come to help him with his book. Baba appeared every night thereafter and cleared his doubts. Seeing that her husband was still at his desk late in the night and hearing conversation in the room his wife asked him about it and he had a hard time to send her away with some plausible explanation. The devotee successfully completed the book and he says that without Baba's assistance it could not have been written. The story sounds incredible but it is from the horse's own mouth and we know where Baba is concerned nothing is incredible, as for instance, the following story.

A woman devotee of Baba in Kolhapur in Maharashtra was reading a book in her drawing room one afternoon when she felt thirsty. She simply said: "Baba, I would like to have a glass of water." It is not known if she meant seriously to ask Baba to get her some water and if it was not just a way of her life to remember Baba at every stage but whatever it was Baba apparently took her seriously. The lady soon found a hand extending to her a glass of water. She was too startled to think of anything but prayed to Baba and accepted the glass and Baba disappeared. She drank the water which was ice cold. When her husband came from office she told him of the incident and he chided her for telling him a cock and bull story. He asked her: "What is the evidence that Baba appeared and gave you the glass of water? If it is true then your throat must have become hoarse." She said the evidence was that her throat had indeed become hoarse after drinking the ice cold water. And he believed her.

Here are some more stories of Baba's lilas gathered from pilgrims during a visit to Shirdi.

A woman devotee from Chandigarh said as the result of an explosion the skin of the palm and fingers of her son were burnt and doctors said a plastic surgery was necessary for grafting skin over the palm and fingers. As she was worrying and praying to Baba she saw in a vision Baba applying udhi to the affected parts of her son's hand. In the next few days she saw signs of skin growing on the burnt palm and fingers. The doctors were surprised at this development and said surgery was no longer necessary. The boy was all right in a matter of days.

The owner of a hotel in Shirdi who has been running it for 40 years said his daughter had been a paralytic and could not walk. She was taken to Baba's samadhi and laid there. Within a few minutes she was seen getting up and walking round the mandir. Later she told her astonished parents that she saw Baba telling her to get up and walk and she found she could get up and walk.

A Bengali who has settled in Shirdi said he had intended to build a house there and needed Rs. 20,000 to complete the construction. He was not able to find this money and was very much worried. One day as he was sitting near Gurustan where Baba had sat under a neem tree a friend approached him and asked him what he was worrying about. When the Bengali told him of his problem the friend asked him if he had prayed to Baba. He said he had, and the friend assured him that Baba would do the needful. Sure enough moments later as the Bengali walked about the temple complex he unexpectedly met an old friend who greeted him warmly. When he heard his problem he gave him part of the money he needed on the spot and promised to give him the rest of the amount later and he did.

A Government official in Delhi and his wife had purchased tickets to and fro to Shirdi. When they alighted at Kopargaon they went to the station master for reservation of berths for the return journey. The station master said the position was difficult and asked them to complete the visit and come back and he would see what could be done. While returning to Kopargaon after visiting Shirdi the husband lost his purse in which he had kept the tickets while travelling in the bus. He reported the matter to the station master and requested him to give duplicate tickets and reservation. The station master regretted his inability to do so as the rules did not permit it. But seeing their plight he offered to purchase the tickets for them spending from his own pocket and they could repay him after returning to Delhi. However, the couple managed to collect enough money for the fare on their own and reached Delhi safely. The official wrote a letter to the railway authorities describing the loss of the tickets on the return journey and his purchase of new ones. He asked for the refund of the value of the tickets lost. The railway authorities rejected the request since the tickets had not been produced. This was in July. To his great astonishment five months later he received a letter from the railway authorities stating that after examining the case they had decided to give him a refund as claimed by him. Curiously enough there was no reference in the letter to their previous rejection of his request. Baba's lilas are truly strange and unpredictable.

In Malleswaram (Bangalore), there is a Sai Baba temple which is run with devotees' support. There occurred an incident which was narrated by the Temple Committee President, Mr Murthy, and the Secretary, Dr Nagesh. They said the management received numerous pictures of Baba for being installed in the temple and it became a problem how to accommodate them in the limited space of the temple. Therefore it was decided not to accept any more pictures of Baba and this decision was announced on the notice board. Shortly after the anniversary of the temple was being celebrated. As the functions connected with the celebration were going on a sadhu, hugging a big portrait of Baba, suddenly barged into the temple and told those present. "This picture must be installed here." He placed the picture in their midst and walked away as swiftly as he had come. No one knew who he was and where he came from and

184   *God Who Walked on Earth*

why he wanted the picture to be installed there. Try as they
might the temple officials could find no trace of him afterwards.
The management decided that the portrait should be installed in
the Meditation Hall and this was done.

11

FAREWELL: "MY TOMB WILL SPEAK"

S AI BABA attained samadhi on October 15, 1918, Vijayadasami
Day, in Dwaraka Mayi in Shirdi. He breathed his last leaning
on the shoulders of a devotee who did not realise that Baba had
shed his mortal coil until a few minutes later. It was the second
time Baba had died, apparently this time for good. He had left
the body once before in 1886 and like the Resurrection of Christ
returned three days after. However, while Christ sacrificed his
life on the cross Baba left the body voluntarily, after telling his
devotee he would come back.

The story of this unbelievable but true incident was told to
his son, Martand, by Mahlsapathy. According to Martand who
recorded the episode in his memoirs of his father, one day in
1886 Baba came to Mahlsapathy and said, "Arre Bhagat ! (as
Baba called Mahlsapathy), I am going to Allah. You had better
guard this body for three days. If I return thereafter I will get
into the body. If I do not you may thereafter have the body
interred in that place" (pointing to a place near the neem tree
where he used to meditate). Baba then reclined on Mahlsapathy's
shoulders and soon ceased to breathe. Body heat disappeared
and the colour of the body turned livid. Baba was dead.

Soon the news spread and village officials and the police
arrived at the mosque. An inquest was held and Baba was
certified dead. The police asked Mahlsapathy to bury the body
as it should not remain in the mosque. Mahlsapathy told them
what Baba had said to him and added that he would wait for
three days as instructed by Baba. The police failed to persuade
him to change his mind. He told them that Baba was a yogi with
wonderful powers and it was possible for him to come back

alive in three days. Mahlsapathy won his point and he was allowed to retain the body which he protected with the help of other devotees.

After three days they noticed that suddenly a finger of Baba's body moved, then his eyes opened. The next minute Baba rose and sat in his usual way and looked around. The resurrection was complete and Baba was back among his devotees, alive and kicking. To the end of his life Baba never spoke about this incident nor does it appear that any devotee questioned him about it. The devotees must have taken it for granted. For anything was possible to a saint of Baba's stature and capabilities. What is surprising is that it did not obviously produce any reaction among government officials, both at the lower and higher levels. The fact of Baba's death must have gone into the village records but was it changed when Baba returned to life? Official apathy and lack of curiosity was in line with the spirit of the times when people led a life of poverty and misery not questioning anything. But we, living in a scientific age, have to ask the question: how did he do it, why did he do it? Where was he in those three days? And finally, why and how did he come back? A dead body gets disintegrated within a matter of hours and begins to stink but in the case of Baba his body was well preserved and in good condition when life returned to it. This is a miracle which we have read in our *Puranas* and mythologies but that it happened in real life in the presence of reliable witnesses is hard to believe but an inescapable fact. The questions will remain unanswered like so many other questions about Baba's life.

Baba used a peculiar phrase to describe death. He called it the "crossing of the frontier". When Rege's child died and his wife became inconsolable and Rege had the dead child on his lap Baba appeared before him and asked: "Do you want me or the dead child? If you want me to revive the child I will but then you will have me no more with you. If you do not want it to be revived you will have many more children in due course." Rege later said he told Baba that he wanted him. "Then do not grieve," said Baba and disappeared.

Baba did revive a dead person on two known occasions. The first was during his stay with his guru, Venkusa, when a disgruntled disciple who tried to harm the guru and Baba himself fell dead and the other disciples pleaded with the guru to revive him. The guru said he had transferred all his powers to the young Baba and it was for him to revive the dead man. The disciples then prayed to Baba who, uttering his guru's name, touched the man's body and it came back to life. On the other occasion, Malanbai, daughter of D. R. Joshi Devgaonkar, died of tuberculosis. Earlier the girl had asked to be taken to Shirdi and placed before Baba. Baba asked her to lie down on a blanket and take nothing but water. She carefully followed these instructions but after a week she died early in the morning.

Baba was then in the chavadi and for the first time he did not leave the chavadi though it was past 8 a.m. The girl's parents with a heavy heart were making preparations to remove the body for the funeral when suddenly they saw that Malanbai was breathing. She then opened her eyes and looked around. Then she said: "A black person was carrying me away. Very much frightened I cried out to Baba for help. Baba took his staff and gave him a good beating. He snatched me away from him and carried me to the chavadi." She had not seen the chavadi before but gave a correct description of it. Just at this time Baba left the chavadi bawling out, and stamping the ground with his stick, he came to Dixit's house where the girl's body had been kept.

It is a faraway cry from bringing back to life a diseased girl to helping a lawyer devotee who was overworked, to sign hundreds of documents in time. And this is what Baba did when he came to the rescue of the lawyer who narrated the incident with awe and reverence. The lawyer was the chairman of the Nashik District Board and he had to sign hundreds of papers every day which interfered with his profession and reduced his income. Every day a peon brought these papers to him and he had to sign them and return them the same day. One day a visitor came and took much of his time and he could not sign the papers brought to him, so he sent them back without his signature. When the papers came as usual the next day he found to his surprise that the previous day's papers which he had sent back unsigned were not there. When he asked for them he was told that they all bore his signature. He could not understand who could have signed those hundreds of papers. The only conclusion he could come to was that Baba had come forward to lighten his burden and protect his name.

In yet another instance Bayyaji Apaji Patel revealed that during the last years of his life Baba paid him daily Rs 4 and advised him not to lend it or make a gift. The devotee invested the money in real estate and was able ultimately to purchase 84 acres of land out of Baba's daily payments.

Seven days before Baba passed away a bullock cart came and stopped before the mosque. A tiger was in it tied by chains. One could see it was in great pain and agony. Its keepers were taking it from place to place and exhibiting it to the people and making money. They had tried all methods to cure it of its illness but did not succeed. They then came to Baba. They led the tiger to the front of the mosque and kept it there. People gathered to look at it but it was restless. The keepers went to Baba and told him about the sick tiger. Baba asked them to bring it before him. As the tiger ascended the steps of the mosque it hung its head and met the eyes of Baba with affection. It hit the ground with its tail three times, then collapsed and died. A samadhi was built over it later in Shirdi.

Baba was once asked about his native place. He said: "I came here (Shirdi) from Aurangabad. My maternal uncle (mama) brought me here." Baba was asked: "What is the name of that mama? Where is he now?" Baba replied: "He was a mad man having no name. He must be living somewhere now." He told a devotee on another occasion: "I was at the battle in which the Rani of Jhansi took part. I was then in the army." The Rani of Jhansi, it will be recalled, was the heroine of the war of Independence in 1857. To another devotee he said: "I was here (at Shirdi) on the banks of the Godavari eight or ten thousand years ago." Baba said on one occasion: "When I was young I went out one morning and suddenly became a girl and continued to be so for sometime thereafter." Baba said: "My mother greatly rejoiced that she got a son, that is, me. I was for my part wondering at her conduct. When did she beget me? Was I begotten at all? Have I not already been in existence? Why is she rejoicing over this?"

G. S. Khaparde reported that Baba was steadily ruining his health for the sake of his devotees. He could not but respond to every appeal made to him night and day and as a result his digestion got upset, his general strength weakened and he knew this would continue up to the time of his leaving the body. He told Khaparde :"I do not care for my life. I care for my bhaktas."

When a woman devotee rushed to Baba and asked for udhi to save her dying husband Baba said life and death were equally manifestations of God's activity and were inseparable. Bodies when worn out were cast away like worn-out clothes. He told the devotee: "Let him go. Do not stop him. Do not ask for udhi. When death arrives do not grieve. The wise ones do not grieve for death. The five pranas are lent for use during life. Now the lender claims them back and insists they are returned. Air goes back to air, fire to fire. Every one of the five elements goes back to its place. The body is made of earth. The return to earth is not a thing to be moaned."

Baba helped both the living and the dying. With his incomparable love and power he stood besides the dying persons even though he might be thousands of miles away from Shirdi and helped him to move into a new sphere, Baba being the guide in this world and beyond. To the survivors who mainly thought of worldly disadvantages entailed by their bereavement he gave the assurance that he would look after them and their interest. He was always as good as his word.

Protection of the good (virtuous), punishment or reformation of the wicked, establishment of dharma or its hold on the people are the functions of divine personalities and Baba performed all these functions. He adopted every *marga* (path) but it has to be noted that in his methods the predominant elements were not rituals or Vedic study but to live in consonance with the supreme manifestation of divinity in one's self. His mission was to help everyone, that meant everyone capable of benefitting, not those who came in an unreceptive mood. He used to quote his guru's dictum that "as he had received liberally from his master he must similarly distribute liberally among those who approached him." Baba was not merely distributing wealth, worldly reliefs and comforts but also spiritual gifts and spiritual blessings to all who were capable of receiving those benefits.

Baba checked vice and weaknesses in men and gave them purity and strength enabling them to progress spiritually. It is related that he appeared once in a dream to a very wicked man who was addicted to drink, sat on his chest and told him: "Once or twice I will give you warning. If no heed is taken of the warning then I will leave you to your fate." The man gave up liquor and reformed his ways. Narasimha Swamiji says Baba was not only a teacher but a controller from within—the ever watching guardian angel. Baba had in him the all round perfection of divine qualities in such a manner as to fulfil our idea of God."

Baba's vast control over people's minds was directed to secure summary justice for those who placed their faith in him. With Baba all things were possible. There are thousands of people who get into some trouble or other and cast their eyes in every direction in quest of relief. They ask in distress: "Is there no God? Is there no saint? Is there no mantra? Is there not anything that will come to my rescue?" At such moments when there is some person or other in the neighbourhood connected with Sai Baba then that person runs up to Baba with the assurance (born of need) that he is not only living and will help but that he is the only person who can help in such moments of crisis. There is no other person, says Narasimha Swamiji, known to have such superhuman power and intent solely on benefitting all those who put their trust in him. Narasimha Swamiji says: "Baba is showing all people irrespective of religion, caste, creed, age and sex that he is that superhuman beneficent power that people call their Ishta Devatha or gurudeva and that he is available to any earnest soul and responds to every earnest call."

Baba said he would give up his life to save those who were constantly thinking of him and were absorbed in him. He told a disciple his health had been impaired and his food intake reduced to bread and water due to worries of looking after innumerable devotees. He said that in spite of these infirmities he must go on doing his duty up to the time of his departure from this worldly thing, whatever be the consequences. In this connection we may recall the incident (which has been mentioned in a previous page) about how Baba put his hand in the dhuni at Dwaraka Mayi to save the life of a child of a blacksmith which had fallen into a fire at some distant place. When asked about the pain and burn caused by his action Baba said he had saved the child and God would cure his burn. It was widely believed at the time of Baba passing away that Baba gave his life to save that of an intimate disciple who was seriously ill and given up for lost.

At the time of World War I in 1914 Baba was an old man, frail by comparison with his earlier years. His health deteriorated and he suffered from severe asthma. His hair was short and concealed beneath a piece of cloth tied around his head. Only in his old age did he relax his severe discipline of begging for his food and partaking of food offered by visitors. He did not possess any spare clothing and it was useless to present him new clothes as he would immediately give them away. His kufni remained on his body until it was torn and some devotee forcibly removed it and made him wear a new garment. He was known to repair the old ones using a needle and thread. During the war he regularly visited the temple in the village. While he attended the worship his face was said to have been suffused with a radiance which was noticeable to all those who witnessed it.

Halfway through the war in October 15, 1916, Baba was in a frenzy shouting that it was his day of "crossing the frontier". Uncharacteristically he tore his clothes and moved about naked for two hours until his mood subsided. He passed away exactly on the same date and month two years later. His illness on Vijayadasami Day (October 15) was serious and rumours spread that he was going to die. His devotees conducted prayers with mass poor feeding at Shirdi for his recovery. Fortunately Baba recovered. At one stage Baba asked Babasaheb Nimonkar who had come to Shirdi on his way to Pune to stay with him, bury him and go. Baba was similarly ill in 1915, suffering from asthma and hard breathing.

There was a bad omen 10 or 12 days before the dasara festival in 1918 which indicated for Baba that the time had come for him to shed his mortal coil. While sleeping Baba used an old brick as his pillow. The brick was believed to be the one given to him by his guru, Venkusa with a torn cloth. Madhav Fasle, an attendant of Baba, handed over the brick to Mahlsapathy every night and along with it the tattered cloth to be placed over it. Madhav prepared the bed by placing the brick at the top and then spread the cloth over it and more cloths to make it soft. Then it happened. As Madhav took the brick to hand it over to Mahlsapathy it slipped from his hands and fell down breaking into two pieces. Baba asked who broke the brick and when he was told that Madhav Fasle had done it he got very angry. He put his hands on his head and said with a touch of sadness: "Sobat tutali" ("the companion is broken"). The next day one of his disciples, H. S. Dixit, said there was no need to deplore the breaking of the brick. He would join the pieces with silver. Baba said: "Even if you join them with gold what is the use? This brick is my *sobatya* (companion) and its being broken betokens evil." He added: "This is my guru's gift, my life companion. It is not the brick that is broken now but my karma is what has snapped. I cannot survive the breaking of the brick." He told Nana Chandorkar who had also offered to cement the broken pieces :"The worth of this brick cannot be reached even if you made a lakh of pillows. This brick was given to me by my guru. Its value is greater than that of the universe. This brick is the object of my meditation and is also my meditation. This brick is my visible life. If this is lost then this body of mine must die. When I was with my guru in a forest in the district of Paarbhani near Selu some wicked men hurled bricks and stones at us with murderous aim. That stone which was aimed at me struck my guru's head. This is that brick. But my guru's power was wondrous. This brick was suspended in the air for one and half hours. It could have continued to be suspended in the air but its force had to terminate by hitting something. My sadguru gave his head to the stone and received it for my sake. He saved me but he himself suffered. That shows that saints always take on themselves suffering to relieve others' suffering. They have power within themselves but will not manifest their powers. I took the brick and placed it at my guru's feet and my sadguru gave it to me as his gift. As my guru's feet had touched this brick I place my head on it and make it my pillow My good guru Gopal Rao entered into it and became Venkatesa. The footprints of that Venkatesa are on this brick. Therefore I call my guru Venkusa. Such is the greatness of this brick."

Devotees said from that day Baba became dispirited and lost interest in life. He told one devotee: "I will be going somewhere in a few days from this mosque." But even before this incident Baba had given a hint to Mahlsapathy that his end was near. While Mahlsapathy was lighting his pipe one day Baba told him: "Arre Bhagat ! In a few days from now I will be going somewhere. After that you come at night for two or four years." Mahlsapathy did not understand clearly what Baba meant. Baba passed away on October 15, 1918, and Mahlsapathy was able to do his nightly puja to Baba only for a short time as he passed away on September 11, 1922.

Baba fully anticipated his death on Vijayadasami (October 15). He had a devotee read the scriptures at the mosque and sent Rs. 250 to a Muslim saint Shamsuddin for the performance of Muslim prayers. He also sent word to another saint Babbamea that he would be passing away on the 9th day of the 9th month (probably Muslim calendar). "The light that Allah lit he is taking away," he said. In the morning he distributed gifts. He paid Rs. 5 from his pocket and then another Rs.4 to Lakshmi Bai Shinde who was daily preparing and giving him food and was being paid Rs. 4 every day. A few days earlier Baba had sent Rs. 200 for the feeding of fakirs and the chanting of prayers with drums beating at a holy place.

During his illness Baba asked Vagne, a devotee, to read to him the *Ramrajya*, a sacred book written in Hindi, once a week. Baba made him go through it a second time nonstop day and night and it was finished within three days. A third round was also completed when the devotee appeared exhausted. Baba let him go and observed silence for the rest of the day. Baba went on his begging mission as usual, helped by some devotees. However, he had to give it up after some days.

Mrs M. W. Pradhan, a devotee, had a dream a few days before Baba's samadhi. In the dream she saw Baba passing away and she cried :"Baba is dead." Baba appeared in the dream and corrected her. He said that saints did not die. The term to be used in their case was that they attained samadhi. "Saints never die," Baba said. He told another devotee who was frightened at the prospect of Baba passing away: "Mother, I do not die. Wherever you are if you think of me I am there at any time you please (whether I am in the body or out of it)."

When it was still four days to go for Vijayadasami, the day which Baba described as the day of his "Seemalanghan", Mrs Andu Marwadi, a local devotee, was sitting before Baba and he told her :"Bai, I am tired of being in Dwarakamayi and chavadi. I will go over to Buty's wada where big people will look after me." At that time Baba's health was very bad. He stopped his morning trips to lendi and the begging rounds and confined himself to the mosque. His close devotees, Dixit and Buti, remained with him all the time and were taking their meals at the mosque.

On Vijayadasami day, which also happened to be ekadasi day, his intimate devotee, Tatya Patil, became very ill. His pulse was becoming weaker and weaker. Baba also was seriously ill. He sat up in his bed and distributed gifts. After the morning arati Baba asked all the devotees to go home for lunch. Only a few devotees stayed with him. Baba said he did not feel well and asked the devotees to take him to the *degdi* (stone) wada of Buti where he would be all right. His last words were :"I am going. Carry me to the wada. All Brahmins will be living near me." He leaned on the shoulder of Bagoji Shinde, his leper devotee, and breathed his last. Bagoji burst into sobs and cried: "Baba is dead." Nana Nimonkar poured some water into his mouth but it came out and he started weeping.

On the same day Baba appeared in a dream to Das Ganu Maharaj in Pandharpur and said: "The mosque has collapsed and the *telis* and *vanis* (merchants and oil vendors) have harassed me a lot. So I leave the place. I therefore came here to inform you. Come and cover me with babul flowers." Das Ganu rushed to Shirdi with a group of devotees.

Devotees have recorded that Baba attained samadhi at 3 p.m. and that he was conscious till the end. His body was taken in a procession from the mosque to Buti's wada as per his wish. Devotees wept inconsolably and the simple villagers who joined the procession were seen weeping loudly.

The disposal of Baba's body became a matter of controversy between the Hindus and the Muslims. The popular belief among both the Hindus and Muslims was that Baba, living as he did in the mosque, was a Muslim. Muslims led by Bade Baba gathered round the body and wished to take care of it. This was opposed by the Hindus who wanted to perform the last rites to Baba. They said they were in a majority and they should have the privilege of putting Baba to rest. The Muslims were few in number and they did not have the means or influence to erect a suitable tomb for Baba. While the discussions were going on the Mamlatdar of Kopargaon arrived on the scene and both parties submitted their petitions to him. It was not known what was Baba's wish in this matter. He never talked about it. But at one stage during his illness he had said: "Carry me to the Buti wada." Buti, a millionaire of Nagpur and an ardent devotee of Baba, had built the wada in what was formerly a garden watered and nurtured by Baba. He had intended to build a temple there. He was willing to spare this site for, burial of Baba and raise a tomb over it.

The Muslims came to an agreement with the Hindus that Baba's body should be buried in the site intended for the temple and that the management of the tomb should be with the Hindus, with Muslims being allowed free access to it. The Mamlatdar accepted the agreement and passed the necessary official order. Baba's body was then buried in the wada.

Baba's body was deposited within the stone building near the vault which had been dug and prepared by Hindu devotees. The last rites were performed according to the Hindu custom. Baba's body was not stiff and his apparel was removed easily. He was bathed and worshipped. He was laid in the samadhi pit which was covered by camphor and incense. Buti's wada or stone building which was originally intended for a Krishna temple became the resting place for Baba. The final rites were performed according to one account by Upasani Baba and Balasaheb Bhate in the presence of other devotees.

Das Ganu and other devotees did bhajan before Baba's tomb the whole day. Das Ganu prepared a beautiful garland of babul flowers and placed it on the tomb. He organised mass feeding on October 18. On the 13th day funereal rituals were performed by Balasaheb Bhate and Brahmins and the poor were fed. Upasani Baba and Jog went to Prayag and performed the final rites for Baba on the banks of the Ganga. After the 20th day Muslims took out a sandal procession in Shirdi. The *Quran* was read and namaz done.

In the pouch which he carried and which he never allowed others to touch it was found that Baba had kept the green kufni and cap given to him by Kashiram Shimpi many years earlier when had came to Shirdi with a marriage party. As Baba died intestate without any heirs his property was taken over by the Kopargaon magistrate. It consisted of Rs.16 found in his pocket. Soon after the religious rites a committee was formed to carry on Baba's puja and worship. The committee consisted exclusively of Baba's devotees including H. S. Dixit, G. R. Dabolkar, Prof. Narke, Tatya Patil and Nana Chandorkar. Bapusaheb Jog was the chairman of the committee. The committee started a fund called Shri Samartha Sainath Kothi which later came to be known as the Kayam Fund. The committee claimed possession of Baba's properties and a suit was filed in the court of the District Judge, Ahmednagar. H. S. Dixit submitted a scheme to the court for the administration and upkeep of the tomb and this was accepted by the court. And this was how the Shirdi Sai Sansthan came to be established and the administration of the property was vested in a board of trustees with a managing committee of 15 members. Dixit became the honorary Secretary of the Sansthan in 1922. Later, owing to factions in the Sansthan its administration was handed over to a Receiver on Court orders and some years later the court appointed a Board of Trustees with an executive officer to look after the day to day administration.

Narasimha Swamiji says Baba left no successor to his seat. He says: "There is no seat to succeed to and there is no person living who can be recognised by all as having the entire Sai spirit or soul in his body who can be regarded as the avatar of Baba. Baba told his devotees he was going to be reborn birth after birth."

One devotee said Baba was present everywhere. For him there was no question of distances. He could be simultaneously present in Bombay, Shirdi and somewhere else. It was not necessary for him to see or hear. Without seeing or hearing he had the power to know for his nature was pure *chit* and his *pratibha* (power of illumination), unrestricted by the ordinary limitations that bind ordinary mortals, enabled him to see and hear at the same time what went on in different places and make use of that knowledge for the benefit of his devotees. He had the ability to assume any form he wanted. He appeared before the brother of a devotee in hospital in one form, at his house in another form and at Shirdi where the devotee saw him in a third form. Once Baba complained to a devotee that he had beaten him when he went to his house as a cat to drink his curds in order to save the devotee from a disease which made it risky for him to take curds. And Baba showed the devotee a weal on his shoulder corresponding to the place where the cat had been beaten by the devotee.

Narasimha Swamiji said that while in the case of ordinary mortals an anniversary of death was a day of mourning, in the case of saints it was a day of rejoicing. "From beyond the veil they are more clearly perceived as God or as fragments of God that will continue to guard, guide and save their loving devotees and answer their prayers." Damodar Rasane told Narasimha Swamiji that after Baba's mahasamadhi in 1918 he saw the physical, living and moving body of Baba with his own eyes any number of times and had talked and moved with that body.

Saipadananda Radhakrishna Swamiji said Baba was a doctor of both mind and body of the people who went to him and also their guardian angel, who prevented mishaps and provided all the blessings essential for their progress. Each of the devotees had his full share of Baba's love and all the benefits that flowed therefrom. That love was equally intense and powerful whether the devotee was in his presence or hundreds of miles away. That he could single-handedly attend effectively to the concern and welfare of thousands of his devotees whether in Bombay, Pune, Shirdi, Delhi or Madras or elsewhere was manifested in hundreds of ways. " This is the mark of divinity perfect," the Swamiji said.

Baba adopted every *marga* (path) but in particular one might note, Swamiji said that importance was given in his methods neither to rituals nor for Vedic study but for living in consonance with the supreme manifestation of divinity in himself. "His mission is to help everyone, that means, of course, everyone capable of benefit, not persons who come in an unreceptive mood." Baba did not influence his devotees mainly by any specific teaching. He moulded his children as he called them from inside and he used not merely words but also his gaze, his touch and even his aura or the will-power to remove undesirable tendencies and influences and replace them by useful and holy ones. Swamiji said Baba's teachings are so simple and common that when set out they may look like copybook maxims and some may wonder why these should be set out at all when they are so self-evident. What Baba taught was not something new or strange. What he taught was the same old truths of morality and spirituality that had to be rubbed into each soul and lived up to. Therefore Baba placed the truth before devotees at the appropriate time.

How old was Baba when he attained samadhi? Nobody knows and nobody is certain. Das Ganu Maharaj said Baba's age was something one could not fix. Das Ganu said forty years previously he had seen an old woman, Salubhai Shelke of Shirdi, who was then about 65 years old. She told him that when she was married (which was at the age of eight or ten) Baba came to Shirdi looking as he was when Das Ganu saw him in 1895, forty or fifty years old. Another old woman, Sai Bai, said that Baba came to Shirdi as a lad. Das Ganu said he believed that Baba must have been over 100 when he attained samadhi. But one is tempted to say this is not the final answer to the question of how old Baba was. Readers will recall Baba told a devotee that he was in the army of the Rani of Jhansi who fought in the war of independence in 1857. He did not say how old he was then. It is curious no one asked Baba about his age nor did he volunteer the information. But to his devotees he is ageless, a *chiranjivi,* beyond death and mortality.

As mentioned already, after Baba's samadhi his property was taken over by the government since Baba did not leave any will or nominate any successor. A report of the Mamlatdar and magistrate of Kopargaon dated October 19, 1918 to the Collector and District Magistrate of Ahmednagar said: "The only course open therefore is to take charge of the property pending the framing of a proper and responsible committee for the management as no will was left by Sai Baba nor any disciple named and appointed."

The preamble to the Rules of Shirdi Sai Sansthan in force since October 1, 1941 says: "H.H.Shri Sai Baba of Shirdi" known to be a saint of all-India fame but of unknown origin, came about 86 years ago to Shirdi, a small village abutting on the Agra trunk road, about eight miles south of the town of Kopargaon in Ahmednagar district, and day by day being found to be a person of great sanctity, happened to be worshipped by Hindus as well as non-Hindus. On October 15, 1918, Tuesday, Vijayadasami saka, ekadasi saka 1840, he died intestate and his remains pursuant to his wish (which were held in reverence by all the villagers as well as his bhaktas) were buried in the stately wada which was then nearing completion and which the late Shriman Gopalrao Mukund Buti, a millionaire of Nagpur, had built with the consent of H.H. As H.H. had a large number of devotees his shrine was going to be a permanent institution of worship by people of all classes and it was therefore deemed necessary to have a body to manage the same. A committee was formed to continue the worship of the deseased as a saint.

"Das Ganu Maharaj, by his hundreds of kirtans, both in Bombay, its suburbs and outside Bombay greatly helped the committee by enlightening the general public about Sai Baba's saintly entity since 1910 and is doing so up-to-date. This committee started from Bhandara day, that is, October 27,1918 at Shirdi, a fund for continuing the worship in the mandir, masjid, chavadi, etc., as in the lifetime of Sai Baba, which by the grace of Sai Baba has up-to-date risen to half a lakh and is steadily growing."

Baba remained a mystic and a mysterious person all his life. He never revealed himself except as an extraordinary soul of love and compassion and possessed superhuman power and energy which transcended human imagination and belief. He brought succour and relief to thousands of people far and near, who had only to think of him to receive instant response. He was a tremendous storehouse of power whose depths and origin were unfathomable. It was unsafe for anyone to approach him with any thought of doubt or hesitation. He read it even before the concerned person himself was aware of it. Men's minds, wherever they may be, hundreds or thousands of miles away, were an open book to him and he could spell out the thinking and actions of men and women simultaneously as though it were second nature to him. His revelations were spontaneous, effortless and almost casual. There was the case of the man from South Africa who was taken against his will to meet him. His Ishta Devatha was Rama and he said he would not bend his head before a Muslim fakir. But what he saw as he ascended the steps of the mosque and looked at Baba was different. He saw Baba taking the form of Rama in all his beauty and glory and rushed in and fell at his feet.

In another instance a Brahmin who wanted to have a dip in the Godavari was told by Baba he could have the Ganga (as he called the Godavari) flowing from his toes and to the great wonder and amazement of the Brahmin water gushed forth from the saint's toes. To us these feats of Baba are miracles but for him they were part of his nature, his very being. He was testing people all the time. When he asked for dakshina it was not the money that he wanted so much as the faith and patience (*nishta* and *sabuni*) of his devotees. He wanted absolute, total surrender from them and he promised to take care of them. And he was as good as his word. Surprisingly it was to the intellectuals, the scholars and learned men and women that he made this demand and they willingly accepted it although some of them never quite succeeded in this process of unlearning. And they were his most intimate devotees. They could not resist his appeal and mesmeric power and to the last they were devoted to him and they saw to it that after his death his devotees were enabled to continue his worship and benefit from his promise: "My tomb will speak."

What was not understandable was that it never occurred to them that Baba belonged not only to Maharashtra but to the whole of India, nay, to the entire world. Until Narasimha Swamiji discovered him much later after his death Baba was practically unknown to the best part of India. While some of these learned devotees openly proclaimed that Baba was their conception of God their zeal and devotion did not extend to the point where they should have announced his presence, his message and his incredible feats of relief and succour to all classes of people, rich and poor, regardless of caste or religion to the entire country and the world outside. It will always remain a puzzle why educated and learned men like them failed in their elementary duty of sharing this divine personality, this man of God, with their countrymen. Was it because they were not sure of his antecedents, was it because they were misled by his garb of a fakir and his residence in a dilapidated mosque? None of them dared to ask him pointblank who he was, whether he was a Muslim or a Hindu. Apparently there was talk and rumours behind his back and vexed by these one day he threw up his clothes and standing stark naked invited the curious to find out the answer to their unasked question. There is no record to show if anyone accepted his challenge and if anyone did he did not talk about it.

The truth of the matter is that in his thinking, in his approach to problems of life and in his teachings and dealings with devotees Baba was cent per cent a Hindu, notwithstanding his disguise as a fakir and his frequent utterances of the name of Allah, which understandably confused most of those who came to have his darshan and his very intimate devotees. For Baba what was important was not the externals but the internal development of man and he concentrated on it. For him Ram, Rahim, Allah and Hari were one, they were the names of one universal being who was the supreme arbiter of mankind, call him what you will.

Baba did not have any Muslim devotee of the calibre of the ones we have described in the earlier chapters. If anybody could be called a true Muslim devotee it was Abdul, his personal attendant to whom he taught not only the *Quran* but also Hindu scriptures. He instilled in him faith and devotion to Hindu deities, especially Maruthi. Baba has said he drew his devotees to him and they never came to him on their own. He spoke of rinanubhanda, of contacts in previous births, his relatives and companions whom he recognised in this birth and as we have seen some of them were animals like goat, frog and snake. But among those whom he called to himself there were no Muslims with the exception of Abdul whom he sent for and would not let him go back when his previous guru asked that Abdul be sent back to him.

Baba spoke frequently of births and rebirths and at one time said that he and a devotee whose name he mentioned were together in seven births including the present. He said he was present during the invasion of Lanka by the vanara sena led by Maruthi for the rescue of Sita. He also spoke frequently of karma and the burden all creatures had to carry from one birth to another. He said no one could escape its effects and they had to be borne with patience and fortitude. But through his extraordinary powers he found ways to mitigate the effects of karma in this birth and brought relief to his devotees.

Thus a devotee, suffering from tuberculosis, came to him for relief and he sent him away with an assurance that he would look after him. That night the devotee had a painful dream in which he was beaten and tortured by the headmaster of a school for a theft he had committed. The devotee cried with pain and had a terrible time. The next morning he found he was feeling better and he was cured in a matter of days. Baba later told him that he had paid the penalty of his karma through the suffering he had endured in his dream.

Baba sometimes used unconventional methods, which others would have considered as risky, in treating patients. An example is when he gave a devotee, suffering from diarrhoea a handful of groundnuts to be eaten, supplemented by cold water. The patient miraculously recovered. In another case when a devotee was suffering from stomachache he had the man sit before him and simply ordered the body to behave and it did and the devotee got up with great relief. He frowned on taboos and superstitions. It was forbidden to orthodox Hindus to take onions more especially on ekadasi day and he made an orthodox devotee eat onion on that particular day. The devotee however insisted that Baba should set an example by eating some himself. Baba obliged him but later played a trick on him by saying that he had not taken onion and to prove it he vomited and what came out were bits of sweet potato, another of his miracles which he enjoyed in displaying to the amusement of his devotees. He had abundant humour and wit which enlivened his contacts and conversations with devotees and visitors.

Baba could be angry too and his devotees were terribly afraid of his loss of temper. But they were not always certain about the reason for his loss of temper and against whom it was directed. He was angry with the elements for inconveniencing his devotees or disturbing a meal and he was angry with the forces of evil which brought disease and misery to his children. It so happened that a devotee, bitten by a cobra, rushed to the mosque to seek relief from Baba. But as the stricken devotee ascended the steps of the mosque Baba shouted: "Don't come, don't go up, come down." The devotee took it to mean that Baba was asking him to go away and stood perplexed. After some time Baba cooled down and asked the devotee to come up and told him that the cobra poison had left his body. The devotee then realised that Baba's anger was directed to the poison which was entering into the bloodstream.

For Baba all creations of God were equal and he gave his love and sympathy to all, irrespective of their status, power and position. Thus he made a top white official and his wife who wanted to see him, wait for some time. When he saw they were in a hurry and impatient he made them wait indefinitely and they left in a huff. He wanted to teach the lesson of humility. On the other hand, when a leper came to have his darshan and painfully got up the steps of the mosque and stood hesitantly he invited him to come near him, and blessed him. The leper who was in an advanced stage of the disease and was stinking embarrassed a woman devotee who was nearby and could hardly tolerate his presence. She heaved a sigh of relief when the man slowly walked back. But Baba called him back and took the small parcel he had in his hand and opened it. There were some pedas which he had brought as his offering to Baba but was too ashamed to give them to him. Baba took a piece and put it in his mouth and gave another to the woman devotee and asked her to eat it. The woman had no other go but to swallow the despicable thing. Baba taught her a lesson of humility and compassion.

A rich man came to Baba and wanted him to show him Brahman or God. He was in a hurry and had a carriage, which he had hired, waiting for him. Baba sent him to various persons to get a loan from a moneylender. The moneylender refused to oblige them but readily gave the money when a devotee, whom he knew well, made the same request to him. The rich man, fretting and fuming at the loss of precious time and the excess fare he might have to pay for the carriage, could not understand why Baba was not responding to his request. Baba told him. "You have got the answer." The rich man was more perplexed than ever and then it was explained to him that Baba wanted to convey that not all could know the Brahman and one had to be qualified for it just as the moneylender would not give the loan to anyone but only to one whom he knew well.

Baba's devotees said they had not seen him read or write and the doubt arose whether he was literate at all. But they were amazed at his knowledge of the Hindu and Islamic scriptures and on many occasions he had entered into disputation with scholars and learned men on what was contained in them and their interpretation. He particularly mentioned *Vishnu Sahasranama* in which he said he saw Hari and kept it close to his chest. It was the Hindu scripture, *Rama Rajya*, which he had someone read to him in the last days of his life again and again day and night till the man who read it felt exhausted and Baba asked him to go home.

Baba's care and attention to his devotees was phenomenal. No one who came to see him could leave Shirdi without his permission. He knew when they should go and why they should postpone their journey although it might be a matter of life and death for the visitor or devotee to keep to their schedule. It so happened that two devotees who were in Shirdi had to leave urgently to catch a train and keep an appointment with an official in another town. Baba said: "Don't go." While one of them implicitly obeyed Baba and stayed back, the other did not want to miss his train and left Shirdi for the railway station. The other devotee was allowed to go by Baba after some time. When the devotee went to the railway station he found his friend still waiting on the platform for the train which had been delayed. In another instance, a devotee who was a deputy collector had to meet the collector at a particular place at a particular time. He was in Shirdi to take leave of Baba who

said: "Don't go today, go tomorrow." The devotee was conscious
that he would be incurring the displeasure of his superior and
perhaps inviting disciplinary action but he decided to obey Baba's
instructions and postponed his trip. When he reached the
assigned place the next day he was surprised to learn that the
Collector had not come the previous day as originally
programmed but was expected only that day. How did Baba
know about the Collector's change of programme? The same
question has to be asked in hundreds of similar cases where
Baba seemed to know everything everywhere and nothing was
hidden from him. Then there is the story of the devotee who
lapsed into evil ways and visited a prostitute thinking, probably,
that Baba wouldn't know about it. But most amazing, Baba did
and he was there at the door when the devotee entered the
prostitute's room. The devotee felt ashamed and took a vow
never to do such a thing.

Baba cured another devotee of his obsession with beautiful
women. A party of Muslim women in purdah visited Baba.
One of his intimate devotees who was present was attracted to
one of them, a young and beautiful woman. The devotee fondly
hoped she would lift her veil so that he could drink the beauty
of her face. However, this did not happen and after the lady left
Baba told the devotee it was an evil thing for him to think of
women as he did. The devotee wondered how Baba had read
his mind and vowed to cast away evil thoughts. Baba never
forgot to take his commission as it were in advance from devotees
who secured promotion in their jobs or got increment through
his grace even when they knew there was no such prospect.
Baba claimed his commission as dakshina from a devotee who
was asked to pay Rs. 50. The devotee willingly paid the amount
but did not understand why Baba asked it of him. As soon as
he returned home he learnt he had been promoted in his job
with an increment of Rs. 50 in his salary. In the case of another
unemployed but well qualified devotee who sought his blessings
Baba repeatedly directed him to go to Pune. The devotee was
mystified for he knew there was no scope for employment in
that place but he obeyed Baba. It was in Pune that he got a job
in a college as professor of geology. Baba never allowed any
devotee or his representative to cheat him of his dues, as a
friend of a devotee who was deputed to visit Baba found to his
great surprise. The devotee had sent dakshina to Baba through

the friend who forgot about it until Baba gently reminded him about the dakshina that had been sent to him through the friend. In another instance when two devotees called on Baba he asked dakshina from only one of them. When the other devotee asked why he had been left out Baba explained that the devotee from whom he demanded dakshina had taken a vow before he got his present job that he would pay his first month's salary to his Ishta Devatha and had failed to do so. Baba now wanted that debt to be paid to him. The devotee admitted his guilt and gladly paid the debt he owed God.

Baba had a way of instilling respect for all God's creations among his devotees. We shall quote only three among hundreds of such cases. A close devotee prepared a cake as *naivedya* (offering) for Baba and asked him to partake of it. Baba returned it to him after some time and said he had tasted it. The devotee did not see him touch the cake and asked him: "But Baba, you have not even touched it." Baba said a fly had sat on it and tasted it and it meant he had tasted it. In another instance, a devotee had similarly prepared a naivedya for Baba and as he was about to leave home for the mosque he saw a sickly looking dog expectantly barring his way. He considered it sacrilegious to give anything to it before offering it to Baba and drove it away. When the devotee offered the prasad to Baba he turned him away saying the devotee had driven him away when he was at his house. The devotee said he had not seen Baba in his house. Baba said he was the sick dog and he had driven him away. The next day when the devotee was again preparing to go to the mosque with the offering he saw a poor emaciated old man of a low caste at the gate anxiously looking at him. The devotee ignored him and went to Baba and placed the offering before him. Baba again refused to take it saying he had been turned away from his house again. The devotee then realised that the low caste poor old man at the gate of his house was Baba himself. In the third instance a sick devotee who was very much fond of curds, had been asked to avoid them in the interest of his health but he could not resist taking curds all the same. One day a cat broke into his house and ate away all the curds. The patient, in a fit of anger, beat the cat which screamed with pain. When the devotee visited Baba the next day Baba showed him the marks of beating on his back. The devotee realised that Baba had come as a cat to save him.

A devotee said Baba conveyed his blessings to devotees mostly through silence. His touch was a potent factor in moulding the minds of those who came to him. He had a way of touching with his palm the head of the devotee. His touch conveyed certain impulses, forces, ideas. Sometimes he pressed the head hard with his hand as though he was crushing out the animal instincts of the devotee. Sometimes he tapped, sometimes he made a pass with his palm over the head. Each gesture had its own effect, producing remarkable sensations and feelings in the devotee.

His devotees worshipped Baba as God as they treated and honoured him as a Maharaja. They assembled all the paraphernalia of a Maharaja and they loved to bathe him in sandal paste and flowers and to adorn him with costly shawls and a golden crown. They made a palanquin with silver accessories, a chariot and bought a horse which was in the vanguard of the procession from the mosque to the chavadi every alternate night. But Baba did not like to be treated as a Maharaja. He declined to be carried in the palanquin which nevertheless formed part of the procession carrying Baba's chappals in it. He walked barefoot and never used footwear except occasionally when he visited the Lendi (garden). He chose to regard himself as a fakir till the last who welcomed poverty and obscurity. He was engrossed in contemplation of his Guru God whom he always called a fakir and in that state of bliss thoughts of food, rest, etc., seldom troubled him. He seemed to follow the principle that a sage should be contented to get just what would keep his body and soul together and to see that his powers of knowing, speech and wisdom might not perish.

In his earlier days Baba did hard manual work. He laid out the Lendi almost single-handedly, sowing the seeds and nurturing the plants, watering them and looking after their maintenance. It is said he baked bread and distributed it to the poor. He cut vegetables and sometimes served meals to devotees with his own hand. He ground wheat flour on a grinding stone. When on one occasion women devotees saw him doing this hard labour they pushed him aside and took the task upon themselves. Baba said the flour should be taken out and sprinkled on the outskirts of the village where a cholera epidemic was prevailing. Devotees said the epidemic subsided after this was done. Baba rarely changed his kufni and had to be forced to discard them after they became totally unfit to use. Devotees have seen him mending his tattered kufni with needle and thread. And the irony was that the contributions made to him in cash by devotees exceeded that of a Governor's salary and at one time the income-tax authorities were reportedly considering levying tax on his income. But Baba never saved any money. He distributed the day's collections on that day itself to the poor, beggars, fakirs and to devotees in strained circumstances.

Baba could be very human on many occasions. When a dear devotee passed away he could not control his tears and followed the funeral procession some distance to bid him farewell. He loudly bemoaned his loss and one devotee has said his lamentations were even heard from a distance. In his earlier days when he was a wandering fakir and thought to be a mad fellow children used to tease him and throw stones but he got hold of them affectionately and gave them sugar candy. He danced and sang in the chavadi at nights with anklets on his feet. Devotees have recorded that he had a mellifluous voice which was strangely soothing. He never admitted he performed miracles. He told a devotee: "I do not do any chamatkars (miracles). You have astrologers. They look ahead and give their predictions, some of which come true. I look further ahead. What I say happens. My art also is a sort of astrology. But you people do not understand this. To you my words look like chamatkars because you do not know the future. So you regard events as proof of my miracle working power and you turn your reverence to me. I, in my turn, turn your reverence to God and see that you are really benefitted."

Baba did not believe that those who treaded the path of spirituality should leave their homes and become ascetics. To a devotee who told him he was sick of *samsara* (family life) he said that samsara, the perpetual cycle of births and deaths, was the result of the law of *prarabdha karma*. As long as there was the body which was the result of prarabdha karma one could not escape going through the results of previous karma. Merely running away to a forest or leaving the family would not enable one to escape the series of events which would make up the present life. Baba said even he was not free from samsara. "As long as there is the body," he said, "there must be samsara. Samsara is binding on me also." Baba said samsara need not be painful if one lived and acted properly. It was possible to escape the effects of samsara, like sorrow and suffering by leading a virtuous life, he said.

To a woman devotee who also expressed a wish to get rid of samsara Baba asked her to ask herself: "Who am I?" He said she should constantly identify herself more and more with sat-chit-ananda and merge in it and that was the only escape from samsara.

Baba was often in ecstatic moods and then words flowed from his lips as if he was God and they reminded one of the Lord's message in the Gita. At one such moment he said: "If one ever dwells on me in his mind and will not even taste food before offering it to me I am his slave. So also if he hungers and thirsts after me and treats all else as unimportant." He also said: "I am the bond slave of my devotee. I love devotion. He who withdraws his hearts from wife, child and parents and loves me is my real lover and he merges in me like a river in the sea."

But these rare moments apart Baba described himself as an agent of God (whom he most often called the fakir) who had been given vast powers. He used to tell devotees who made some requests or other that the fakir had not sanctioned them. Thus one day he was distributing kafnis to a number of people and one of his intimate devotees thought to himself he would like to have one. Baba divined his thought and told him: "The fakir has not sanctioned your request," meaning that the devotee was destined for something else.

To this day nobody knows what was the name given to Baba by his parents and he never chose to mention it. Sai Baba is the name given to him by the people of Shirdi and when a magistrate taking evidence from him in a case asked his name he said :"They call me Sai Baba." He discouraged all questions about his parentage and gave mystifying answers. On one occasion he said his father was *purusha* and his mother *prakriti*. His mystifying remarks to a devotee led to a calamity. Baba one day told this rich devotee of the village: "Thieves are entering the village. Take security measures." The devotee took Baba's word literally to mean that the village was being threatened by thieves and he strengthened the security around his residence. But the thieves proved to be an epidemic of cholera and the rich devotee became its first victim. Baba however controlled it after saying it would claim seven victims and that was what happened.

Considering the various stages of Baba's life it could be seen that there was a marked difference between his life before 1886 and the life thereafter. Before 1886 the stress was on doing good to those who were near to him and connected by rinanubhanda (pre-natal obligations). The mass of devotees came to benefit after 1886. According to one writer the main benefit was the unification of the Hindu faith within itself and of Islam within itself. Baba's aim was by purification and refinement of both religions to build one common central religion or faith that could be a world faith. It would have also resulted in helping to solve India's national problem of unifying conflicting faiths. Baba did not live long enough to achieve this goal fully. He envisaged a world brotherhood of man unspoiled by religious fanaticism and conflicts, a world where man will live in peace and amity with all creations of God. He did not believe in rituals and advocated the bhakti marga and prescribed nama japa and devotion to Guru as the talisman for spiritual advancement. For him Guru was God and there was nothing that could not be achieved by guru worship. And this he was at pains to repeat again and again with examples from his own experience under a Guru. He never gave any discourse nor whisper mantras into the ears of his devotees. He laid stress on a pure and orderly life and the do's and don'ts he prescribed for his devotees were what everybody knew and had heard but never followed. The pity was that very few people came to imbibe his teachings, they came to him seeking material benefits and relief from sorrow and suffering. Many of them did not understand him at all. The right approach or mentality that was necessary for understanding a saint was wanting in many of them who met him and Baba himself said: "They were coming for water to the supplier of water but insisted on holding their pots with their mouths down. So unreceptive they were." Baba graphically demonstrated this when he arranged the pots in the mosque upside down. When a surprised devotee asked the reason for his keeping the pots with mouths shut Baba said: "Those who come here do not want to learn." It was not until 1910 that Baba achieved respectability and more and more people came to receive his blessings and benefits. Before that he was still being considered as a mad fakir who had unusual powers.

But even after 1910 his appearance in the garb of a fakir and his invoking the name of Allah did not remove the strong impression that he was a Muslim. But with all that they worshipped him for to them whatever might be his faith he was God, a living God, who did for them what they were daily praying to their own deities. Some of them called him "Muslim Vishnu". It was during the period of eight years that his real worth was recognised and his name and fame were at their peak.

A devotee wrote: "Sai Baba was a unique and perhaps one of the strangest of known spiritual personalities adorning the earth during recent times." But to millions of people all over India today Sai Baba is more than a saint. He is God who lived on earth like Rama, Krishna, the Buddha and Christ to promote human brotherhood and love and compassion and to instil faith and confidence and inspire them to progress towards divinity which is vouchsafed to every man and woman. Aurobindo envisaged a time when man will become superman and then progress to divinity. Baba was such a personality who became God while being born as man. Like God his origins are mysterious, like God his powers are vast and like God he is immortal for although he has left his body he is still alive in his tomb and in the hearts and minds of millions of his devotees and in the shrines and temples built for him all over the country. He has become part of the Hindu pantheon responding to cries for succour and protection from wherever it comes and taken the role of the guardian angel of those who fall at his feet and seek his guidance for a safe journey through the vale of tears which is this world.

12

SHIRDI TODAY

A VISIT to Shirdi was an exciting, spiritual experience, the memory of which will last a lifetime. From the moment one got down at Kopargaon railway station and took a taxi to Shirdi, 18 kilometres away, one was consumed with anticipation and a feeling of exhilaration that one would very soon set foot on the sacred soil of Shirdi; one would be enveloped and awed by the aura of a great guru god who charmed and ennobled the lives of thousands of devotees far and near for over a decade, and continues to do so even after he shed his mortal coil 76 years ago.

To one who was familiar with Sai Baba's life and the times in which he lived, Kopargaon was an important name with which was associated many incidents connected with Sai Baba and his devotees. If one remembers Sai Baba one has to remember Kopargaon too, for it was there that the devotees came first on their way to Shirdi. It has been the scene of some of Baba's miracles as we have seen in the earlier chapters. It was also the place where for some time the station staff was antagonistic to Baba and tried to dissuade people from visiting Shirdi. But they could not stop the flood of pilgrims to Shirdi and realised their mistake much later.

Shirdi may have changed in the last 60 years or more but Kopargaon apparently has not. It remains an antiquated and undistinguished wayside station with hardly any sign of its greatness by being associated with Sai Baba. Anyone who got down there unaware of its history had no means of knowing it was the gateway to Shirdi except for a signboard hidden behind the platform which said: "Alight here for Shirdi." There is no mention of Baba, no picture of Baba and no poster to attract pilgrims. One felt that the railway authorities were not conscious of the importance of the station as a pilgrim centre which might fill their coffers and also of their responsibility to satisfy the needs of the growing number of pilgrims to Shirdi. How far they are ignorant about the importance of Kopargaon can be understood from the fact that until a few months ago no express or mail train stopped there and long distance passengers were put to hardship by not being able to detrain at Kopargaon to go to Shirdi. It was only after repeated appeals to the Railway Minister, Mr Zaffer Sharief, that mail and express trains have been permitted to stop at Kopargaon for a few seconds. It is now possible for pilgrims from the south to come to Bangalore and board an express train in the evening and alight at Kopargaon the following afternoon round about 4 p.m. This is the shortest and safest route to Shirdi but this is still not widely known.

From Kopargaon to Shirdi it is less than half an hour's journey. There is not much traffic on the road which is well maintained. It is as you approach the outskirts of Shirdi that one sees the bustle and hectic activity all round. Flower sellers and petty shopkeepers cry out their wares and seek to attract customers. One has to walk through lanes and bylanes with shops on either side almost touching you and carrying on roaring business. In such a narrow space one occasionally finds a car or a motor cycle trying to share it with you but no one is bothered and the vast crowd of Sai devotees simply moves on. The old village of Shirdi with about 100 mud houses is gone and what is there today is the vast temple complex ringed by hundreds of big and small shops and big and small hotels. All that one could identify with the old Shirdi are three or four houses where some of Baba's intimate devotees lived. These are the houses of Mahlsapathy, Baba's oldest devotee, Lakshmi Bai and Shama. We will refer to a visit to these houses later in this narrative.

The most important building in the complex is the Sai Baba Samadhi Mandir. It was originally built by a Nagpur millionaire, a devotee of Baba, Bapusaheb Buti, and was called Buti Wada. Sai Baba's body was interred in the site reserved by Buti to build a Krishna temple and Baba's samadhi has come up here. The samadhi has been built with white marble stone. Around the samadhi railing one can see ornamental decoration. In front of the samadhi are two pillars with decorative designs in silver.

Also in front are two marble *padukas* of Baba and the brick which was broken and led to Baba predicting his death, is kept near the samadhi. Just behind the samadhi is Baba's statue, made of Italian marble. It shows him seated on a throne with his right leg thrown on the left in the familiar posture which thousands of his devotees all over the country know and worship. The statue was made by late Balaji Vasant alias Babusaheb Talim who made it out of a sheer sense of gratitude. The idol statue was installed on October 7, 1954 by Swami Saisharanand, an ardent devotee from Ahmedabad. Before that Sai Baba's picture was placed beside the samadhi and worshipped. Overhanging the statue is a silver umbrella and the back of the statue is Prabhaval (hinterland) made of silver and with swastik signs depicted on both sides. Above the statue on the wall is engraved this couplet:

Raghupati Raghava Rajaram
Patita Pawan Sainam

On the high ceiling behind the statue is also this inscription:

Sachidananda Sat Guru Sai Maharaj Ki Jai.

It is in the big hall facing the samadhi that thousands of devotees take part in the daily arati performed four times a day. It is a delight even for the gods when prayers go to Baba from a thousand throats in union in an atmosphere surcharged with emotion and ecstacy.

In the Samadhi Mandir in a separate enclosure are kept in view articles used by Baba and the various items of paraphernalia which formed part of the durbar held by Baba who was treated and feted as a maharaja like the royal umbrella, silver mace, whisks and other symbols of royalty.

Not far from the mandir is Dwaraka Mayi or the masjid where Baba stayed all his life after he came to Shirdi. It was then a dilapidated mosque which was not used by Muslims and it was in such an awful condition that parts of it were crumbling all the time. Baba's devotees offered to build for him another residence but he would not agree to move from the place nor would he agree until the very last moment to repairs being made to make it habitable. But today it has been renovated and does not look like a mosque at all. It is a very small place hardly 30 feet by 15 feet and one wonders how Baba would have lived there with so many devotees and visitors occupying the limited space. Baba called it Dwaraka Mayi (he also called it once "A Brahmin Mosque") to respect Hindu sentiment. As one enters Dwaraka Mayi one notices on the left the dhuni which Baba created from the moment he settled in the mosque and which still burns as it did throughout his lifetime. It was by the side of the dhuni that Baba sat and received devotees and visitors and to mark the spot a portrait of Baba has been installed on the side of the wall. In the front above the steps are two pillars where Baba used to stand in the evenings and greet passersby and talk to them. In one corner on the right is a large stone on which Baba sat while taking a bath. Further inside on the right at the extreme corner is the grinding stone which Baba used for grinding wheat into flour and by its side is kept a closed rack with stored wheat. On the opposite side, on the left, is preserved the mud pot in which Baba kept the alms he got daily and placed it outside the mosque to enable crows, dogs and beggars to share the food with him. A big open shed has been put up in front of Dwaraka Mayi to serve as a prayer hall and place of meditation. Here opposite to Dwaraka Mayi there is another picture of Baba and below it is the famous stone on which Baba sat in comtemplation. The picture of Baba in this posture is the one seen in the homes of thousands of devotees.

A short distance, less than 200 yards, from Dwaraka Mayi is the chavadi, another landmark of Shirdi. Baba slept in the chavadi on alternate nights. He was taken in procession there and there was an elaborate ceremony before Baba retired for the night. The chavadi also has been renovated and it looks neat and clean. It is a very small building, actually a hall 20 feet by 15 feet with a partition which served as Baba's bedroom. In the bedroom there is a picture of Baba and a notice warns women from entering it. In the hall on one side there is a cot on which Baba's body was placed for a sacred bath after his passing away. On the other side is a chair mounted with wheels. An inscription says it has been there since Baba's time but it does not say if Baba ever used it. The chavadi, it may be recalled, was the village guest house and Baba had taken part in entertainments there in the early days of his arrival in Shirdi and he had been seen singing and dancing.

Another landmark which has been preserved is the neem tree under which Baba sat when he first came to Shirdi in the latter half of the 19th century, some say, as a lad of 16. A mandap has been built round the tree and it is called Gurusthan.

To protect the tree from its bark being peeled off by devotees the trunk has been covered by a shield. There is always a long queue of devotees doing pradakshina of the tree and its sacredness is exemplified in this prayer: "I bow down to the Lord Sad Guru Sainath who by his constant abode at the foot of the margossa tree, whose juice though by nature is bitter and distasteful has turned it nectar-like sweet because he has exalted the tree above the legendary Kalpavriksh (wish-fulfilling tree)." The reference to the juice of the neem tree in the prayer is attested by devotees who say that some of the leaves of the tree taste bitter which is its natural quality while some others taste sweet which is unnatural.

In between Dwaraka Mayi and the chavadi is the Maruthi Shrine where Baba used to stand for a minute or two making mysterious signs on his way to the chavadi. The shrine has also been renovated and the granite stone figure of Maruthi is imbedded in the wall.

At some distance from Gurusthan is Lendi, the garden which Baba laid with his own hands, digging and planting trees and watering them. He repaired to this garden in the morning and evening and no one was allowed to go with him except his personal attendant, Abdul.

On the other side of the national highway to Agra is the Khandoba temple where Baba was refused shelter by Mahlsapathy, its priest, on the ground that he was a Muslim. It was then that Baba decided to make the dilapidated mosque his home. Mahlsapathy later realised his mistake and became an intimate devotee of Baba. When Baba left his body for a short while in the early years of his stay in Shirdi it was to Mahlsapathy that he entrusted it. Mahlsapathy guarded the body and refused to surrender it for burial in spite of pressure from the officials and the local people. Baba came back to life after three days. Khandoba temple is very small and Khandoba himself, engraved in granite stone, looks like any wayside god we see in the countryside.

Not to be missed in the temple complex are the samadhis of Shyamkarna, the horse which was in the vanguard of the procession to the chavadi and back and for the unknown and unidentified tiger which, brought before Baba by its keeper to cure it of its sickness, breathed its last at his feet. Tiny memorials have been erected over these samadhis enclosed with a small horse and tiger statuettes.

The daily rituals at the Sai Samadhi Mandir consist of four *aratis* (worship), the Kakad arati before sunrise at 5 a.m., the noon arati, the evening arati at sunset and the night arati at 10. The devotees participate in these aratis, joining in the prayers and singing in unison. The congregational worship lasts 30 minutes at the end of which arati is performed with lighted kindled cloth wicks dipped in ghee and wrapped round wooden sticks. Camphor, so familiar a part of temple worship in south India, is not used. At the end of the worship the devotees march forward one by one and offer their homage to Baba's footprints and the samadhi and disperse. There is perfect order and discipline and silence which is amazing considering the large number of devotees, men, women and children who pack the prayer hall. At night Baba is ceremonially put to bed after the arati with a mosquito curtain fitted above his head. Readers will remember Baba had refused to use a mosquito curtain at the chavadi but ultimately had to yield to pressure from devotees. The symbolic practice is continued today. At the early morning arati Baba is given a sacred bath with milk which is later distributed to devotees.

The prayers to Baba in the early morning arati are intended to wake him up and seek his darshan. "With folded hands I lay my head at your feet, oh Sadgurunatha, please listen to my entreaty," says the devotee in his prayer. "Irrespective of feelings I have come to you, please look at me mercifully, Sadgururaya. Since I desire to be at your feet always, give me shelter, leaving aside all reservations."

The devotee then asks Baba to wake up. "Arise Panduranga (Vithal of Pandharpur), it is now dawn. Vishnu's devotees have gathered in large numbers on the Garud Para (eagle-shaped platform found in Vaishnava temples). Arise, Arise, Shri Sainath Guru, show us your lotus feet.

"Tide over and relieve us of all mental tensions, physical tribulations and temporal problems and save us all.

"Oh, Lord Sainath Maharaj, you are the sun that destroys the darkness of ignorance of this world. How ignorant we are! We have no words to describe your greatness. Even the great poets are exhausted in their attempt to describe it. Mercifully, therefore, give us the ability yourself to sing of your greatness.

"The faithful devotees who follow you with good intentions and feelings to have your darshan are waiting at your doors. We are filled with contentment to see you in deep meditation but we are eager to drink from you the nectar of your teachings.

"Open your lotus eyes, Lord of the poor and the destitute, Lord Ramakanta (Vishnu) and look at us mercifully as a mother looks at her child. Your amusing sayings in a sweet voice take away all our sufferings, Sainatha.

"Arise, Panduranga, now give your darshan to all. It is sunrise now and the time to sleep is past.

"The saints, sadhus, sages all have gathered together. Now leave the comfort of your bed and show your lotus face.

"A big crowd is gathered in the pandal up to the main gate. Everyone is eager at heart to see your handsome face."

The devotee then speaks of his own spiritual growth.

"I have compressed and entwined lust, anger, ego and envy and made them into a wick for the lamp and soaked it into the ghee of asceticism that I have poured.

"I have lit it with the spark of devotion for Sainath Guru. After burning up the vices the Guru has shed the light on me. Destroy the darkness of duality and merge me in the self. Show me. I do arati. Show me.

"How shall I describe your greatness? Who can extol it? Even the tremendous sin of killing a thousand brahmins is washed away by your mere darshan."

The devotee calls upon all saints and sages and devotees to wake up.

"Wake up all, saints and sages. Achieve your own welfare. The human body is perishing every moment. After it is gone we can never achieve self-realisation.

"Wake up! Wake up! Let us go quickly to the Lord's palace. The heaps of sins that we sinners have committed will be burnt if we reach there in time."

At the noon arati the following is part of the prayer:

"Meditation upon your name removes the worldly sufferings of all. Unfathomable is your action. Show the path to the unfortunate ones.

"In this age of kaliyug you are the true Brahmta avatar that has taken form and descended on this earth. You are also Swami Datta Digamber (Dattatreya).

"Just as the chatak bird desires to drink pure water so give
me knowledge directly, oh Lord! And kindly give me your
assurance.

"You take avatar whenever dharma declines and even the
atheists begin to believe in you.

"You show different types of lilas in your innumerable forms
and remove the difficulties of your devotees, day and night.

"You have not distinguished between Hindus and Muslims.
In the present human form you have taken again you look at
Hindus and Muslims with the same love and show how
comprehensive are your powers, Oh Sai.

"My body, my speech, my mind and all my senses, my
intellect, my innate being—all these I offer to you.

"Whenever people remember you they should touch your
feet with pure hearts and full faith always. If at all we live and
become known it should be as your devotees, thus earning
salvation not only for ourselves but for our parents and families.

"Thou art my mother, thou art my father
Thou art my brother, thou art my friend
Thou art knowledge, thou art the embodiment
Of love and tenderness
Thou art everything, my Lord, my Lord.
My body, my speech, my mind and all my senses
my innate being—all these I offer to you, Narayana

"All those who meditate on you diligently have
Lakshmi, the goddess of wealth, dwelling in their homes
Day and night uninterruptedly
You also protect them and remove all their difficulties
Such art thou Baba.

"I bow down to the Lord Sadguru Sainath
Who is truth incarnate and always rooted in consciousness
And bliss, the Lord who is the cause for the creation,
Existence, destruction of the world and who has come to
        this
World in a human form for the sake of his own devotees.

"Sai is the avatar of Raghav (Rama) the Lord
Who fulfils the desires of his devotees for the
Purification of their infatuated and deluded hearts

And minds—to whom I pray, day and night
Untiringly and blissfully.

"Sainath! You are my God whom I worship
I extol your praises. Let my mind dwell lovingly
On your lotus feet just as the bee hovers over the
Lotus flowers enticed by the desire for honey."

The following are part of the prayers sung by the
congregation in the evening arati at sunset:

"My darling mother may be annoyed with me or even
My father, My wife may be annoyed with me or even my
     son or my daughter, my sister or brother may be
     annoyed
With me or even my father-in-law and mother-in-law but
     never
Dattaguru, my mother Sai, be annoyed with me.

"My daughter-in-law may turn away from me or even
My brother's wife; my dear ones, kith and kin may turn
Away from me, or even my own people or my relatives
But never my guru, my mother Sai, be annoyed with me.

"Deer, birds, insects, the entire animal and bird world
May be annoyed with me. The trees, stones, mountains,
     rivers,
Seas may be annoyed with me. The sky, wind, fire, water,
     earth-
The five elements may be annoyed with me but never
My Dattaguru, my mother Sai be annoyed with me.

"Let my reasoning, speech and fickle-mind be annoyed with
     me
Let my own body, all the ten directions, be annoyed with
     me
Let all-pervading time be annoyed with me. Let the entire
World, the universe be annoyed with me, but never my
Dattaguru, my mother Sai, be annoyed with me.

"Let people call me a fool and laugh. Let envy not sting me.
Let me delight at the touch of the feet of the Lord
Let me not get trapped by the mire of the world

Let not the fort of chivalry topple down
Let me not wish evil upon anyone
Let me be angry with the worldly affairs I am engaged in
Let me be disinterested and let that indifference
Stay firmly in my mind

"Let me not be contemptuous of anyone
Let me have no desires
Let there be only Sai in my heart, intellect and meditation
Let my love be oozing towards the Lord's feet
Wherever I look in the world I should see him only
My Lord do not deny me these above mentioned entreaties."

At the night arati when Baba is put to bed the devotees make this prayer :
"Holding the lamp in my hands I do arati and
Pray to you with all my love
Hail! Hail ! Sainath! Now come and lie down in the temple
For those devotees who have sufferings
You endure their problems by taking them upon
Yourself thus removing their difficulties
For those who are dedicated to the Lord you quickly
Give them darshan
You must be terribly troubled in your body
Forgive us and lie down on that beautiful flower-decked
Bed. Please accept some of the services your devotees
Render in your worship
I offer you the light of good intentions lit with
The five elements of my body
This servant is offering you the attar of love and also
Fragrant water.

"Sai, it saddens us to leave your feet and go away
At your command we go with your blessings as prasad
To our own homes
We are going now but we will come again to be near your
          feet
To awaken you, Sai mother, and to achieve our own welfare

"The swing-bed of faith and devotion has been suspended
          from

The rafters in my heart. Baba, I have hung it from the
rafters
With a pure and virtuous mind I have made your bed"
(The reference to the rafters in the song is to the wooden plank
which Baba had hung up from the rafters of the mosque for his
bed. See earlier chapter for details.)
"Inconceivably absorbed in divine contemplation
Baba wrapped in a delicate pair of shawls
Perfect light of knowledge, Sadguru Swami
Rest and sleep in your bed

"Now Swami sleep well
Gopala, kind Baba Sai
Our desires are now fulfilled and
We go now to our own homes
We shall wake you up for our own needs
To destroy the torment that is ours
Due to our fate caused by our good and bad actions."

Every Thursday night before the arati Baba is symbolically
taken in a procession from Dwaraka Mayi to the chavadi where
he used to sleep every alternate night. His padukas and portrait
are placed in a palanquin after worship and the procession
wends its way to the chavadi which is hardly a stone's throw
away. The procession has all the marks of royalty and the
paraphernalia associated with it. At the chavadi there is an
elaborate ceremony before Baba is symbolically put to bed. He
is fed and his clay pipe put to his mouth for him to have a puff
or two, everything symbolically of course.

Sanstan officials said there were three official festivals every
year and they are Sri Rama Navami, Guru Poornima and Dasara
or Punya Tithi. Each of these festivals is celebrated for three
days with cultural and religious functions. An interesting fact
about the visit to Shirdi is that the devotee has not to pay
anything at any time. Darshan of Baba is free and so are visits
to Dwaraka Mayi and the chavadi and other important places
associated with Baba. Hundi boxes, called Dakshina Box, are
kept in the Sai Samadhi Mandhir where devotees can make
their contributions as part of their homage to Baba but there is
no compulsion. Close circuit TV sets outside the mandir and at
Dwaraka Mayi enable the devotees to watch the arati ceremony.

At the conclusion of the morning arati Vishnu Sahasranama, a favourite of Baba, recorded by M. S. Subbalakshmi on a cassette is broadcast.

There are not many contemporaries of Sai Baba alive but residents of Kopargaon where Baba roamed in the forests after he came to Shirdi in the early years said there were some centenarians in their midst who had seen Baba and talked to him during his visits to Kopargaon. There is a big park in Kopargaon which is named as Sai Baba Park to mark the place where he did penance.

In Shirdi itself by some good fortune one was able to meet a 90- year-old devotee of Baba who said Baba played marbles with him when he was a boy of eight. He is Uddhau Madhava Rao Deshpande, son of Deshpande alias Shama, an intimate devotee of Baba who acted as a kind of private secretary and confidant of Baba. His name has appeared frequently in this chronicle. Udhau Madhava Rao identified himself as the small boy with a cap on and holding a sceptre in his hand in the photograph of Baba with his devotees taken on his way to the chavadi. In the picture where Baba is seen clutching his kufni with his left hand and a royal umbrella held over his head he is flanked on either side by two children and the child to his right is Deshpande's son. Udhau Madhava Rao, who lives in the same house occupied by his father, was too old and feeble to talk much but he was anxious to let the visitor know of his intimate contacts with Baba who had visited his house only once. That was when his father was bitten by a snake. Baba had then come and applied udhi on the affected part and asked Shama, as he affectionately called him, to come to the mosque the next day for arati. He said their house was so near the mosque that when his mother shouted at home Baba could hear her. Bal Gangadar Tilak came to their house and Shama took him to Baba. He said Baba was a multi-linguist. He conversed in the language of the visitor, be it English, Hindi, Urdu or Marathi. He said he had heard Baba speak in English. He mentioned that when Baba took his bath the swastik sign was formed on his head with vilvam leaves. After the bath Baba's face was "strikingly brilliant". He said Baba was tall and his hands touched his knees like those of Rama. Madhava Rao was 15 when Baba attained samadhi.

Nearby is the house of Mahlsapathy who passed away four years after the samadhi of Baba. His granddaughter lives in the house sanctified by Mahlsapathy who was the first to call Baba "Sai Baba" which has now become a mantra in millions of homes throughout the country. Baba's padukas presented to Mahlsapathy by Baba were shown to visitors. These padukas are lent to various Sai shrines in various parts of the country for devotees to pay homage.

Not far away is Lakshmi Bai's house. Lakshmi Bai was an ardent devotee of Baba and she was one of the privileged persons before whose house Baba stopped and asked for alms. A few days before he passed away Baba called her and gave her nine coins to preserve and worship. These coins are imbedded in the heart of a statue of Lakshmi Bai kept in the centre of the house.

Other landmarks in the temple complex which remind one of the times of Baba are the samadhis of Tatya Patil, a favourite child and devotee of Baba whose mother Bayyaji Bai used to chase Baba in the forest and hills to feed him and who Baba claimed was his sister in a previous birth, and that of Abdul the personal attendant of Baba who served Baba faithfully till the last and became a yogi himself, ministering to the needs of Baba's devotees.

An interesting person one comes across in the temple complex is Swami Sivanesan, who hails from Coimbatore in Tamil Nadu. He is dressed like a fakir and speaks only in Hindi. He has been in Shirdi for 41 years and is doing service to Baba in a silent and unobstrusive way. Not many will notice him, he is so unassuming and keeps himself away from the crowd. It was difficult to meet this 68-year-old yogi but after some persistent efforts he agreed to talk and invited the visitor to his shack which was a lumber room under a staircase with little or no ventilation. He was requested to speak in Tamil to which he agreed after some hesitation. He told the story of an atheist young man disillusioned with life who left home in search of peace of mind and landed in Shirdi where he found in Baba what he craved for. In Coimbatore, Sivanesan who had read up to the IX standard had asked the question, what is religion, what is God, why go to temples. But he was puzzled by a vision he had of an old man sitting on a rock and he could not understand its meaning. He left home and came to Bombay and met a number of saintly persons, including Swami Nityananda and Swami Krishna Chaitanya. A sanyasi appeared in his dream and advised him to go to Shirdi. Not knowing where Shirdi was and being penniless he walked along the railway line and subsisted on the scraps of food thrown from passing railway carriages. A sympathetic station master put him on a train bound for Nashik and told him not to bother about not having a ticket. From Nashik he walked to Triambakeshwar where he met a Tamil sadhu who took him under his protection. But Sivanesan's aim was to go to Shirdi. He left the sadhu and trekked to Shirdi. He arrived in Shirdi in 1953 and has been there ever since. At that time Shirdi was still undeveloped. He made himself useful by cleaning up Dwaraka Mayi, the chavadi and other places and lived on offerings made by devotees. Shama's son, Uddhau Madhava Rao came to Dwaraka Mayi for puja every day and he undertook to feed Sivanesan. This helped him to pull on for six months. The Court Receiver who was in charge of the Sansthan assigned him work and he was assured of boarding and lodging. But things became difficult when this sympathetic official was replaced by an Executive Officer who created problems for him. But Swami Sivanesan had created a niche in the hearts of Baba's devotees and he became part and parcel of the temple complex serving Baba and the devotees in his own simple way. The Sansthan now feeds him and has allotted the lumber room for his residence. Swami Sivanesan who has graduated from an atheist to total surrender at the feet of Baba said he conducted bhajans and discourses at the chavadi in the evenings. He said Baba had appeared before him in the Lendi garden once and he had a number of experiences of Baba's grace and protection.

Quite an unusual devotee of Baba one meets in Shirdi is a 30-year-old black American, Christine who has settled there for eight years now. From what Swami Sivanesan said one learnt she came from California in the United States. She was studying in college and one night she saw Baba in a dream. From that moment she was overpowered by her desire to go to India and to Shirdi. She expressed her wish to the Principal who allowed her to go and helped to collect the air fare from her fellow students and she also paid from her own pocket. She arrived in Bombay and after being misdirected and losing her way often, managed to reach Shirdi where Swami Sivanesan gave her protection and shelter. She had told him Baba had sent her to him. Swami Sivanesan said she had gone hungry for many days and suffered many hardships. She suffered from some stomach trouble but that did not prevent her from doing service to Baba. She told him she had seen Baba in visions after coming to Shirdi. She did not mix with the pilgrims and was rarely seen in the temple complex. She barged into the swami's room like a a flash of lightning while he was being interviewed and before one could notice her she dashed out. She was dressed in a heavy skirt which looked more like a sack cloth and it appeared she did not care much about it at all. The Swami said she was sometimes out of her mind but she was very much attached to him. One noticed her at the bhajan conducted by the Swami at the chavadi in the evenings where she was found to be completely lost in contemplation of Baba. It required much effort and persistence to catch hold of her. At last as she was darting in and darting out of the Swami's room she was waylaid and she willingly stopped and smiled, a smile that was born out of peace and contentment. She would not talk but only smile. She would not say anything about herself except that she was "Om Sayi" and Christine was not her name. In reply to a persistent question she said she saw Sai Baba's presence all the time and clutching the ballpoint pen which was presented to her as a memento she fled with that captivating smile.

Officials of the Sansthan said on an average 15,000 to 20,000 pilgrims visited Shirdi daily and the figure went up to 1,00,000 on Sundays and holidays. The largest number of devotees came from Andhra Pradesh. According to one pilgrim from Andhra Pradesh 70 per cent of the devotees were from his state. Maharashtra came second and Tamil Nadu was not far behind. Prasad was given to 5,000 to 6,000 people daily and there was free feeding also. Pilgrims belonged to all religions and among them were Hindus, Muslims, Christians, Sikhs and Parsis. Hindus constituted the majority and Muslims were very few. A Sansthan official said hundi collections for 1993-94 were Rs.14 crores and the average daily collection was Rs. 1 lakh. The Sansthan provided all basic amenities for pilgrims such as accommodation, canteen food, transport and medical facilities. It runs a full fledged hospital with latest equipment in all departments. It runs a high school too. But Shirdi lacks an information centre which can help pilgrims to plan their visit to Shirdi and to know much more about it and facilities for worship of Baba than are provided to them now. Even in Shirdi itself there is not much guidance to pilgrims who have to fend for themselves. A newcomer is likely to feel at a loss and it may take some time for him to find his bearings. Curiously enough there are no welcoming banners and notice boards to greet pilgrims to Shirdi at Kopargaon railway station, not even a picture of Sai Baba. Kopargaon gives the appearance of an ordinary wayside village station and there is no indication that it is a legendary place connected with the life and times of Sai Baba. It is a pity that the Sansthan has not interacted with the railway authorities to make Kopargaon railway station worthy of its fame and proximity to Shirdi, the home of Sai Baba. The hotels and eating places in Shirdi are no better. For all the information and literature they provide about Shirdi and Baba to their customers they might as well be in some foreign city. No information is given about the daily worship and the timings and the facilities available for pilgrims.

A talk with the Executive Officer of the Sansthan, who is the chief administrative official, revealed that there was much work to be done to put Shirdi on a wider map of India. The Executive Officer had taken charge only recently and he said he was willing to hear reasonable suggestions to make Shirdi more widely known. As we have seen in an earlier chapter after the passing away of Baba in 1918 a trust was formed in 1922 to conduct the daily worship of Baba and carry on the day to day administration. An elected body was constituted in 1952 which functioned till 1960. Then it was caught up in litigation and a civil court in Bombay appointed a Receiver to take over the administration of the Sansthan. The Receiver functioned till August, 1984 when a 22- member Board of Management was nominated by the Maharashtra government to take over from the Receiver with an Executive Officer in charge. From the very beginning the Sai Sansthan had a very limited conception of the scope of its work and responsibilities. Readers will recall that when Narasimha Swamiji approached the Sansthan with funds for propagation of Baba's life and teachings it cold-shouldered him and Narasimha Swamiji took it upon himself to carry on Baba's prachar throughout the length and breadth of the country. With the assistance of Radhakrishna Swamiji, he organised propagation of Sai ideals and worship and hundreds of Sai mandirs and Sai samajams sprang up all over the country. Today it is they who are the backbone of the great Sai movement, who have kept alive the message and worship of Sai Baba in the hearts and minds of millions of our countrymen. The Sai Sansthan has little or no role to play in the noble task of taking Baba to every home in the villages, towns and cities of our country. The Sansthan's journal, *Sai Lila,* which was started by Dixit and other devotees with the idea of spreading the Sai message has fallen on evil days. Its publication is erratic and its material poor.

The question of Sai prachar was taken up with the Executive Officer and he agreed that much remained to be done in this department. When it was pointed out to him that there was total ignorance about Shirdi Sai Baba in foreign countries especially in western countries and America he conceded that propagation of the message of Sai Baba abroad was an urgent necessity in the context of certain developments in the religious scene in India which has created confusion among deeply religious people abroad who look to India for spiritual uplift. Except, Christine, the American black woman for no foreigner was seen in Shirdi and this was strange seeing that hundreds come to India in search of peace and love which Baba provided to his devotees and continues to provide today. Baba stood for universal brotherhood and a universal religion and this is the message which the world needs so badly today, battered as it is by turmoil, violence and hatred.

One was surprised to learn that the Sansthan has no contacts with the various Sai temples and samajams in the country and especially with the All India Sai Samaj in Madras founded by Narasimha Swamiji. The Samaj has 40 to 50 associate samajams all over the country working with it and it has helped in the construction of 52 Baba temples in various parts of the country. It publishes a monthly journal *Sai Sudha* started by Narasimha Swamiji in 1941 and its mandir in Madras draws thousands of devotees daily.

The Sai Spiritual Centre in Bangalore, founded by Radhakrishna Swamiji and built entirely by devotees, is also doing good work and thousands take part in the worship of Baba. It is said that the largest number of Sai temples are in Andhra Pradesh. What is required is one central organisation which can channelise all resources and manpower into a national and international movement for the spread of Sai faith. The Sai Sansthan can and must help in this effort with its resources and prestige. As a first step it must establish contact with the All India Sai Samaj, the Sai Spiritual Centre and similar organisations and explore the possibility of convening an All India Sai Devotees' Conference under its auspices in Shirdi which could map out a strategy to make Sai name a national and world faith and a potent instrument of peace, harmony and brotherhood.

Too much emphasis is laid on ritual worship of Baba and too little on the moral and spiritual values inculcated by Baba. It was ironical that before the start of the arati daily at the Sai Samadhi Mandhir devotees are warned to protect their pockets and their ornaments as anti-social elements (in plain words pickpockets) might rob them. That such anti-social elements could dare enter the sacred portals of the living God reveals that much work remains to be done to develop character and moral values which are so dear to Baba's heart. Ritual worship and spreading the message of good character, love and compassion must go hand in hand and we would be nearer in achieving the task set before his devotees by the immortal Sai Baba.

Bibliography

Acharya E. Bharadwaja, *Sai Baba the Master,* Shirdi Sai Publications, Vidyanagar, Andhra Pradesh, 1978.

Arthur Osborne, *The Incredible Sai Baba,* Orient Longmans Hyderabad, 1957.

B V Narasimha Swamiji, *The Wondrous Sai Baba,* All India Sai Samaj, Madras.

———, *Significance of Baba's Mahasamadhi,* All India Sai Samaj, Madras 1965.

———, *Devotees' Experiences of Sai Baba,* Akhanda Sainama Sapthaha Samithi, Hyderabad 1989.

———, *Life of Sai Baba* Vol. I to IV., All India Sai Samaj Madras, 1955.

———, *Introduction to Sai Baba,* All India Sai Samaj, Madras

———, *Baba's Charters and Sayings,* All India Sai Samaj Madras, 1954.

H. B. P. Das Ganu Maharaj, *Sai Harikathas,* All India Sai Samaj, Madras, 1968.

Kevin R. D. Shepherd, *Gurus Rediscovered: Biographies of Sai Baba and Upasani Maharaj of Sakori,* Anthropographia Publications, Cambridge, 1985.

M. V. Kamath and V. B. Kher, *Sai Baba of Shirdi — A unique saint,* Jaico Publishing House, Bombay 1991.

Nagesh Vasudev Gunaji, Shri Sai Satcharita: *The Wonderful Life and Teachings of Shri Sai Baba,* Shri Sai Baba Sansthan, Shirdi, 1991.

Rangaswami Parthasarathy, *Apostle of Love.* Saint Saipadananda, Sai Spiritual Centre Bangalore 1981.

230 God Who Walked on Earth

Rao Bahadur, M. W. Pradhan, *Sai Baba of Shirdi*, Sai Baba
Sansthan, Shirdi, 1945.

Sai Sitaram Anand, *Sri Sai the Superman*, Sai Baba Sansthan,
Shirdi Prakashan, Shirdi, 1988.

Swami Saipadananda, *Sri Narasimha Swamiji (Apostle of Sai Baba)*,
All India Sai Samaj, Madras, 1973.

T. S. Anantha Murthy, *Life and Teachings of Sai Baba of Shirdi*,
Bangalore, 1974.